EMPIRE'S NOBLE SON

By
Daryl Moran

A catalogue record for this book is available from the National Library of Australia

Copyright © 2019 by Daryl Moran

All rights reserved. No part of this book may be reproduced or transmitted in any form or by any means, electronic or mechanical, including photocopying, recording, or by any information storage and retrieval system, without permission in writing from the copyright owner.

Publisher:
ASPG (Australian Self Publishing Group)
P.O. Box 159, Calwell, ACT Australia 2905
Email: publishaspg@gmail.com
http://www.inspiringpublishers.com

National Library of Australia Cataloguing-in-Publication entry

Author: Moran, Daryl

Title: **EMPIRE'S NOBLE SON**/*Daryl Moran*

ISBN: 978-1-925908-67-1 (print)
    978-1-925908-68-8 (eBook)

Dedication

To Lyle Buntine

A Noble Son whose life was tragically cut short.

Acknowledgements

This book would not exist had it not been for the dedicated work of Walter and Bertha Buntine and their children and immediate family who treasured and preserved so much of Lyle's letters and memorabilia. For a family grieving over the loss of their eldest son, it must have provided some comfort to have been able to preserve his words in written form, his military artefacts and the many expressions of sympathy and tribute paid to him. I direct my specific thanks to Lyle's nephew and namesake, Carlyle Buntine and his wife Elspeth, who were the loyal custodians of the material for so many years and who eventually gifted 'The Buntine Collection' to the Caulfield Grammar School Archives in the early 1990's. At Caulfield Grammar School, members of the School Council, including its then President Lindsay Cuming and Roy Hoult, a long-standing Council member, who saw the value of the precious material and arranged secure, safe-keeping measures. Succeeding CGS Principals, Rev Angas Holmes, Mr Stephen Newton, Rev Andrew Syme and Mr Ashleigh Martin have generously allowed me to have full access to the CGS Archives and the Buntine Collection for research purposes which has assisted greatly in the production of this publication.

In turn, Ms Judith Gibson, the current Archivist, has ensured that the entire Buntine Collection has been preserved, catalogued and made available for research purposes. It is to her credit that the material is still in such good condition even a century after its creation and is accessible for use by staff, students and researchers. Judith has always been a great source of information about the Buntine Collection and ever ready to assist me in producing this book, especially in the gathering of photographs, lists and checking of facts and names. Author of the CGS History of Sport, Dr Ian Wilkinson has also provided valuable advice and knowledge, especially in the area of the school's sporting achievements and its underlying philosophies.

During the lengthy process of preparing this book for publication other researchers have also provided material for me to use. Ashley Mison was invaluable in carefully checking facts and for providing me with sound advice and was always able to add that extra piece of missing information which helped to round out the story. Lt.Col Neil Smith AM, undertook research in the National Archives (UK) and was able to bring a sound knowledge of military matters to his findings. Author Jill Bush (UK) who has written about another 11 Squadron pilot, shared her research and discovered hidden insights into Lyle's life with the squadron as well as uncovering additional details about Lyle's MC winning action. I also express my thanks to Lt Col Marcus Fielding, President of Military History and Heritage Victoria, and Dr Andrew Kilsby for allowing me to present Lyle's story to a MHHV Speaker's Meeting and to receive valuable feedback and advice in return. Dr Peter Bennett brought insight and a keen eye to my work and provided thoughtful suggestions and gentle criticisms to help improve the written word. Dr Tom Heenan and Dr David Dunstan of Monash University provided sound advice to help place the story into the context of the times and to help further explain the concept of 'War and Memory,' especially as it applied to CGS. Bob and David Buntine, grandsons of WM Buntine, ensured that names, facts and details to do with the family were correct.

To my long suffering family, who have listened patiently to the story of Lyle Buntine over the past many years, I thank you for your patience and good humour. To my wife Jenny, who knows how long this 'passion project' has taken and has absorbed my time, I express my deepest appreciation. Thank you for giving me the chance to tell Lyle's story.

Dr Daryl Moran 2018
The author can be contacted at djjamoran@gmail.com

Contents

An Introduction 1

Chapter 1: Setting the Scene for Raising a Noble Son 7

Chapter 2: A Noble Son is Raised 24

Chapter 3: The Voyage to England 46

Chapter 4: Early Days in England 62

Chapter 5: A Tourist in England 77

Chapter 6: Officer Training in the British Army 105

Chapter 7: Training in the Royal Flying Corps 114

Chapter 8: Life at the Front 139

Chapter 9: Aerial Combat at the Battle of the Somme 156

Chapter 10: A Wounded Hero Returns Home 184

Chapter 11: Life Just Before Death 204

Chapter 12: His Death and Immediate Aftermath 221

Chapter 13: 'Years May Pass On, But Memory Remains' 253

Published Sources 269

Archival Sources 274

Notes 276

Photographs 282

Index 293

An Introduction

NOBLE – *'Having or showing fine personal qualities or high moral principles and ideals.'* **Oxford Dictionary**

The Beginnings of a Story

It was the early afternoon of June 4th 1992 when I drove back to Melbourne from the sleepy Victorian Western District area of Darlington. My thoughts were still trying to comprehend the worth of the historical treasures I had stored in the back seat and boot of my car, having just spent the night at the home of an old Caulfield Grammarian. But this was no ordinary Old Caulfield Boy. His name was a reminder of his strong family connections with the school and the tragic death in the Great War of his decorated pilot uncle. The Old Boy was named Carlyle Buntine and his grandfather Walter Murray Buntine had been the owner and Principal of Caulfield Grammar School (CGS) from 1896 – 1931. Walter's eldest son, Walter Horace Carlyle (Lyle) Buntine, had been the Royal Flying Corps pilot tragically killed in a flying accident in Scotland in 1917. Old Boy Carlyle Buntine had been named after this late uncle and I had just been to see Carlyle Buntine on school business. During the early years of the 1990's I held the position of Director of Development at CGS, essentially a 'fundraising and friend-raising' role amongst the school community, its supporters and its alumni. It was in the latter capacity that saw me appointed Executive Director of the Caulfield Grammarians' Association (CGA) where amongst other tasks my duties involved liaising with the various state branches and sporting clubs as well as organising major class and chapter reunions. In addition, the stewardship of the School Archives fell under my responsibilities. I had invited Carlyle Buntine to speak to a gathering of Old Boys about his grandfather, the former school's principal Walter Murray Buntine. He obliged, delivering a fine paper to the Buntine Chapter Luncheon which shed further light on this revered man. During my conversations with Carlyle he mentioned that he had some archival material he wished to donate to the School Archives, however, I would need to visit him at his Western District farm so that he could officially deliver the material to me. He briefly outlined the contents of the material stating that in giving it to CGS, he felt as if a heavy burden of responsibility had been lifted from his shoulders. Essentially, he was donating to the school the entire contents of what later became known as the 'The Buntine Collection' and which in the first instance consisted of many rare papers, photographs and artefacts belonging to former Principal W.M. Buntine. However, the second part of the gift was the most astonishing, as it consisted of the personal effects, correspondence, photographs and artefacts connected with the life and death of his pilot uncle, Lyle Buntine, W.M. Buntine's eldest son and Carlyle's namesake.

At the end of the Great War Nations, organisations and institutions chose to remember their war dead in a variety of ways and families were no different. The Buntines, however, perhaps through the lack of the usual method of mourning at a grave side, strove to preserve the memory of Lyle by the keeping of artefacts, letters and photographs as a shrine in the family home to preserve the memory of 'noble' Lyle. His medals, badges of rank, and other objects were mounted and displayed in a professionally built glass-fronted display case which held pride of place in the family home. This case, along with other numerous documents connected with his death, including a copy of the Royal Flying Corps inquest, newspaper tributes, letters of condolence, poetry and magazine articles were amongst the donated items. Also, amongst the artefacts were his medals and badges and flying gloves and helmet. There was also a memento of the action where he was wounded and subsequently awarded a Military Cross for bravery, the shattered propeller tip and the German machine gun bullet that had seriously wounded him. The collection was significant for a school which had been raised on the Buntine story as his name was listed on the Caulfield Grammar Honour Roll and he had a House and Speech Night prizes named in his honour. The immediate family, however, had chosen to remember him in its own way by saving all of his letters. Most remarkably, all of Lyle's correspondence over his two-year military service, nearly 200 letters, was collected and over time typed into a readable and useful form. This well-documented record of an Australian flier and his experiences as a member of the British Army and the Royal Flying Corps is uncommon amongst Australian servicemen. The circumstances behind the Lyle Buntine story had been forgotten in recent school history until 2010, when my younger brother Rod, then a Housemaster at CGS, suggested it as the name for the trophy for the Caulfield Campus Inter-House Competition, thus bringing the name of the dead war hero back into common circulation. With the heightened interest in Australia's war history, this renewed interest in Buntine has been reflected in other ways, as the Buntine Collection is now used by CGS History teachers for reference purpose when students are researching the Great War. In April 2014 his photograph and story appeared in the school's quarterly magazine to mark Anzac

4 ✧ Empire's Noble Son

Day and an entire display case devoted to his story and artefacts was assembled in the school's Heritage Room display marking the Great War service of its Old Boys.

Lyle Buntine's short life and legacy provides a notable and well documented example of how his former school and family dealt with his loss. Remembered as *'A Noble Son of Empire Fall'n to Earth,'* in a tribute poem published in the June 1917 CGS magazine, Lyle Buntine's correspondence and associated papers reveal him to be very much an 'Australian-Briton,' whose short life and death were held up as an example to all at Caulfield Grammar School, an institution whose ethos very much reflected the traditions of Empire. This story, mainly told in his own words, will explore how the life of Lyle Buntine very much reflected the ethos of the school; an ethos based on factors such as athleticism, militarism, muscular Christianity, British-Australian identity and loyalty to God, King and Empire. This ethos was in large part constructed during the pre-Great War period by his father Walter Murray Buntine as the owner/principal of CGS.

This story will also explore the concept of 'War and Memory' at CGS during the conflict and then study the later commemorative war practices instituted at CGS in the context of a Principal mourning for his lost son in the post war years. But most importantly, this story will bring to life again the words of Lyle Buntine himself from over a century ago; words that reflect not only an intelligent and well-educated man, but a young Australian who was a keen observer of his surroundings and who throughout the two years of his military service recorded his life in uncommonly rich detail. These writings may also help to shed further light on some unwritten aspects of his life. Why did he enlist and as an Australian, what factors motivated him to join the British Royal Flying Corps? As this story will also show the Buntine and Gibbs family (his maternal cousins) suffered loss more than most as a result of the Great War, which might help to explain why Lyle's memory has been enshrined at his old school and why his family went to such lengths to preserve his memory through the 'safe-keeping' of his correspondence and associated artefacts. His tragic death was just one amongst the seventy Old Boys of CGS who gave their lives during the Great War, but the complete record of his life that remains today is a testimony to the grief felt by all the families who had suffered such tragic losses.

Dr Daryl Moran 2018

Chapter 1:
Setting the Scene for Raising a Noble Son

*Football has been of great value developing the
character of the Australian soldier.*[1]
WM Buntine CGS Principal 1896 - 1931

On the afternoon of Friday November 10th 1911, the competitors of twelve Victorian private boys' schools gathered at the East Melbourne Cricket Ground to contest the first annual combined sports of the Schools Amateur Athletic Association of Victoria (SAAAV). Students from the Caulfield, Trinity, Camberwell, St Thomas', All Saints' and Malvern Grammar Schools, along with those from Haileybury College and Queen's College were joined by the newcomers to the association Canterbury Grammar, Camperdown Grammar and New College (Box Hill). With some 2000 spectators in attendance and with competitors being cheered on by students from Melbourne girls' schools who had been granted a half day holiday in honour of the occasion, the twenty events were held to decide the Championship, a title eventually won by Caulfield Grammar School (CGS). The twenty-one victorious Caulfield team members competed in events from under 12 to open division, and as a later historian noted, the fact there were only four individual CGS winners, showed good all-round strength and placings in each of the high jump events were a prelude to Caulfield's virtual domination of these contests over the next few years.[2]

What was particularly notable about this group of young Caulfield Grammarians was not just the result, but that by the end of World War 1, of the twenty-one members of that champion 1911 athletics team, sixteen had enlisted and served in the Australian or British military forces, whilst five were too young to serve. Of these sixteen young men, five were awarded the Military Cross and one received a Distinguished Conduct Medal, whilst four of them were killed on active service. Walter Murray Buntine, the Principal of Caulfield Grammar School in his Annual Report in the School Magazine of December 1918 referred to these men and could proudly state, 'From this record will be gathered the importance of athletic training as a preparation for gallant service in the war.'[3] He also reminded his readers that of the undefeated school's champion football team of 1914, fourteen of those eighteen players had enlisted with four paying the supreme sacrifice. What W.M. Buntine failed to mention in any printed or public forum was that his eldest son, Walter Horace Carlyle (Lyle) Buntine was one of the young former athletes from 1911 numbered amongst both the medal winners and sacrificial deaths. Lyle had been educated at CGS and later became a medical student at the University of Melbourne, but the unique circumstances of his father's ownership of CGS ensured that Lyle was certainly raised as a 'noble son of Empire.'

Caulfield Grammar School – Foundation and Its Early Years

Caulfield Grammar School had been founded in 1881 in the then semi-rural location of Elsternwick by Joseph Henry Davies who had served as a missionary in India in 1876 at the age of nineteen. Unfortunately, his work in India was not to last very long at all and he was shortly back in Australia for health and family reasons within a few short years. Aged nearly twenty-five and as the eldest surviving son, found he had to provide for his family upon the death of his father. As a consequence of this circumstance and in order to raise much needed funds, he founded Caulfield Grammar School on April 25th 1881 with nine boys as his first pupils. His evangelical and educational intentions were clear from the outset when he wrote in the first school's prospectus of 1881, that the School would be conducted wholly on Christian principles and regular Biblical instruction of a strictly denominational character would be given in every class. He went further in the 1883 prospectus when he proclaimed that the Bible lesson was to be made the first lesson of each day, and while sparing no effort for the mental and physical training of the boys, the first aim of the Headmaster was that School should be a thoroughly Christian one.[4]

Important as Davies regarded academic success to be, he was aware of the benefits conferred on character by the participation in many games and pursuits.[5] Davies provided a substantial playground for CGS and showed that he, like other late 19th century educators, certainly favoured the idea of boys participating in organized games.[6] Put simply, it was argued that organized games not only helped produce 'fit' young men, but also generated 'school spirit' and taught boys fair play, teamwork and how to win and lose graciously. [7]

But the large playgrounds were also used for other 'team-building' activities and the official establishment of the Caulfield Grammar School Cadet Unit in 1885[8] made it the fifth oldest in a Victorian school. Lt. Col. Frederick Sargood, the Victorian Minister of Defence, was the driving force behind this innovation and as he lived at his 23-acre estate 'Ripponlea' in East St Kilda, was a close neighbour of CGS and his sons were also pupils at the school. Sargood stated that he would look to cadets in the future as furnishing a most important recruitment ground for the militia forces[9] and that his aim in founding school cadets was; 'To bind together in one patriotic brotherhood the youth of this country so that, should occasion arise, they may be able in after years to defend their country with the most telling effect.'[10] The CGS Cadet Unit was reported in 1888 to be participating in regular parades, drilling, participating in musketry training and preparing for the annual camp.

After seven years and eager to return to the mission field, Davies sold CGS and travelled to Korea and although he died from smallpox and pneumonia soon after he arrived, is credited with being one of the founders of the Presbyterian church in Korea.[11] His founding work at CGS saw a philosophy laid down that was fundamentally Christian in outlook, global in vision, and that worked across man-made divisions for the achievement of a higher and greater good. It could be contended that this view extended in a wider context to a loyalty and devotion to the British Empire.

Davies had sold CGS to an Anglican clergyman, the Rev. Ernest Judd Barnett who was its Headmaster from 1888 until 1896. Barnett was a man well suited to the task of broad churchmanship and already deeply committed to the cause of missionary work and he certainly would have earned the approval of Davies' clients. The school magazine of the time also records details about the new Headmaster's intentions upon announcing that CGS was moving to a new site when it stated that,

> 'Lovers of sports, however will be glad to know that there are rather more than five and a half acres of land out of which a good football ground and cricket pitch

can be carved by sacrificing a part of the present garden, which our Headmaster is prepared to do.'[12]

In 1891 CGS Principal Barnett had ensured that his school joined the amateur based Schools' Association of Victoria (SAV) for the purpose of engaging in organized cricket, football and athletics competitions against local boys' schools in Melbourne and surrounds. In this instance, it was thought advantageous to have inter-school games and sporting meetings organized by a single body under an agreed set of rules and conditions.[13] Barnett also encouraged participation at CGS in carpentry, tennis, gymnastics, music, self-expression activities such as acting, public speaking and the maintenance of high academic standards. Importantly he continued to support the school's cadet unit and actively promoted and encouraged its activities. As a later observer noted, Victorians of the time were much concerned with military preparedness and CGS willingly played its part.[14]

In time, Barnett, like his predecessor Davies, also offered himself for overseas missionary service, eventually becoming the Anglican Archdeacon of Hong Kong. During this time, he founded St Stephen's College (for boys), Trinity College Canton and took a leading part in establishing Hong Kong University.[15] As he departed for Hong Kong, Barnett undertook the sale of CGS to a man who for the next thirty-eight years would consolidate its educational and social position in Melbourne. He would take the key foundation principles of Davies and Barnett as epitomized in the practices of sport, spiritual matters, academics and military training and ensure that they and their allied philosophies became the bedrock of CGS into the future.

That man was Walter Murray Buntine and Barnett wrote to the CGS parents at the time of the sale, 'I have no doubt that under the strict, but kindly discipline of the new Headmaster, the

School will continue to flourish even more than it has done in the past, and it will be a satisfaction to parents to know that the foundation stone of the School – a working spirit of Christianity based upon the daily lesson from the Word of God – will be left untouched.'[16]

Some Background Educational Conditions

At this time in Australia and especially Victoria, the vast majority of schools were privately run, as was Caulfield Grammar School. As historian Brown contends, 'the years preceding the Great War featured the consolidation of Australian versions of the British public school in Victoria and New South Wales. Central to the curricula of these schools was the powerful and addictive ideology of athleticism.'[17] Brown argued that, 'the ideological foundations of athleticism had been advanced initially by a generation of British public-school masters who began to arrive in Australia during and after the 1860's. Their educational philosophy and practices were founded on the Arnoldian concept of a Christian education which was based on the development of character by means of 'playing the game' – literally and figuratively.'[18]

Noted social historian Mangan saw a wider agenda in schools than merely just the attainment of commonly accepted educational goals to do with socialization, literacy and numeracy. He noted, 'In later Victorian and Edwardian Britain, to an extraordinary degree both sport and war were welded together into a fused expression of sublime middle-class heroic manhood with one as preparation for the other.'[19] Mangan contended that imperialism, militarism and athleticism in the last quarter of the nineteenth century became a revered secular trinity of the upper middle-class school. McIntosh agreed and wrote that, 'By the end of the century it was not the public-school system in general, but the playing fields that were associated with the imperial battlefields.'[20]

Other writers concurred and Meyer for instance stated that, 'the encouragement of competition was based on the moral grounds that games were a preparation for the battle of life and that they trained moral qualities, mainly respect for others, patient endurance, unflagging courage, self-reliance, self-control, vigour and decision of character.'[21] Some writers called this view of the prevailing religious ethos of the British Empire, Muscular Christianity and which had been viewed in the following manner by one of its early proponents, the English writer Charles Kingsley, who saw through the medium of sport the potential for spiritual, moral and physical development;

> 'In the playing fields boys acquire virtues which no books can give them; not merely daring and endurance, but better still, temper, self-restraint, fairness, honour, unenvious approbation of another's success and all that 'give and take' of life which stand a man in good stead when he goes forth into the world and without which, indeed, his success is always maimed and partial.'[22]

Muscular Christianity's call and chance to 'vindicate obligations 'and to carry out gallant service to the Empire at the outbreak of the Great War in August 1914 was built upon many long standing social and educational practices in Australia. Perhaps the best of these examples was in the spread of the Church of England, the adoption of sports such as cricket and rugby football, the copying of military uniforms, customs and practices in the army and the reproducing in the 'colonies' of the English Public School and its associated culture and trappings. The ethos of these schools was based on the English public-school tradition with its amalgam of learning, sport, military service in cadet units and loyalty to King, Country and Empire. In the context of Britain and implicitly the British Empire, Mangan in *Manufactured Masculinity* suggested that, 'imperial masculinity was methodically 'manufactured' by means of a cultural 'conveyor-belt' set up eventually throughout the empire with varying degrees of efficiency and with variable responses. Central to this was the Empire's influential public-school system, with its emphasis on muscular Christianity.'[23]

The public-school boy of England and Australia had been trained to do his duty by the Empire and because of the passion for games and athletic excellence which swept these institutions, it encouraged boys in particular to further develop those qualities needed to rule the state and Empire.[24] In time of war it then became an easy transition from loyalty to one's House at school to the same devotion directed towards one's regiment in the greater game of war. Boys in particular were taught that success in war depended upon patriotism and military spirit and that preparation for war would strengthen 'manly virtue' and 'patriotic ardour.'[25] In the Empire's view, war was not an evil thing, but was the greatest of all games, a sport at which the 'home team,' the British Empire, invariably excelled.[26] At countless prize-giving's, schoolboys were told that their schools were providing just that training in character and body which made future officers and leaders of men. Behind the creation of the officer, rifle and cadet corps was the new conception of the social citizen and the nation-in-arms.[27] Indeed, Henry Newbolt's poem *Vitae Lampada* written in 1892 and set in the grounds of his old school, Clifton College, was one of the best-known examples of combining sporting metaphors with an underlying 'call to arms.' With its catch-cry *'Play up! play up! and play the game,'* it was one of many such vehicles used in the education of the young members of the Empire to teach them about the merits of a life of selfless commitment to duty.

In Victoria, influential headmasters such as L.A. Adamson of Wesley College, emphasized the importance of excellence in sport for his students and extolled the effects on character of training and preparation for military service.[28] He claimed that, 'the British love of games had proved a magnificent asset to the Empire producing unselfish, devoted leaders, able to endure hardship and discomfort. Schoolboys might well continue with their games, even in times of war, because sport equipped them to take their places at the front if this was necessary.'[29]

But where did the new owner of CGS base his standpoint in light of these principles?

Walter Murray Buntine

Walter Murray Buntine was born in 1866 near Rosedale in Victoria and grew up in Gippsland before becoming a boarder at Melbourne's Scotch College for the final two years of his education before completing a Bachelor of Arts at the University of Melbourne. He became the owner and founding headmaster of the inner suburban Hawksburn Grammar School in 1893, but by 1896 had merged this enterprise with Caulfield Grammar School when he took over the school's ownership and Headmaster's position. Buntine saw great advantages in merging Hawksburn Grammar School with that of CGS which was located in the semi-rural location of Elsternwick. The premises and grounds were more spacious and attractive than those at Hawksburn, and in addition Caulfield had premises specifically designed for a school with a spacious dwelling house set in five acres of land with another ten acres under its control. A school of twice the size could be conducted with a higher rate of profit on the Caulfield site rather than at landlocked Hawksburn.[30]

Buntine, the owner/principal of Caulfield Grammar School (CGS) from 1896 – 1932 had as a schoolboy at Scotch College in 1884 – 85, come under the influence of the Principal, Scot Dr Alexander Morrison whose influence was later found in the way in which Buntine moulded the ethos and practices of CGS. The manner of how he would operate and organize CGS was answered in part by Horace Webber, the author of the school's centenary history and a former staff member who had worked under WM Buntine in the 1920s. Of his former Principal, Webber wrote that after Buntine had experienced as a boy the Headmastership of Dr Alexander Morrison of Scotch College as a matriculation pupil in 1884 and 1885,

> 'He, like many boys who sat under Dr Morrison, had great respect, not to say veneration, for the ways and person of this patriarch among schoolmasters in Victoria. To Walter Buntine, it must have been axiomatic that the way Scotch College was run was the proper way to run a school.'[31]

Dr Morrison was the Headmaster of Scotch College from 1857 - 1903 and took up the position from Hamilton Academy in Scotland where he had also held the Head's position and in coming to Australia was seen as one of the 'new breed of educational missionary who came to the colonies.'[32] His influence can be borne out in the words of the historian Sherington who stated, 'Eventually, in Australia as in Britain, athleticism, militarism and imperialism became enmeshed. Playing fields prepared boys for the battlefields of empire.'[33] Australian writer McKernan agreed and stated, 'It was seen that the middle class in Australia accepted sport because of the values that it taught the young and reinforced for spectators of all ages; values such as loyalty, determination, unselfishness and team spirit. Sport was a preparation, a training ground for something higher; he who succeeded in sport equipped himself to lead in business, politics or the professions. Little wonder that sport attained such an exalted place in the private schools.'[34]

By way of example the CGS prospectus of 1912 stated that the aim of the school, 'is the fullest development of strong manly character, through such channels moral, intellectual and physical as a well-organized, well-equipped and well-staffed school can afford.'[35]

Walter Murray Buntine was described as both a gentle man and a gentleman, of great integrity, with an honest face and someone who had faith in himself and in CGS. He had the walk of a British Guardsman and the complexion of an Englishman; he was an ardent Christian, an Empire man, and a true-blue conservative. His pupils were taught respect for the British Empire, the King and the King's representatives in Australia. He was always known as 'The Chief,'[36] and was a patriot of patriots who even stood to attention when the evening radio broadcast concluded with the National Anthem.[37]

During his life Buntine was also instrumental in the founding of Ridley College at The University of Melbourne as well as the Church Missionary Society. He served in many voluntary capacities including on the Council of the University of Melbourne, the Melbourne Church of England Girls' Grammar School and the Council of Public Education.

Buntine's imperial outlook and a hearking back to the 'Mother Country' saw itself manifested in a variety of ways as outlined in various school magazines of the time. In 1909, for example it was written, 'Following the example of some of the old public schools of England, a record of yearly increasing interest is to be kept in our corridor. A large slab of beautifully prepared timber has been erected so that old boys and senior present boys may inscribe their names. Already one hundred and thirty-eight spaces have been marked out and most of them very tastefully carved.'[38] The death of King Edward VII on 7th May 1910 found that, 'Buntine assembled all the school, and a suitable and impressive ceremony carried through, which will live in the minds of all who were present as the great qualities of our late beloved Sovereign, were highlighted and all boys were urged to uphold their duty of loyalty to the new king, George V.'[39] By December of that year and the relocation of CGS to its new site in Glen Eira Rd, East St Kilda, a flagpole and plaque were erected in the late monarch's honour.[40]

Buntine was also aware that new ideas were being developed in education[41] and as an Empire man he embarked in 1906-07 upon a fact-finding mission to England where he visited Eton, Rugby, Charterhouse and Heriot's School in Edinburgh, schools then regarded as some of the finest in the world. On his return, and with the passing of his mother in his absence, he bought ten acres of land with her legacy on Glen Eira Rd, Caulfield so as to relocate CGS from its small suburban site. He had seen the gracious estates of the great schools of England and realized that if Caulfield was to become a considerable school, it must be established on a sufficient area of land[42] and he saw this development as his greatest legacy to the school. Buntine reflected like-minded ideas to those of his fellow Headmaster of Wesley College, L.A. Adamson and saw that the sort of boy emerging from the school was the most important outcome of all, his academic training being only a necessary part of a wider whole.

However, he was also mindful that most boys' schools helped provide for the physical development and well-being of their students by devoting at least some time each week in their extensive playgrounds and sporting fields for military style drill. Buntine maintained his strong support for school cadets. Militarism in Australian schools had seen the establishment of cadet units which had arisen or been established in the 1860's and essentially grew out of the practice of students undertaking various forms of military drill mainly in the form of marching. Stockings states, 'Of particular importance, was the appointment of headmasters to prominent private schools in the colonies, men who believed earnestly in the moral aims of the British public-school system, to produce boys fit to take leadership in a Christian state and Empire, which tacitly at least, made them very receptive to the concept of cadets.'[43] After Australia became a Federation in 1901, the cadet movement largely remained under the control of the individual colonies until 1906 when the Federal Government formed the voluntary Commonwealth Military Cadet Corps (CMCC).[44] In 1909 the Prime Minister Alfred Deakin issued an invitation to the British Army's Field Marshal Lord Kitchener to come and inspect the existing state of Australia's military's preparedness and make recommendations for its future. As a direct result of Kitchener's visit, on 1st January 1911, the compulsory provisions of the *Defence Act (1909)* made Australia the first modern English-speaking country to demand universal and mandatory military training in times of peace.[45] Obligatory Cadet training for all boys aged 12 – 18 meant that 12 – 14 years olds became Junior Cadets. All 14 – 18 years olds had to serve in the Senior Cadet Units, which could be raised within schools if those boys were continuing their education and in Victoria these units from the private schools were all held within the 2nd and 3rd Battalions.[46] These moves were greeted enthusiastically by educators and schools such as CGS.[47] The CO of the CGS Cadet Unit, Lt. McCullough, wrote extensively in the 1911 school magazine to outline the changes in the cadet scheme, to remind boys of the seriousness of the work they were about to undertake, to point out that they had a Record Book in which to record their service and to single out those boys who were to seek promotion through the scheme. 'Having decided this, that Australia must prepare to defend itself, we must have the best system of defence, and the best training it is possible to get. The system that it has been decided to adopt in Australia is one of universal training.' Having control of their own cadet units meant that the military activities could be tailored around the busy life of a school thereby ensuring that academic studies could be undertaken as well as the busy sporting programme. Perhaps Lt McCullough and his training staff provided something out of the ordinary for the CGS cadets, because he reported in the 1913 Speech Day programme, Lyle Buntine's final year at CGS;

> 'The school company of the Senior cadets has succeeded in winning the Battalion competition for 1913 and this entitles our company to represent the Battalion in the Brigade competition to be held early next year. The honour of being the champion team of the Battalion has thus been secured (by CGS) for the third year in succession.[48] (The unit also won again in 1914 for their fourth successive victory.)'

War Declared

Given the general ethos and practice of CGS up to 1914, it was not surprising that the school magazine under the heading 'For King and Country' should adopt a supportive tone upon the outbreak of war.

'August 5th was the date upon which Britain declared war against Germany. For days, the whole Empire had been waiting the decision of the British Cabinet, and the tension was considerable. At last the decisive step, which would involve many lives and much treasure, had been taken and people everywhere accepted the situation quietly and loyally. The nation's honour demanded that Germany's aggression should be stoutly resisted.'[49]

The CGS Cadet Unit had won the 46th Battalion competition for the fourth year in succession in 1914 with the team excelling in rifle shooting and on the declaration of war eight of these Senior Cadets were immediately called for duty. The School Magazine reported that on the very day upon which the declaration of war was announced, many young citizen soldiers were called upon to shoulder their rifles and answer the country's call to defend Australia. 'Eight from the school – four-day boys and four boarders – received notice that they were required to present themselves at the Drill Hall, in McWhae Avenue adjoining the school at an early hour next morning. A day's supply of rations was to be brought and they were to be in readiness to proceed to an unknown destination. Some little excitement prevailed as kitbags were hastily packed, and, for the first time, the youthful soldiers anticipated that they were ready to take part in the real business of war. The following day was spent in strenuous drilling exercises, cheerfully undergone, but at the close of the day most of them were ordered back to don civilian dress once more. This new order occasioned some surprise, and perhaps regret, for the enemy had undoubtedly advanced considerably beyond his western frontier, and was threatening Belgium, France and perhaps England; and young Australia was quite prepared to offer a stout resistance in the name of the King.'

The school did become directly involved in the early war effort three days later, when some two hundred officers and men were unable to use the adjacent McWhae Avenue Drill Hall due to recent asphalting works. They were offered the hospitality of the CGS classrooms where they spent the night on the floor of the classrooms before marching into the city the next day.

Life at CGS in 1914

School life continued on as usual despite the war and its impact upon society in general. The first school Debating Society was formed, over 30 students attend the weekly meeting of the

Christian Union, whilst over £23 was raised to support an Old Boy missionary in India and students staged a performance of Oliver Twist. Boys were actively encouraged to take part in the range of sporting and extra-curricular activities with participation being clearly seen as a measure of success. In 1914 CGS had won the Schools' Amateur Athletic Association of Victoria (SAAAV) Athletics championship for the fourth year in succession, whilst the 1st XVIII won the SAAAV football premiership for the second year in a row. Old Boy Bertrand Coombes was the first ex-Caulfield student enrolled at the Royal Military College Duntroon and just 13 days before the declaration of war arranged a football match between the 1st XVIII and visiting Duntroon Cadets. In late 1914 the 1st XVIII defeated the Old Boys team in the annual Past and Present match; sadly, before the war's end, five of these players (from both sides) would be killed on active service. It should be remembered that throughout the Empire that the games tradition was a central part of schools such as CGS and was clearly seen as a preparation for the bigger game of life, in particular that of war. The school's activities during the Great War however, were not just based around sport and the usual academic program but were also directed towards supporting the war effort in a variety of ways and means. On the declaration of war, a charity concert was arranged and £5 was forwarded to the Patriotic Fund. It was also decided at this time that no silver trophies would be awarded to winners at the annual athletics sports held late in the year and the resultant £15 savings was directed towards the Red Cross.

Many past students of the School left no doubt as to where their loyalties and actions lay as reported in the ARGUS a month later on Friday 4th September 1914. 'Old Boys of the Caulfield Grammar School assembled at Sargent's Café on Friday night to bid farewell to former scholars who had volunteered for service at the front. Mr W.M. Buntine M.A., Principal of the school, presided. In welcoming the guests, Mr Buntine said that he was proud to see that the old pupils of the school were to the fore in this, the greatest of wars. Many of the Caulfield Grammar Schools boys had fought in the South African war and in the fight now in progress they would uphold the honour of their school. (Cheers.) He wished the volunteers a prosperous voyage, success on the continent of Europe, and a safe return. (Applause.) Mr A.M. Lonie, President of the Old Boys' Association, in proposing the toast of the volunteers, said that the high example set by the British soldiers should incite the old Caulfield Grammarians to the strongest efforts in the task in front of them. In responding on behalf of the Old Boy volunteers, Captain Fowler said that the school could depend on the old pupils doing their best for the Empire. He hoped they would uphold the confidence which had been placed in them. (Cheers.)[50]

The first troop transports of the AIF began to leave from Australia in September 1914 and many Caulfield Grammarians sailed together as they had joined the same Battalions or units.

The educational and philosophical background to this story is therefore well reflected in one such school, namely Caulfield Grammar School, that both extolled and exemplified all of the manly virtues taught by the school couched in athleticism, imperialism, militarism and Muscular Christianity. The personal background to this story is reflected in just one individual who exemplified all of these manly virtues, namely, Lyle Buntine, the eldest son of the CGS Principal, Walter Murray Buntine.

Chapter 2:
A Noble Son is Raised

Lyle's School Days at Caulfield Grammar School

Walter Horace Carlyle (Lyle) Buntine was born at Toorak on 10th August 1896 and was the eldest son of CGS Principal Walter Murray Buntine and his wife Bertha Florence (nee Gibbs). They subsequently had four more children, Richard Murray (b 1897), Martin Arnold (b 1898), Bertha Mary Gladys (b 1901) and Robert Douglas (b 1906). Lyle entered the CGS Preparatory class in 1903 aged seven and showed his all-round prowess as an accomplished student from his very first year when he was placed 2nd in the Preparatory School running race and on Speech night, also collected the Preparatory Prize for Reading, Dictation and Spelling. Collecting a similar prize in 1904, he showed his versatility by being placed 3rd in the Under 12 100 yards race and on Speech Day being awarded prizes for French, Drawing and Music. In 1908 he was placed 3rd in the High Jump and completed a 'double' by being placed in the same position in the Egg and Spoon race! He collected prizes in subsequent years for Latin, French, Music, English, Bible, Science and for securing a high place in the year's academic marks in 1908. He figured prominently in the results for Science and Gymnastics gaining first place in Form Vb in 1910 for both areas of endeavour. A similar pattern emerged until the end of his schooling in 1913 with prizes won in a wide variety of academic disciplines including French, Latin, Science, Music, Bible and Drawing.

His senior sporting and extra-curricular career blossomed in the final three years of his time at CGS in 1911 when he was named amongst the best players in the 2nd football XVIII against Brighton Grammar School; 'new players Duckett and Buntine L did all that was required of them.' The same magazine article reported that Lyle had represented CGS in the open events at the Combined School's Championships on Friday 10th November 1911. This was the same team whose war service was later extolled by his father in 1918. In addition, the magazine noted that Cadet L Buntine had been named as a member of the CGS cadet shooting team versus Trinity Grammar School. The 1912 issue of the school magazine also gave an example of his perseverance and determination not to let down his school and his team-mates.

> 'WHC (Lyle) Buntine was a member of the (winning) CGS Athletics team at the Combined Sports and was 3rd in the 120 yards hurdles and 4th in open high jump. In his heat for the hurdles, WHC Buntine had the misfortune to bring one down, but with considerable presence of mind he rose from the ruins and continued his course, thereby gaining a place in the final.'[51]

He was for three years a member of the first eighteen premiership football teams at CGS and of the premiership athletic teams which represented the school at the combined sports which included the noted 1911 Athletics team. The school football team of 1913 in which he played would begin a winning sequence of unbroken premiership wins for CGS until 1931. In 1913, he won the 100 yards breaststroke at the combined swimming sports and was second in the school athletics championship, being a member of the winning Combined Sports Athletics team as they achieved their third of four consecutive premierships.

Elected a Prefect in the first term of 1913, he was also active in the Debating Society and tied with the School Captain, who had also been the school dux of 1912, for the Debating Prize. A member of the Cadet unit since 1908 and aged 12 at the time, Lyle experienced first-hand the significant changes in training that took place in the movement following its take-over by the Commonwealth Government and continued his cadet career and became one of the first qualified non-commissioned officers in the new Senior Cadet scheme in 1912 – 1913, his final years at school. The Commanding Officer of the CGS Cadet Unit wrote in the school magazine of 1913 that, 'Seventeen boys in the school have realized that there is something more serious than cricket or football. They may be seen any lunch hour at half past one; they parade then, they have done so practically since the beginning of the year. Some of them will soon be noted in their Record Books as among the first non-commissioned officers of the Senior Cadet Forces of Australia.'[52] The list of seventeen boys contains the names of six of the Champion 1911 SAAAV Athletics team and of the seventeen cadets listed by the CO, sixteen of them enlisted in WW1 with four of them being killed, amongst them Lyle Buntine.

He was seen in many ways by his CGS peers and his school community as a model student, an academic scholar of high standing, with cultured tastes, a very talented and all-round sportsman and a recognized and qualified leader in the cadet unit. He certainly fitted the mould of the ideal well-rounded product of CGS that his principal father W.M.Buntine was aiming for as a Caulfield Grammarian. By the time Lyle Buntine left Caulfield Grammar in 1913, he had experienced a unique set of family, educational and social circumstances which had all combined to help shape his life and attitudes. His father, Walter was a committed Christian, of conservative views and a thorough Empire man. The school he owned was organized in such a way to ensure that the boys who attended were encouraged and prepared to serve Australia and the Empire by having been exposed to an underlying imperial ethos and curriculum, involvement in sport and a commitment to the ideals and practices of school cadets; Lyle Buntine had indeed been immersed in a diet of imperialism, athleticism and militarism, all wrapped up in 'muscular Christianity,' and when he left CGS at the end of 1913 aged 17 he began his tertiary studies in the Medical Faculty of the University of Melbourne.

Lyle and Athletic Pursuits

In August 1912, the Caulfield Tally Ho Harriers Club was established at a meeting designed to 'form an amateur Athletics Harriers Club in the Caulfield district,' and Lyle became a member. After leaving CGS at the end of 1913, Lyle continued his sporting pursuits and, on the Melbourne, Cricket Ground on February 17th 1914, he tied with R.R Templeton (sen) in a pole vault handicap, when he cleared 9ft 2 inches. Two weeks later on 30th March 1914 he represented his club at the Victorian State Athletics Championship held at the MCG and with a jump of 9ft 6 inches came second to R Rodgerson (9ft 9ins) in the pole vault. In addition to following field athletics he was a member of the Melbourne Swimming club and was recognized as a good gymnast and wrestler.[53]

Harry Hawker Flies at Caulfield

No record exists to tell us where Lyle gained his later keen desire to become a pilot, but perhaps he was heavily influenced by the exploits of the famous Australian pioneer aviator Harry Hawker who visited the Caulfield area in early 1914. Hawker was born in the nearby suburb of Moorabbin and following a move to England eventually became the chief test pilot for the Sopwith Aviation Company, later the builders of the famous Great War fighter plane the Sopwith Camel. To promote the company's then current model the Sopwith Tabloid, which he had helped to design, Hawker undertook a five-month promotional tour of Australia. On 19th January 1914 he was feted at a civic reception at the St Kilda Town Hall, the first of many such functions. A number of local dignitaries were invited to such an event, and it is more than likely that W.M.Buntine, headmaster of CGS in East St Kilda was present at the luncheon.

A week later Hawker flew the Tabloid for about 20 minutes over Elsternwick in what was described as a beautiful exhibition of flying. Incredibly on 2nd February as reported in the *ARGUS* newspaper, Hawker flew the aeroplane from Elsternwick and landed on the lawns of the Federal Government House in Melbourne where he was greeted by Lord and Lady Denman, the Governor-General and his wife. But Saturday 7th February saw the highlight of Hawker's flights when he gave a flight demonstration from the nearby Caulfield Racecourse. Such was the public interest that the Collingwood Citizen's Band was engaged to entertain the crowds and special trains and motor buses were organized to help transport over 40,000 spectators to the event. Hawker took a paying passenger aloft with him, but was prevented by the crush of the crowd in landing on the straight of the racecourse, so diverted to the nearby Elsternwick Golf Course, where unfortunately the plane was damaged on landing. With the plane repaired, Hawker undertook more flights during the next week taking aloft a number of passengers including Senator Millen the Defence Minister and other paying members of the public. Eventually the plane was entrained for Sydney where Hawker attended more receptions and undertook more demonstration flights, in the hope that the fledgling Australian Flying Corps would make orders for the Sopwith Tabloid; sadly, not to be. The Press reported that large numbers of people witnessed not only the flying exhibitions from the Caulfield Racecourse, but over the Caulfield and Elsternwick area in general. Although there is no mention in any of Lyle's papers about the display, as a resident of the area he must have seen the spectacle and in all likelihood witnessed the flights at the racecourse. Perhaps it was this exposure to these early days of aviation in Australia that sparked his interest in flight and that later saw him change his life direction so dramatically away from medicine to that of a pilot.

Lyle Enlists

After leaving CGS Lyle Buntine became a medical student at the University of Melbourne in 1914. This institution, as with Australian secondary schools reflected the influence of England, the 'Mother Country' in both approach and staffing. Most of the men who governed and taught at the university had absorbed the values of imperial Britain at its source. They brought these values with them to the 'colonies' as part of their social inheritance and responded passionately to the crisis of war, seeing Australia's need as inextricably linked to the Empire's needs. For many of the native-born Australians the choice seemed equally straightforward. Their parents and the politicians who governed them, their schools, newspapers, laws and language had made Britain 'home.' Australia was 'a Britain overseas,' Harry Allen, the

University's Dean of Medicine declared, and he turned to poetry to express his emotions;

> 'Britons we in blood and bone and nerve,
> Britons in speech, Britons in thought and deed.
> May God forget us in our utmost need
> If in her peril from her side we swerve.'[54]

War was declared on August 4th 1914 and as a first-year medical student, Lyle Buntine tried to enlist and presented himself at the Drill Hall, Commercial Road Prahran with the first batch of volunteers, but being only 18 years of age, he was advised to wait until at least his 19th birthday on 10th August 1915. At that time, the legal age of adulthood was 21 and young men who enlisted under that age had to receive permission in writing from their parents so that they could be sent for overseas military service. Lyle was forced to exercise patience and as most young men of the time did, perhaps try to quietly convince his parents that he should enlist. But medical students were also placed in a difficult position. Whether they should volunteer at all was problematic as students in the later years of the course were being encouraged by the University of Melbourne to complete their medical degree before volunteering.[55]

But as events transpired, Lyle Buntine did eventually enlist in the AIF on May 15th 1915, at a time when revenge for uncivilized German acts of war was in the air. Lyle's writings do not indicate what factors persuaded his parents to allow him to enlist before his birthday, but a number of elements may have come into play. Certainly, the use of poison gas at Ypres on the Western Front by the Germans on 22nd April and the loss of 1,198 passengers in the torpedoing of the passenger ship *Lusitania* on 7th May by a German U-boat had served to negatively influence world opinion. To this could also be added the bombing of innocent civilians in

London by Zeppelins on 31st May and beyond. Historian Diana Preston wrote that, 'Part of the attraction of the new weapons to the German authorities was indeed the potential of their 'frightfulness' to cause mass panic not only among troops but also civilians, thus forcing their opponents to make peace.'[56] In the face of a completely altered landscape of war where civilians were now considered as targets and rules and conventions of war no longer applied, Preston noted that the French press declared, 'the German's divorce from civilization is now complete.'[57]

To this factor could also be added Australia's very direct and ongoing involvement in the Great War. Although Australian sailors and soldiers had seen action already in the capturing of German New Guinea in September 1914 and the sinking of the German raider *Emden* by the *HMAS Sydney* in November 1914, it was the ANZAC landings at Gallipoli on 25th April 1915 that had dramatically captured the attention of the nation. It was reported in the Australian press a week after the action, by the English journalist Ellis Ashmead-Bartlett who provided, a thrilling description, full of stirring phrases which told the Australians that their men had performed just as they had expected.[58] 'There has been no finer feat in this war than this sudden landing in the dark and the storming of the heights. General Birdwood told the writer that he couldn't sufficiently praise the courage, endurance and the soldierly qualities of the Colonials (Australians) who were happy with themselves because they had been tried for the first time and not found wanting.'[59] The legend was already being born of Australians as natural soldiers, with skills and toughness acquired from generations of struggle in the bush, with war seen as the supreme test of manhood and also a test of national character and it was a test which Australians felt they had passed with flying colours.[60] In addition, in early February notices had been placed in the nation's newspapers calling for medical officers and nurses to join the colours. The medical faculties of the universities had also been approached for recruits from amongst the ranks of their medical students.

But perhaps closer to home it was the death of fellow Caulfield Grammarians at Gallipoli that influenced the circumstances of Lyle's early enlistment. By the 15th of May when he signed up, seven Caulfield Old Boys had died, including four at the landing on the first day and one, John Melvin, had been the Secretary of the Caulfield Grammarians' Association, the body representing ex-students. Given the number of his former students who had already died in such a short space of the war, Lyle's Headmaster father Walter must have held mixed feelings as he wrote on CGS letterhead on the day of Lyle's enlistment, 'My son, WHC Buntine, who has already been medically examined, I understand has the permission of his parents to enlist for active service with Australian Expeditionary Forces.' Lyle also signed the paper underneath a message written in his own handwriting. 'I certify to the above as my father's signature.'

By June 1915 the enlistments in the AIF had doubled from the April figure to 12,000 men for the month.[61] In fact, in July 1915 a highly-organized recruitment campaign in Victoria saw 21,698 men enlist in just that one month; the highest ever achieved for any state in any month in any year of the war. Australians were seen to be fighting for the high ideals of God, King and Country in 1914-18 and most, even those who declined to enlist, would have believed in the lofty principles enunciated from time to time by their leaders and other public figures. They fought for defence of national freedom and integrity, way of life, standard of living and the well-being of their families and friends, as well as for the liberation of Belgium and France.[62]

No matter the particular reasons for his enlistment, Walter Horace Carlyle (Lyle) Buntine, (No. 243) a University of Melbourne second year medical student aged 19 and 9/12th years joined the Australian Imperial Force (AIF) in Melbourne on 15th May 1915 and undertook the 'Oath to be taken by Person being enlisted.'

> 'I, Walter Horace Carlyle Buntine swear that I will well and truly serve our Sovereign Lord the King in the Australian Imperial Force from 15th May 1915 until the end of the War, and a further period of four months thereafter unless sooner lawfully discharged, dismissed or removed therefrom; and that I will resist His Majesty's enemies and cause His Majesty's peace to be kept and maintained; and that I will in all matters appertaining to my service, faithfully discharge my duty according to law. So, Help Me God.'

The enlistment form noted that he was a natural born British subject and had served 2 to 3 years as a member of the Volunteer Cadet Corps and a further 4 years as a Senior Cadet at Caulfield Grammar School. He was required to have his father's permission to join the AIF as he was under the age of consent, which was then 21 years of age. He stood at 5 ft 6 inches, weighed 10 stone 6 pounds with a fresh complexion and brown hair, and his distinctive marks were listed as '2 vaccination scars on his left arm, a scar below the left hip and another one below the right thigh.' With a chest expansion measurement of 34I/2 - 37 inches he was passed fit for active service and therefore as a result of his university medical student background, Walter Horace Carlyle (Lyle) Buntine, Service no. 243, was posted to 'Hospital Ship Details.'

Lyle's Military Life Begins

But in reality, instead of the Hospital Ship, he was sent to the Broadmeadows Depot for initial training the very same day. Whilst none of his letters from this aspect of his training remain, his time there can be imagined and reflected in the observations and experiences of others about the problematic Camp. By virtue of his university medical training he was promoted to Corporal just two months later.

The Australian War Memorial holds a copy of a photograph of him taken during this time along with three other unidentified medics, all pictured in their training uniforms. Lyle is confidently standing with his medic's red cross badge and corporals' stripes proudly displayed on his right arm.

A reference about Australian Military Units from the Australian War Memorial notes in part; 'Broadmeadows, a rural settlement (18km) to the west of Melbourne, was the site of the main camp for the reception and training of recruits for the AIF from Victoria early in the First World War. Broadmeadows had been identified as a possible site for military training in 1913, but no facilities had been established. The camp was further established in August 1914 at 'Mornington Park,' a property loaned to the government by Mr R.G. Wilson. Early on, Broadmeadows was predominantly a tented camp and conditions were quite spartan. These facilities, combined with wet weather and poor drainage resulted in a rapid increase in sickness among recruits in autumn 1915. By mid-May 1915 various newspaper articles and Letters to the Editor were highlighting a number of problems with the Broadmeadows Camp, particularly after three deaths there from pneumonia. This resulted in a decision in May 1915 to re-establish the main Victorian training camp at Seymour, approximately 100km north of Melbourne. Broadmeadows Camp remained in use throughout the war, however with facilities being progressively improved.'

Consequently, the *ARGUS* was able to state on Friday 28th May 1915, 'An immediate commencement is being made with the work of shifting the military camp to Seymour, and while the authorities at Broadmeadows are completing the plans of their part of the undertaking, a staff at Seymour is marking out the selected site, arranging the water supply and attending to the thousand and one details that have to be attended to make the place habitable. Those acquainted with Seymour told the authorities that after rain the weather invariably cleared and the rolling ground drained quickly. The complete transfer should be made within six days and about 5,000 men will be moved to the new site. Although the permanent buildings at Broadmeadows are not to be removed, it is understood that a number of the hospital huts will be taken to Seymour, so that proper accommodation will be available for cases of sickness. The fact that the tents that have been in use at Broadmeadows are to be taken to Seymour will mean that the new encampment will not be entirely free from possible sources of infection in cases of minor infectious illnesses, but the bracing air of the hills, coupled with a drier camping-ground, is expected to lead to an improvement in the general health of the troops.'

By Monday 14th June, the preliminary arrangements for putting the site in order were proceeding rapidly with a large gang of men involved in stump clearing in anticipation of the arrival of 2,000 men the following Wednesday. The Seymour Council decided to spend £100 on repairing the access road to the camp and at a meeting of enthusiastic residents, it was decided to form a vigilance committee to co-operate with police and military authorities to keep undesirable persons out of the town during the existence of the camp! The Railway Commissioners were asked to reduce the train fares to Seymour and to run an additional daily passenger train. The Water Trust decided to supply water free of charge to the encampment and as about 10,000 gallons were required daily, this was a considerable contribution to the War effort. Postal arrangements were put into place with deliveries and dispatches to take place twice a day and extra officials being provided. The camp was connected to the telephone, tradesmen arrived, a site for the YMCA was selected and all buildings suitable for the housing of motor vehicles were requisitioned. In the case of the latter it was noted that as they were not numerous it was expected that temporary sheds would be speedily erected.

Colonel Featherston the Director of Army medical supplies, also stated that men afflicted with illness of a non-infectious character would be brought back to Melbourne and treated at the new hospital, where the old police barracks stood in St Kilda Rd, near the Princes Bridge. This institution would hold 400 patients and would comprise part of No. 5 General Hospital. He also said that no man showing signs of a serious complaint would be kept at the camp longer than 48 hours at most and these patients would be removed to the hospitals in a special ambulance railway van. Those suffering from infectious diseases would be placed in a separate compartment in this van. Coincidentally, Lyle was later to be very thankful for both the innovation of the hospital and the special van as tents would be used at Seymour for housing sick soldiers until they were removed to one of the hospitals.

It was reported that the Seymour site was rapidly becoming ready for use by the troops and that the work of erecting tents was being pushed ahead. The clearing of the ground and the installation of the water service was almost completed and some five hundred men were expected to soon arrive with many more to follow the day afterwards. Motor transport wagons from Broadmeadows had arrived and were beginning to cart the camp materials to their designated positions. Noting this fact, the Seymour Shire Council decided to strictly enforce the by-law in relation to the carrying of lights after sunset to ensure safety to persons travelling by road.

It was with these background factors in place and a move away from Melbourne that Lyle began his correspondence to his family on 5th June 1915. No doubt given the controversy surrounding the Broadmeadows Camp, especially with the deaths through illness of a number of young soldiers, both Lyle and his family were pleased that the camp was to be relocated. His many letters over the rest of his two-year military service to his parents, brothers and sister provide a unique insight into the life of a young Australian ready for adventure, eager for action and prepared to do his duty for his King and Country. During his previous eighteen years he had been well prepared to 'fight the good fight' and so Corporal Lyle Buntine AAMC prepared to relocate from Broadmeadows to Seymour.

Lyle at the Seymour Clearing Hospital

He reported his move from Broadmeadows to Seymour in clear detail and highlighted a number of circumstances that prevailed to make his experience a memorable one. Informed at 11.30pm the night before that he and his comrades were going to entrain for Seymour the next morning, 6th June 1915, Lyle tried to phone his parents to inform them of his departure, but was unsuccessful and indeed then found himself put in charge of loading the baggage into the train. As events unfolded another corporal had been originally put in charge of this task, but just as the train was leaving, he was called off the train and Lyle was handed the task. As a consequence, he had no list or any description of placement or indeed knew on which carriage the baggage had been placed. Upon arrival at Seymour he tried to send his family a telegram, but his duties with the baggage prevailed as he had been instructed to get everything together and get to the camp as quickly as possible. It was then that he discovered that the baggage had been spread in a variety of trucks all over the train and although the train had arrived at Seymour at about 1 o'clock in the afternoon, it took until 7.00pm that evening to restore some semblance of order from the chaos. In addition to beginning the day at 5.00am at Broadmeadows, the whole situation had been compounded by the fact that one of the medical sergeants had met a number of old friends and they had all retired into the refreshment rooms with the result that he had emerged as worse than useless. Lyle recorded that, 'It was a pity because he is a fine chap otherwise.'

Lyle was soon writing to his parents whilst on Guard Duty and Fire Picquet, even if it was 3.00am the next day! 'The camp at Seymour is looking very nice and the Clearing Hospital is right on top of a hill so we get beautiful fresh air. The country is dry and gravelly up here with not much mud. We put no men on tonight as we weren't sure of them. My hours of duty were from 2.00am to 5.00am and I really prefer the guard work up here to sleeping in a tent. I believe we are 1600 ft up and the air here is beautifully clear and sharp. I am at present sitting in front of a fire with a big overcoat and scarf on, so am quite warm. The night is absolutely perfect and there is no wind and all the stars are out and no moon. There is not a cloud in the sky and the stillness is broken only at intervals by the noise of a train at Seymour or a cough from one of the tents. However, colds will soon get right up here in this beautiful climate.'

How wrong about the 'beautiful climate' the young medical student proved to be as two days later he wrote to his family from the new Military Base Hospital near Princes Bridge in St Kilda Rd, Melbourne where he had been admitted with influenza. He wrote a reassuring letter to his younger sister outlining the visitor's hours and explaining that he had had rather bad luck in being sick again, but that it was not a bad condition, just a cold. In contrast to some current practice, visitors were only allowed for one hour each day on four days of the week with two hours being permitted on Sunday afternoon. Lyle noted that his new abode was a nice little hospital with nurses as well as orderlies.

He was indeed also fortunate that the military authorities had made provisions for such medical eventualities and had provided not only a hospital, but also a special train to carry the patients to Melbourne from Seymour. Being a medical student and a member of the army medical corps, he must have felt some sense of irony and anti-climax that after all the chaos involved in getting to Seymour, that he had returned to Melbourne in such a short time and in such circumstances.

Measures at the Seymour camp to combat disease were put to the test in the months immediately after Lyle embarked for overseas service in mid-July 1915. By 18th July, the *ARGUS* was reporting that fresh outbreaks of cerebro-spinal meningitis had been reported in three camps, including amongst the men still remaining at Broadmeadows and that the isolation of the Seymour camp was being maintained with measures being taken to check the spread of the epidemic. Despite these actions some 400 cases of sickness were reported at the Seymour camp in June alone. In addition, shortly after Lyle's time at the camp came to an end, a large outbreak of meningococcal disease did occur with 644 cases being recorded with a mortality rate of 52%.

Lyle's condition improved and after a few days he was discharged from the hospital and was back at the Seymour camp, where he received the news from Major Maguire, a superior officer, that he might allocate Lyle to the next hospital ship sailing from Melbourne. In a letter to his mother Lyle lamented that he had to return to Seymour before seeing his father again and also asked for a money belt and vest pocket Kodak camera to take overseas with him. He was particularly anxious to get the Autographic model which cost about two pounds 10 shillings and had a special place in it for writing the picture's title on carbon paper placed between the film negatives. 'Try and get up soon in the car or for a week end and bring up the camera if you can, because there are some wonderfully pretty spots up here and also some very amusing and interesting scenes about camp. One thing that has come into fashion lately is the use of charcoal burners by the men and by jove they are great if you keep the door of the tent well open.'

After the few days of convalescence, when he returned to the Seymour camp from Melbourne and had been able to move into a tent with some friends from the Broadmeadows camp he noted that they rose at 6.30am, had physical exercises for half an hour and then breakfasted. He observed once again that there had been no rain during his absence and that the camp grounds remained quite dry and as became increasingly apparent throughout his correspondence, he always looked beyond his surroundings and viewed the world in a different light.

Sensing that he was to be posted overseas soon, he continued to encourage his family to visit him and provided them with details about the timetables, especially the special trains running on Sunday. Extra provisions of food were also a priority with soldiers and he noted that the father of one of his tent mates had brought in a good supply of provisions so they had been able to supplement their rations. Lyle took the opportunity to remind his parents that if they were to send him a box of provisions, not to forget a couple of pounds of butter as they were quite short of it in the camp.

'Today was warm and sunny. What was it like in town? If all the days are going to be like today, then life in camp won't be bad at all. Of course, it is chilly in the morning, but physical exercises soon warm you up. When I got up this morning it was lovely and warm and standing at the door of one of the wards about half past seven in the morning you look out on a most beautiful view. In front on the side of a hill are the tents of the reinforcements with the cook's tent a little larger than the others and as it is a beautifully still morning the smoke goes straight up and the scene looks for all the world like the pictures of the Israelites camped before Sinai with the cloud over the temple. Behind the tents is a range of hills, blue in the distance and with mist driving through the valleys and looking wonderfully beautiful. All the sky is tinted and rosy red by the rising sun and the moon has not quite gone out. Behind is the isolation camp with 3 fires going and the smoke rising straight as an arrow to heaven. In fact, we couldn't wish for a better morning.'

Despite this idyllic scenery, it was however, noted by the Official War History that at this stage of the war there was little opportunity for systematic training of medical personnel. For the most part both officers and other ranks, such as Corporal Lyle Buntine, were prepared for service overseas very much by the system of training being part and parcel of performing routine camp duties and picked up 'as they went along.' Consequently, the duties of a Medical Corporal were many and varied and Lyle as a young medical student was exposed to an interesting array of injuries, sicknesses and situations to deal with during his six weeks stay at Seymour. As a 'new chum' to the field of medicine each experience brought him new insights and an increasing sense of what his duties might entail once he was exposed to the real business of war.

'I have had quite a busy day today. I was in charge of the whole hospital and had 5 wards to look after. There were of course a couple of orderlies in each; but I had to supervise the work. It was pay day today and I drew £3 - 10 for about 10 days' work. Not bad was it eh? However, I have quite settled down to work again now. We had a case of diphtheria in today and I was present while the doctor injected anti-diptheria serum. He seemed to put about a pint into the chap's arm. In one ward, today a chap who was down with influenza suddenly developed measles and we had to take him down to the measles ward. I am writing this in the measles ward so I hope that you don't get measles through reading it.'

Life at the Seymour Camp was full of interest and excitement for young men and amongst the entertainments available was the provision of football and boxing matches at the camp's 'Stadium.' Lyle described what took place when he watched one of the latter exhibitions and also related another 'fighting experience' with a patient in the hospital. Lyle seemed to be quite suspicious of this patient's symptoms, actions and motives.

'I went the other night to the Depot and saw some scraps at the Stadium. By Jove! They make it willing. There were two bread and jam fights which were very good, both fought to a finish. In both cases neither man knew anything about the game, but made up for it by a desire to hurt the other chap. You may judge how willing they make things by the fact that last night a man came into the hospital and had to get three stitches put in his eye and also had two teeth broken. But he was the winner of the fight and knocked out the other man all the same. On the whole though the fights are the funniest things you can imagine, mostly chopping and round-arm swings. We had a little bit of excitement in one ward last night. A man suddenly went mad after acting very queerly for most of the day. He foamed at the mouth and struggled so hard that it took 8 men to hold him down and then he managed to bite the sergeant on the finger and while a corporal was doing something else, he bit him in the backside and nearly took a piece out. By Gosh! It was funny. All the same I think he came the bluff stakes a good deal and the doctor seemed to think so too.' Lyle was gaining a great deal of experience, both in life and in preparation for his forthcoming military medical duties.

'This afternoon a call came for the motor ambulances and they were sent out in a hurry and we waited anxiously to see what was wrong. They came in with 4 men who were terribly cut about. They had been blasting some stone and had an accident and two of them were very badly hurt and the other two had been peppered with small pieces of stone. I was on ward duty and so had to attend to them. The two who had got off lightly, bathed themselves and I fixed up the other two. One had a splinter of stone in his right eye and will lose the sight of it. The doctors were at dinner and so I had to bathe them and administer first aid and bandage them up and send them to town in the motor ambulance. The doctors came in and just told me to bandage them and left them to me. It was gruesome work; but I don't suppose so bad as I will get in time to come. The other chap had a very deep cut in his head full of gravel that had to be got out. So, what with explosions, motor accidents, and boxing matches I am getting a great deal of valuable experience.'

Lyle, as with many others took the chance to visit the YMCA tent and often wrote his letters from this welcoming atmosphere. The Salvation Army also had a similar facility, although they were also used for Salvationists' meetings and Lyle wrote about one such experience. 'Please excuse any mistakes in this letter, but I writing in the Salvation Army tent and they are holding a meeting at the same time and singing hymns and most of the men are singing the camp versions of them. They have also all the popular songs made up into hymns. The music is provided by a very much cracked cornet which persists in keeping out of tune and time with the singers.'

Another aspect of his time at the camp was the number of young men from his old school, Caulfield Grammar, that he kept encountering. In addition, a number of his fellow Melbourne University medical students were also training with him in the AAMC. Thus, he mentions Billy Cole, Hal Nelson, Norman Eadie, George and Cyril and Billy Rankin, Lionel Chinn and '...a man called Green from Brighton, also an old boy.' In addition, fellow Old Boys and other medical students Edmanson, Purbrick, and Buzzard were also with him. Naturally for a young soldier to get on with the adventure of his life that lay ahead of him Lyle was eagerly waiting for news of his departure and his letters highlight his anxious eagerness. As with many undertakings of such a large and dangerous nature, some indecision and change of plans was inevitable.

> '16/6/1915 – I saw Major Maguire and he said he might put me on a hospital ship. 18/6/1915 – I have some good news. A hospital ship is going on the 27th of this month and I am going with it. I spoke to Major Maguire and he said he was putting all the Med. Students, of which there are quite a number out here on it. There are quite a little squad of some seven 2nd year Meds. here now so I will be quite all right. 20/6/1915 – Major Maguire told me today that he thought I would get away on July 5th on the *Orsova*, but don't bank too much on it.'

In reality, the *Orsova* did not sail from Melbourne until 17th July 1915 and Lyle's story of the voyage is told in the next chapter. There is a gap in his letters from the end of June until his departure and it is more than likely that he returned home to East St Kilda for two week's leave before sailing overseas. His letters already reveal a young man with a keen insight into his surroundings and circumstances. He has a measured approach to matters military and does not display a jingoistic or emotional response to the happenings of the war. He also shows a different tone in his correspondence to the females he writes to, i.e. his mother and younger sister ('girlie'). 'I am your loving son/brother/your affectionate brother,' is different to the signature in his letters to his brothers, 'Well goodbye and write when you have the time.' Swept up in the events of the time, when the world was not quite a year into the 'War to End Wars,' it is poignant to note the enthusiasm and zest for life and all that it holds as displayed by Lyle Buntine. In particular, his insights into his surroundings and circumstances reveal a sensitive, aware and educated young man who was keen to serve his country, follow his medical calling and embark upon the greatest adventure of his life.

Chapter 3:
The Voyage to England

On Board the *ORSOVA*

On Saturday 17th July 1915, Lyle along with many other personnel from the Hospital Transport Corps, eagerly awaited their departure on board the ship *Orsova* from Station Pier Melbourne. Troop transports were requisitioned by the Commonwealth government for the purpose of carrying the AIF overseas and one such ship was the Orient Steam Navigation Company's *Orsova* which was retitled HMAT A67. At 12,036 tons the ship was a two-funnelled passenger liner built in 1909 and had a capacity of some 400 passengers and in 1909 made her maiden voyage from London to Australia. Although she was later torpedoed in 1917 near the Eddystone light, she survived the war and resumed her London – Australia route in 1919 eventually ending service in 1936.

Also sailing with the men were a considerable number of army nurses and quite a few of them had their photographs taken on the pier prior to departure. The following notice also appeared in the *ARGUS* newspaper at the same time and named amongst these young men was another Caulfield Grammarian, John Gardiner.

'The University of Melbourne Medical Students. The following second and third year students from Melbourne University are leaving with the Army Medical Corps for the front. These young students are giving up their studies. L.G. Male. W.R. Richards. H. Hampton. T.J. Watt. F.J.A. Grant. J. Buzzard. R.H. Hardy. D.D. Mc Cowan. H.R. Walker. W.H. Nelson. W.H. C. Buntine. J. Gardiner. All these students embarked on the H.M.A.T. A67 *Orsova* on the 17th July 1915.'

The various fates of this cross-section of medical students proves interesting to follow, especially as Lyle mentions a number of them in his correspondence. Of these twelve University of Melbourne students who sailed on the *Orsova*, ten of them completed their medical commitments in Egypt and then returned to Melbourne later in 1915. Of the ten who returned, four resumed their medical studies whilst the remaining six re-enlisted into the AIF and were allotted to the same unit, the 3rd Division's Medium Trench Mortar Battery. Only Lyle Buntine and Douglas McCowan did not return to Melbourne but instead continued their journey to England. McCowan was eventually discharged from the AIF in January 1918 to resume his medical studies. Ultimately both Lyle Buntine and John Gardiner would become Lieutenants, win the Military Cross and be killed; Lyle in the RFC, John in the AIF. William Nelson was gassed and lost his right eye and was awarded the Military Medal. Frank Grant was severely wounded in the arm and back and was discharged from the AIF as medically unfit for service. Willie Richards was wounded in action and received a Meritorious Service Medal. Thomas Watt became seriously ill and spent much time in hospital being treated for scabies and other ailments as well as influenza. Frank Grant and Lindsay Male eventually served as doctors in the AAMC during World War 2.

The Kyarra Returns

The *Orsova* had its departure from Melbourne delayed on this fateful Saturday by the return of the Australian hospital ship *Kyarra*. This was the first such vessel to return to Australia from Gallipoli with sick and wounded soldiers and was accorded special entry to Melbourne. This converted liner had left Suez with four hundred and seventy eight men on board comprising fifty-eight wounded, one hundred and two cases of venereal disease, four prisoners, two of whom were officially designated prisoners of war and a number of disciplinary cases. Some thirty cases had been unloaded at Fremantle whilst another thirty were officially reported to have escaped from the ship. The ship arrived off Port Melbourne before daybreak on Saturday 17th July, but it was not until it was cleared by the quarantine officer that by 12.45pm it drew alongside the Town Pier at Port Melbourne.

The Argus of 19th July reported that the pier had been absolutely barred to the public and that in addition to barriers at the entrance a military guard had been placed at the gates. Despite these measures, such was the interest in the returning soldiers, that some two to three thousand people had gathered outside to witness this event, the first return of wounded soldiers from the Dardanelles. Curiously, perhaps as a mark of respect for the seriously wounded men, the crowd refrained from cheering, instead allowing those who were mobile to leave the ship through an almost silent throng. In addition, the crowd were unable to differentiate between those men who were genuinely heroes and those who were disciplinary or venereal cases. The correspondent observed to his chagrin that the real heroes of the Dardanelles, thus were deprived of being welcomed in a manner befitting their deeds. Ironically the four soldiers who were prisoners were marched off under a strong and imposing armed guard, and were mistaken for real heroes and loudly cheered by the crowd.

The Argus noted however, that with befitting dignity, the one hundred and twelve seriously wounded cases were removed through the crowd to the St Kilda Road Base Hospital, the same one where Lyle had been hospitalised with influenza earlier in the year. It was noted that most of the wounded had received injuries to limbs from shrapnel or shell fire. Wounds to some of the notable officers were especially described in some detail, both as to the extent of injuries and the circumstances in which the injury had occurred. The Queenslanders followed by the New South Welshmen and South Australians marched through the crowds to the station prior to boarding their express trains for Brisbane, Sydney and Adelaide respectively.

In conclusion, *The Argus* report stated that, 'Lists of wounded cases will be published, probably today and this will indicate those who actually saw service at the Dardanelles. Such a list is desirable for at Fremantle, deserters who had never left Egypt have regaled newspaper representatives and the public with tales of their own heroism at the front. While on Saturday groups of these 'never-have-been' heroes were posing for photographs on board the *Kyarra* until superior officers exposed their spurious claims. The public are entitled to such a safeguard as the promised list will provide.'

One of these 'never-have-been' heroes who had deserted in Fremantle was arrested and sentenced to three months having been charged with disorderly conduct. It was stated that the former soldier from South Australia had addressed a crowd of people, claiming in part, '...that he had been treated like a dog by the army and hoped that the Germans win right through and that all the Australians at the Dardanelles would be shot.' Given the anti-German feeling prevalent at that time he appears to have been lucky to only be arrested and not dealt with by the crowd!

The Voyage Begins

Lyle's parents had hired a motorboat to visit the ship and wave and farewell him on his journey. He did regret that he was not allowed to disembark to see them, but the security surrounding the return of the *Kyarra* had prevented this from happening. The *Orsova* finally got under way and Lyle and the others from the AAMC found themselves on the lowest of the six decks in the steerage section. In a letter to his parents he invited them to imagine his position, but with fine weather, a great trip on the first day and a concert that night, he sent them a cheery telegram, 'Arrived Heads Alright. Goodbye.'

As can often be the way on sea voyages, conditions soon changed and before too long Lyle was reporting that they had run into some real Australian Bight weather. 'It has been horribly rough, in fact as bad as I have ever seen the ocean and of course most of the men suffered from mal-de-mer. I have found my sea legs, so can enjoy things a bit. As I write there is a terrific swell and everything is sliding about. I was up at the fore-peak last night and watching the ship take the waves and had hardly been back five seconds when she took a sea right where I had been standing. We are all well and most of the 'Shop' (university students) lads have found their sea legs by now.'

The ship encountered heavy weather for most of the voyage to Fremantle, but on the second day Lyle was appointed as the orderly corporal and as he had to work didn't find time to be sea-sick. By July 22nd the ship had reached Fremantle and he sent a telegram to his family advising them of his good health, and then followed up with a series of letters detailing a number of events and incidents in the early part of the voyage. He found the food on board the *Orsova* to be excellent and a tremendous advance on what they experienced at Broadmeadows and Seymour. 'Just finished a real good three-course dinner with fresh bread, good butter and fish! Just think of it and well-cooked too.'

He had his first sight of land at Western Australia when the ship rounded the 'Corner' and he saw the lighthouse just before they sighted Rottnest Island and arrived at Fremantle at about 2.00pm on 22nd June. *Orsova* anchored out in the stream and a favoured few were given shore leave; but not Lyle and most of the soldiers. Not to be deterred, about four hundred of the troops, but not Lyle, clambered overboard onto a coal lighter and then into rowing boats and finally ashore. Most of them were able to return before the ship sailed in the early hours of the morning of 23rd February 1915, but it would appear that a large group were left behind on the pier, whilst many of those who did return were mostly drunk and proved to be noisy and boisterous. The big swell they encountered in the Indian Ocean soon quietened them down and the boat continued to roll and pitch as it made its way ahead.

In the Indian Ocean

Lyle recorded that his limited experience as a sailor did not permit him to make an informed comment about whether the sea conditions he encountered were rough or smooth. There were white tops to the waves which appeared to be in a ceaseless ocean swell which made the boat roll continually and he remarked that it was quite funny to try to eat a meal with the dishes rolling from one end of the table to another. His ship board experience was further enlivened after a parade in uniform and a full kit inspection. 'We had some orders this morning. Guess what they were! You can't? Well, all the men have to appear close shaved and officers and NCO's have to grow moustaches. I have started but a very feeble effort so far. Also, everybody has to have a close crop haircut. I went down yesterday and got an ordinary close crop and today was told I must get more off. So, try and imagine me with no hair at all and a tooth-brush on my lip. Won't I be a beastly dawg? Eh what!' A few days later he wrote that his moustache was still going slowly and he was undecided as to whether the style would be a la the Kaiser, or Charlie Chaplin, with Lyle eventually concluding that it would be latter as he had always admired that style.

As they reached higher latitude, the weather took a turn for the better with Lyle reporting lovely evenings and beautiful colours in the sky. He had more chance to view the daylight as he had been put on night duty in the hospital for the next week. It was here as a medical student that he had his first encounter with nurses and reported that he found it quite strange as he didn't quite know what to do in their presence. One of the nurses, a veteran of the Boer War however, showed her fortitude when she appeared with her hair in plaits and in her dressing gown when the first of the fire alarm drills was held. He also encountered a number of other nurses such as Nurse Bull from Bairnsdale who knew a lot of the Buntine's family friends and Nurse Sproule from Kew, who was 'very nice indeed.' In addition, he met Nurse Vines, who was an aunt of Ernest and Geoffrey Vines, boys who had attended CGS.

Amongst his shipboard friends and acquaintances were Joe Warnock who was a sergeant in the Army, Buzzard and the boys from the 'Shop'. Others present were Dr Allan, Major Wood, Captain Jamieson and Captain Sam Fitzpatrick, who got off at Suez, Roy Hardy who was on duty with him at nights, Nelson, Ernie Phillips and Captain Cade, a doctor from the Boer War who knew his Uncle Robert.

Shipboard life on a long voyage was punctuated by a number of special events to help relieve the monotony of the trip and the first one Lyle reported was a celebration of Australia Day. It was not until at least 1934 that 26th January was universally accepted as the official Australia Day. During World War I, however, July 30th 1915 was designated as Australia Day, as a means of fund raising for the war effort by drawing on the pride that Australians had in their soldiers' achievements at Gallipoli and on their growing confidence in being Australian. Although Lyle was on Ward Duty and had to sleep during the day and miss the festivities, he reported that there had been all sorts of games and sports on the ship to mark the occasion.

The ceremony of 'Crossing the Line' took place the next day and although his hospital duties prevented him participating in events, he wryly reported that he didn't feel any bump as they crossed over. A fancy-dress ball was held for the officers and nurses to celebrate the occasion and although as a humble corporal he was not part of proceedings, he still managed to see some of the women's pretty costumes. At about the same time he remarked on the advantages of rank, as the sergeants lived in a nice saloon with afternoon tea, whilst he and his fellow corporals had an awful den.

Thoughts of his family were not far away, especially as the 1st of August was his father's birthday and although he wished him many happy returns of the day, Lyle wondered how he was getting on and if he was worried about the running of the school, but ruminated 'Still, I expect he will know that I am thinking of him.'

As a landlubber enjoying his first sea voyage many aspects of the journey and his surroundings provided a great fascination for him. 'The sea is wonderfully calm today with hardly even a swell. There are lots of flying fish about and some of them do some really good flights. Last night the sea was phosphorescent and we could follow the track of fish, mostly sharks. One of the boys caught a flying fish today as several of them flew aboard, or rather were blown aboard. We have run into a beautiful monsoon and most people are sick again. I have not succumbed yet, thank goodness. It is quite interesting to sit by the rail and watch the ship's screw coming out of the water.'

Enjoyable though these events might have been the realities of life on board a troop ship were ever present and he reported on 2nd August, just a few days before they reached the port of Aden of the death of one of his ship mates. 'A burial at sea. One of the most solemn ceremonies there is. A poor man in one of my wards died last night and was buried today. Laid on a plank, sewn up in canvas, the service was read, the plank tipped up, the three last volleys fired and then the 'Last Post' played on the bugles, a hymn by the band and all was over.'

Aden and the Suez Canal

Eventually after a voyage of fifteen days from Fremantle without sighting land, they anchored in the harbour at Aden. As they had approached the port they were surprised to find locusts being blown on board from some distance out from the land and apart from the occasional passing ship, these insects provided the only other example of terrestrial life they had encountered since leaving Australia. The men were not allowed off the boat and so once again Lyle was resigned to making more observations from his ship board perch as they spent some time in Aden and then made their way up the Red Sea towards the Suez Canal.

'It is night now and we are anchored in the harbour at Aden. I got a couple of photos of the rocky coast just outside of the harbour. It is beautiful here riding quietly on the waters with the pretty lights on the water and the natives coaling the boat. They are awfully funny and come around in boats and did a brisk trade in cigars and cigarettes. There is an auxiliary cruiser here (*The Empress of Asia*) with eight 4.7 guns on her. A camel corps went out of the town just now with about five hundred camels so it looks as if there is fighting near here. It is an awfully hot night but today has been lovely. We got under way at half past four this morning and about 10 o'clock got to the Straits of Beb-el-mandeb. We are now well in the Red Sea and it is quite keeping up its reputation for heat. It is great to get back to the steamer track again after being off it for such a time. The steamers are passing fairly frequently now and look very pretty at night coming up out of the darkness like a great phosphorescent whale and passing by and disappearing again quickly with a few flashes of the lamp to tell us who she is. It is very funny here at present living in our native garments with a pair of trousers and perhaps a singlet, though even that is too much. It is a bit hot for writing so will leave off and go to my bed which consists of a blanket spread on deck to lie on. The different colours of which the sea is capable is wonderful and today it is a rich indigo blue. The heat has considerably moderated owing to a head wind which keeps things beautifully cool.'

A variety of concerts was held for entertainment purposes and to support Australia Day on Friday July 30th. Amongst the many items were listed the following;

- *Recitation 'The Irish Fire Brigade' Gunner Brown*
- *Patriotic Song by Nurse Burkitt*
- *Trio with Violin Obligato 'I'd like to live in Loveland' by Mrs Malloy, Mrs Money and Miss Holdsworth*
- *Fancy Jumping by Sgt Woods the Champion High Jumper of the World*

Lyle also reported that the AAMC gave a sacred concert on one Sunday evening which was 'very nice indeed.' The 10th of August was his twentieth birthday and as to be expected his thoughts turned to his friends and family. He mused that he was certain that although they were a long way from him he knew that he would be held in their thoughts. As proof he remarked that had just received a wireless message for his birthday to that effect from his parents. Regarding it as a good omen he viewed Mt Sinai on his birthday and was able to celebrate his special day with a few boys from the 'Shop.'

Meanwhile the ship continued its slow passage to Suez and when they finally arrived the next day Lyle described the various scenes he witnessed. 'When we woke up this morning we were at Suez and anchored out opposite the entrance while we took on water and coal. The sea here is a wonderful blue and looking across it to the golden yellow of the sand makes it a very pretty picture. All the morning we were surrounded by the canoes and triangular shaped sails of the boats selling curios and souvenirs to the soldiers. During the afternoon the *Mongolia* came up and went off during the evening up the canal. She had a load of passengers including the wives of some of the officers and looked very pretty moving off. A beautiful day and it seems to be some Arab festival as all the town is decorated with flags. At eight o'clock this morning disembarkation began and the baggage was taken off and some of the infantry who were going by the early train to Cairo got off. The rest and the AMC are going by the afternoon train. Sam Fitz. is getting off here and I wish he was coming on with us. The boat moved over to the wharf and ran a gangway ashore so I got nearer to Suez than father did when he came through.'

It was at this point in the voyage that the other ten medical students disembarked to take up their duties at various AIF hospitals, with only Lyle Buntine and Douglas McCowan remaining on board. Lyle's letter at this stage give no hint as to why he had decided not to do the same, but the military world of regulations being what it is, some official reason must exist for the two of them to be able to continue their journey to England.

'In fact, since I wrote the last sentence I have been ashore. It is very funny watching the natives diving in for pennies which the boys were throwing in to them. They reaped quite a harvest and some of them went in with nothing on and then the black policemen would come along and chase them out of the water. Then again there were English and Australians who live here riding around on donkeys, so some of our boys hired donkeys and had a race. Would you believe it took all day to disembark about 600 troops and a few nurses? Anyway, we are in the canal now and leaving Suez further behind every minute. The Canal is different to when father passed through it as there are trenches and barbed wire entanglements all alongside, also a guard of Indian troops on the Arabian side. On the evening of the 12th we passed through a lot of the Canal and I did not see much. At the Suez end there was just the sand on either side and little oases in the shape of railway stations all along. This morning, 13th August we have got to a very pretty part of the Canal and although I thought the Canal was just a bare ditch all along its length here it is very beautiful. All along the Egyptian side there is a line of trees with the railway running between them. We passed an armoured train this morning. A queer little train coloured khaki with the engine in the middle and a couple of guns mounted on trucks. The stations are wonderfully pretty, all so green and fresh looking; quite a contrast to the sand on the Arabian side and a blessed relief to the eyes which have got quite tired looking at the sand around Aden and Suez. Port Said is in sight now, so will finish later. Just as we were coming into Port Said, after completing the journey of the Canal, we saw a sea-plane. It went up in full view of us. The engine started and it began to move slowly at first and then faster and faster along the surface of the water, like a swan taking flight and then rose and soared up into the air. It went out to sea looking for submarines. We spent all day coaling. The blacks running up and down the planks loaded with coal look like flies. There must have been 300 of them employed on the job. We were given leave to have a swim yesterday and I went in for about 20 minutes. It was great to get into the water again; but it was pretty dirty. The natives here are also very keen on diving for pennies. A lot of the men broke leave tonight and went ashore in the face of strict orders that no-one was to leave. A lot of them were caught, but I don't suppose anything will happen to them. The men are Australians and won't be kept in and the officers haven't sufficient go in them to catch them and punish them enough to deter them in future. The next day will be 14th August, and we are still in Port Said. A lot of the NCO's went off with the men last night. Silly fools! It will probably mean losing their stripes, though they may get off with a reprimand.'

Heading for England

August 14th 1915 would prove to be a watershed day in Lyle's life, because for the first time as a serving soldier he was confronted with the human tragedy and cost of the war, as it was on this day that the *Orsova* took on board some 300 wounded British and Australian soldiers from the Gallipoli campaign. These men were described by Lyle as more or less convalescent, but seemed to have every sort of wound and sickness amongst them. Some had lost arms or legs and some had been blinded, but he reported that they were all happy and delighted to be getting home again. Some of these soldiers would have been through the Australian attack and subsequent Turkish counter attack on Lone Pine in early August, whilst others had been involved in the disastrous charges at the Nek. With their tattered and torn uniforms, 'the bottoms of their trousers are not even hemmed,' and being paid only 1/- a day, they could certainly tell some grim tales of the struggle on the Peninsula. Lyle reported that one of the wounded men had been awarded the VC as he had single-handedly captured a Turkish mining tunnel. This was most likely a British soldier as no Australian winner seems to be the candidate.

Meanwhile in addition to sending a telegram to his parents, he prepared for his arrival in England by cabling to his South African cousin Jessie, the eldest daughter of his uncle Dr Robert Buntine, the elder brother of his father. Jessie and her younger sister Noelle were currently attending boarding school at Tunbridge Wells in England.

Portents of the U-boat threat became more evident the further their journey progressed and all portholes were now closed and blackened, all lights had to be out by 7.00pm, no smoking was allowed on deck, all the lifeboats were swung out and ready to be lowered at a moment's notice and rope ladders were suspended over the side. In addition, many of the men had to use life belts as pillows and sleep on deck. 'These preparations seem ominous of a danger that is ever present and we are beginning to feel that we are near the enemy at last. It does seem like a game though and as yet we have seen no cause to be disturbed.'

As any ship board traveller would do, Lyle passed comments on the sights and events taking place around him. He noted the arrival of a French cruiser escort, the sighting of Sicily, the view of beautiful fully rigged sailing ships and the *Orsova*'s receipt of a wireless message from the Eiffel Tower in Paris. His duties as the Orderly Corporal however, meant that he was not able to gain any more experience in the ship's hospital, a matter he quite regretted.

Military precautions when they docked at Gibraltar prevented a repeat of the episode in Fremantle where many Australians soldiers had left the ship without permission. This time they were warned that they would be shot if they attempted the same thing and for good measure the *Orsova* was surrounded by a guard of armed police. Interestingly at this late stage of the trip they took on board a 4.7 gun for protection against submarines; a point reinforced by Lyle's comment; 'We are all on the lookout for submarines. We are fortunate in having one of the best gunners in the service with us – a gold medallist – the sort of man who can hit a periscope at 1000 yards.'

The weather in the Bay of Biscay took a turn for the worse and after the calmness of the Mediterranean Sea, the instances of sea sickness laid many of the men low indeed. Lyle seemed to have gained his 'sea legs' by this stage of the trip, having only suffered at the beginning of the voyage as the ship sailed through the Great Australian Bight. In addition, for the first time he records the disgruntlement that some of his comrades are feeling after such a long confinement on the ship, as well as revealing his thoughts about taking on a new military career. 'There are two men in our corps who have done nothing but growl and argue since we left Melbourne. And the trouble is they don't only growl once or twice a day; but the whole time and they are worst at meal times. If things don't improve soon either they or I will have to go, in fact all the Medical students are anxious to get out of the corps into a field ambulance or a fighting unit.'

As they neared England and the very real threat of U boats was present, all the *Orsova's* watertight doors were shut in readiness for an emergency. Some torpedo boats circled around them all day as they neared landfall at Plymouth. 'Despite the fact that we were doing over 20 miles an hour the first torpedo boat was travelling about half as fast again. These torpedo boats are like little wasps and look like little toys alongside our boat, but mighty useful little toys they are too.'

The potential for disaster was reinforced to them when they learnt that the liner *Arabic* had been sunk by U-boat *U-24* four days before just off the south coast of Ireland with the loss of

40 passengers. Two Americans had been lost in this sinking and US President Wilson threatened to break diplomatic relations with Germany over the incident, although at this stage of the war the Germans still lacked sufficient U-boats to conduct all-out war on the high seas. Consequently, the German government undertook to halt the practice of attacking unarmed passenger ships without warning, however this action was probably based more on practical realities rather than for humanitarian reasons. The sinking had taken place not too far from the *Orsova's* own position and sailing course. In addition, Lyle reported that another boat had been sunk in their path early that morning and it must have been salutary for all those aboard the *Orsova* later in the day to sail through the wreckage from this ship, past an abandoned life boat and to see the bodies of victims in the water. Despite this event they sighted the coast of Cornwall in the mid-afternoon, sailed past the Eddystone Lighthouse and finally arrived safely in Plymouth at about 8.00pm on 23rd August 1915.

Lyle's arrival in England after a voyage of five weeks was the natural progression of his war service in the Australian Army Medical Corps and as a second-year medical student at the University of Melbourne, seemingly a logical choice of military career. But as later events were to prove, it also seemed that he was also amongst those of his medical comrades who wanted to transfer to another area of military service. The circumstances surrounding his initial army service in England and the chance of a life time that came his way were also critical factors in determining the course of the rest of his brief life.

Chapter 4:
Early Days in England

Arrival in England

The *Orsova* docked at Plymouth on 24th August 1915 and all the passengers including Lyle and his companions, were eager to set foot on dry land once again, however they had not received any directions as to how to proceed. Suddenly, about an hour after their arrival they were ordered to put on their marching uniforms and bring their kits on to the deck prior to disembarking. The troops had an awful rush in trying to achieve this and at the same time were told that they also had to unload all the officer's and nurse's kits as well. Lyle and his friends managed to complete these tasks in time to catch a 10.00pm train on which they travelled all night finally reaching the Naval Docks at Southampton at 4.00am the next day. To their shock they found that due to some administrative bungling, they had been loaded onto the wrong train and were now an orphan unit as they should have gone directly to London. 'We have arrived here and will now have to stop. It seems a pity, but really the English officers seem to be more incompetent than the Australians.'

To add insult to injury the AAMC unit was put under quarantine as there had been some cases of measles on board the *Orsova*. The conditions of their confinement were not too arduous as Lyle reported, 'We have finally arrived at the camp in a Park, or Common, as it is called here, which must be one of the most beautiful in England – covered with thick green grass and quite a forest of beeches and oaks, all of a lovely green and it is the prettiest site for a camp imaginable. It is like pitching a camp in the Botanical gardens. There are beautiful green lawns and forests of oak trees with the tents nestled in amongst them and pretty ponds scattered all about. I don't know whether the officers are supposed not to be infectious, but while we are kept here they can wander about the town. I seem to have the bad luck that whenever we go to a new place I am on guard the first night. I was on last night and we had two men to patrol 200 yards of frontage. Of course, a lot of the men went to town as well as some of the Warrant Officers and NCO's. It was the silliest farce I have seen and the English Tommies are very much amused. This morning we all went in for a swim in a cement-lined pond with beautiful white swans on it. We are supposed to be in quarantine; but we are swimming with the other soldiers again showing what a farce it is.' Finally, the embargo was lifted and they were all granted seven days leave, so Lyle went to stay at the Ivanhoe Hotel in London where his Colonel and a number of the unit's officers were also staying. He remarked that the English officers did not seem to be used to having NCO's such as himself staying in the same accommodation.

Travels in England

His surroundings were soon to change, as on his arrival he had received an invitation from his cousin Mima Frame inviting him to Scotland to spend some time with her and his South African cousins Jessie and Noelle Buntine, the daughters of his uncle Robert, his father's brother. He had missed seeing his uncle by only two days, as he had just sailed for South Africa the previous Saturday. Along with Mr Matthew White, his wife and their daughters Hetty and Meg, his relatives were staying at Elie, a little fishing village on the east coast of Scotland just south of Dundee. Lyle travelled by train to Edinburgh, over the Forth Bridge to Kircaldy, caught another train to Glen Leven and finally hired a motor car from the local garage to drive him to Elie. He received a hearty reception and he expressed the feeling that it was just like being at home as they were all so kind to him. Lyle soon did feel at home, although he described the local village as a quaint old place which looked like it had been built in the year one! He enjoyed himself by taking some walks in the summer weather along the beach and rocks and exploring some of the caves and being in Scotland and being relatively close to St Andrews, it was only natural that he also played some golf.

The White family left after a few days and in time Lyle returned to Edinburgh where he continued to take a number of photos and enjoy some sight-seeing. He visited the Castle, Holyrood Palace and walked down Princes Street where he enjoyed a free lunch at Mackies restaurant, courtesy of a woman motorist whose car he had helped to start. She had insisted on paying for the meal, as she said it was a pleasure to be able to do something good for the soldiers.

Returning to London on the night train, he finally had the chance to act as a typical tourist and see the famous city and over the next few weeks he recorded his observations. 'I went around Piccadilly and other places and saw quite a lot of London. Aren't the tubes great things? The moving staircases are bonzer arrangements and they have got a lot of them now fitted with the moving staircase where you go in and stand on the stairs and it moves and takes you up or down, running on an endless chain. The taxis are very handy too as you never have to wait more than half a minute for one. I quite got bushed in London a couple of times, but it is very handy to be able to call a taxi and he will take you anywhere. There are also crowds of policemen who know everything. I came out here on Sunday evening and during the day was strolling around London. I went to a service in Westminster Abbey which is a grand old place and the transept where the service was held was crowded. Then I had a walk over Westminster Bridge and round St James Park and Whitehall, round to Leicester Square, Piccadilly and The Strand. I have now spent five days in London but I hardly know 100 sq. yards of it. If you get into the centre you've got no hope of finding the way out without the help of a policeman. I went out to Hampton Court yesterday and wandered all over the beautiful gardens laid out by Henry the Eighth and Queen Anne. We saw the wonderful grapevines with clusters of beautiful black grapes. The girth of the stem is 5ft on the ground level and 4ft 7in. one foot above. We went also through the picture galleries and saw some famous paintings and tapestries. The gardens are beautiful and I suppose father will remember them, with the ponds and the fountains. I forgot to say I had a trip around the British Museum this morning and it is a wonderful place. The specimens of old Bibles were lovely and all so beautifully illuminated; you can quite believe it took years to copy them out. I also saw Scott's diary of his expedition to the South Pole. In most places his writing is firm and decisive, but, at the last, where he says, 'It is a pity but I don't think I can write anymore,' you can hardly read it as he was so weak when he wrote it. The Egyptian room is very good too with the old mummies and sculpture; but in one corner of the museum I found just one case devoted to Australia.'

Army Life Resumes

When his leave had finished, he returned to the Rest Camp at Southampton and had to adjust to the rigours of military life again. After a short period of recuperation, he soon found himself performing guard duties and a series of route marches each morning, which had to be undertaken at the pace of a forced march. Lyle noted that some of the English officers who were drilling recruits around the camp seemed to think they were at a singing lesson judging by their commands. These same officers called the Australian troops 'A Ragtime Army,' but Lyle noted that some of the English troops he saw were more like the Keystone Comedy Company of slapstick silent film fame. He also delighted in relating a story in which an Australian got the better of an English officer. 'I must tell you a story. All the English officers wear their stars or crowns on their sleeve instead of on their shoulder as in Australia. Well, the other night, when we were standing on the Plymouth Station, Major Woods was standing saying goodbye to some of the nurses, who were going off by an earlier train. The English Embarkation Officer came by, and glancing down at his sleeve saw no stars or crown and supposing him to be a private, grabbed him by the shoulder and said, 'Here, you look a good healthy man, give me a hand here with the luggage and don't stand talking.' The doctor drew himself up and looking at the officer, said, 'Sir, I'm a Major!'

Although he had not as yet seen combat, he was prepared to relate what others who had been through that experience told him. 'There are about ten Australians here going back on No.1 Hospital Ship who have been through the Dardanelles and are going back for a furlough. One of them got in the road of a machine gun and was hit 14 times and still has 4 bullets in him and all of them have wounds to show. The French soldiers seem to have a habit of advancing for 200 yards and then retire

100 English Tommies are catching this habit to the disgust of the Australians, who believe in sticking to a trench once they have captured it. When the word goes around 'Prepare to Charge,' they all crouch down ready and then up and over the parapet and as soon as they get near, the Turks throw down their arms and sing out 'Allah,' but that does not save them. They are good fighters with the rifle, but can't stand the bayonet at all.'

UP in the AIR!

Perhaps it was the solid training with deadly intent he was receiving, or the Gallipoli casualties he had seen, that now influenced him to take charge of the future direction of his military career and embark upon an even greater adventure, for his letters suddenly reveal a new interest. 'It is surprising the number of aeroplanes there are about in England. Even here at Elie, where we are, we saw one yesterday. It came down in a paddock alongside the golf links and we went over to see it. The aviator came down because the oil was splashing about and getting into his carburettor.'

And then literally out of the blue, he told his family of his great experience in an aeroplane. 'On Saturday afternoon, what do you think I did? Won't the boys wish they had been there too? I went out to Hendon and went up in aeroplane and it is a grand sensation. You get into a little seat behind the driver, the engine starts and away you go over the paddock until finally looking down you see the earth isn't quite where you thought it was, but quite an appreciable distance away. There is no jar of any kind when you leave the ground. We went for quite a long way and when we got back had just started to volplane down, when another biplane crossed our bows and we got the backwash from it. The plane stood right on its head and did a dive for about a hundred feet and then came back beautifully on to an even keel. There were a lot of aeroplanes there, some of them capable of taking six passengers besides the pilot. It is great being up and feeling that you have at last thrown off the fetters that hold you down on earth and soared away up among the clouds.'

Whilst the flight was exciting by itself, Lyle then wrote about his plans in a letter of 3rd September 1915 to his mother. 'I suppose you will be wondering what this is all about. Well, the reason is that I am applying for a commission in the British Army with an idea of transferring to the Royal Flying Corps. You know Arthur O'Hara Wood came over here to join it, and I have been thinking of it for a long time. It will be quite a change to mix with gentlemen instead of some of the men whom I have been with on the voyage over from Australia, because, by no stretch of imagination, could some of them be called gentlemen.' He concluded his letter by informing her that he had just that very morning received orders to attend an Officer's Training School on the 19th September and that if he was lucky he would get a transfer to the Royal Flying Corps (RFC) in about two months. Lyle also revealed that he had received a certificate of moral character from Dr Allan, a family friend who had also sailed on the *Orsova* and was now in command of Harefield House Convalescent Hospital in Middlesex. This facility was used as the No. 1 Australian Auxiliary Hospital from December 1914 until January 1919 and originally it was estimated that the house would accommodate fifty soldiers under winter conditions and 150 during spring and summer. At the height of its use it accommodated over 1,000 beds, mainly housing Australian casualties, and was supplemented by a large nursing and ancillary support staff. Lyle had been out to the hospital to see Dr Allan and had been invited to dinner one evening at the Palace Hotel which was only 100 yards from the Ivanhoe Hotel where Lyle was staying.

Colonel Appleton a family acquaintance from Brighton, had known Lyle for the past ten years in Melbourne and had also provided documentation of his good character. In his quest for these references, he had also visited the Commonwealth Offices in London to try and gain an interview with Sir George Reid the Australian High Commissioner and former Australian Prime Minister. Although unsuccessful he did get to meet his son and in addition met Lord Hugh Cecil, the famous statesman and gained an autographed note from him.

Old Boys Reunited

He continued to make contact with former school mates and friends from Melbourne, nearly all of whom had come to England to make their contribution to the war effort. 'You remember when Arnold Young left with his horse to join King Edward's Light Horse. About a month later a number of boys, all sons of wealthy station owners, came over here for the same purpose. I remember hearing of them leaving and it was common talk in Melbourne at the time as they were nicknamed the 'Millionaire Brigade.' Since they came over here they went, not into King Edward's Light Horse, but into the Royal Field Artillery. I met three of them yesterday and they hailed me as an Australian and mate. They were very decent fellows, but they made the money fly too fast for me.' Arnold Young (CGS 1899) was gazetted as a 2nd Lieutenant in the Royal Artillery and served with the 7th Division's T Battery at the battle of Loos, but was later killed on 4th October 1917 whilst serving with the 50th Brigade.

Lyle also recounted meeting up with other Caulfield Old Boys in London. 'I just met Jack Vines, a brother of Ernest and Geoff. He is in the 3rd Light Horse Field Ambulance and was sent to England supposed to have enteric fever, but it did not develop. Vickery, the 'Fighting Parson,' is in the same corps as a private in the nursing branch. Have many Old Boys enlisted since I left? I am going to try and find a news agent, where they keep the Melbourne *Argus* now. It is wonderful how hungry you get for news of home sometimes, and as no letters have come that is the next best thing. As I was walking down past Euston Station this morning, a boy came up to me and said, 'Surely you are Lyle Buntine?' It was Dudley Seelenmeyer. Isn't the world a small place? Think of meeting him over here after all these years. I met Keith Gardiner yesterday morning. He has had quite an exciting time, and after eight weeks in the trenches is now in England, on furlough. He has been ill, but is now quite recovered and is looking well. He has met a lot of the Old Boys out in the trenches and I got their names from him.'

Keith Gardiner (CGS 1910 – 12) had served at Gallipoli and was present at the battle of Krithia, however he became a victim of concussion after prolonged exposure to high explosives. Having served continually at the front for over 13 weeks he became ill, was granted a discharge and returned to civilian life in Australia. Keith's brother was John Gardiner, the fellow CGS 1911 athletics team member and University of Melbourne medical student who had sailed with Lyle on board the *Orsova*.

Zeppelin Raids

Life for Londoners took a tragic turn when the first raids from German Zeppelins hit the city in early September 1915. Due to the fact that the early airships were able to fly in excess of 50mph, operate at more than 9000ft, carry bomb loads of about 100lb and were fitted with 6 machine guns, they were capable of easily outdistancing and out-manoeuvring contemporary aircraft.

At the outbreak of war in 1914 the Imperial German Army had seven Zeppelin airships (prefix LZ) whilst the Navy (prefix L) only possessed two such craft, however a rapid program of expansion was embarked upon by both services. About eighty-eight Zeppelins were used during the war and of the sixty-one operational types, nineteen were shot down, eleven wrecked by weather and eleven destroyed by accidents or were bombed by the Allies in their sheds, about a 40% casualty rate. Both British air services, the Royal Flying Corps (RFC) and the Royal Naval Air Service (RNAS) bombed German Zeppelin sheds early in the war and with the destruction of others through accident and ill planned battle use, the Germans decided to severely limit the use of the airships; the Army limited tactical raids over the front line to darkness whilst the Navy increasingly saw North Sea reconnaissance as its main task.

These factors combined with the blockade of the German High Seas Fleet, saw airships diverted to independent operations and at the beginning of 1915 it was decided that they would be most effective against targets in England. London had also been chosen as a target, although the Kaiser had forbidden attacks on royal residences or other historic sites and only sanctioned bombing raids on strategic military and industrial targets. The airship's captains however, forced to fly at night, over cities and potential targets in a blackout and with limited navigational aids and bomb aiming devices, faced an impossible task in limiting their attacks and inevitably non-military targets were hit. London was also easier to reach than Paris, as no military front lines had to be flown over, and the German High Command reasoned that they would be able to bring terror to the civilian population and therefore weaken the will of the English people and politicians to continue the war. In this policy it was the first in history to attempt to defeat a country by attacking non-combatants rather than their armed forces.

The first attacks began against east coast British towns on January 1915, but it was not until the night of September 8th and

9th 1915 that London was bombed by the L.13 commanded by Kapitanlieutenant Heinrich Mathy, which resulted in twenty-two people being killed and eighty-seven being injured. Although Lyle was at his Army camp in Southampton at the time of the raid, a few days later he was an eye witness to the damage that had been caused. 'All England is pretty excited at present owing to the Zeppelin raid on London last night and on the eastern counties a couple of nights ago. Some of our men were in London at the time and helped to take some of the wounded to the hospitals. In London there were over one hundred victims and about fifty killed. It makes me wish I was in the Flying Corps now instead of having to wait. I went to the British Museum yesterday and in the evening went around with Meg White, who is in London to have a look at the damage caused by bombs from Zeppelins. In one place, one fell in Queen's Square and all the windows nearby are broken and holes smashed through the walls of all the houses. One bomb fell on a motor-bus and you can imagine how much was left.' Lyle's report of the casualties unsurprisingly, does not tally with the official figures.

The L.13 had been picked up by searchlights and had been fired at by all of the capital's twenty-six anti-aircraft guns but had remained unscathed. In total the capital was attacked some twelve times by Zeppelins between 1915 and 1917, when Britain's air defences improved to such an extent that the Zeppelins were replaced by the Gotha fixed wing bomber.

By the end of the war England had received fifty-two Zeppelin air-raids that had dropped some two hundred and twenty-five tons of bombs, had killed five hundred and fifty-seven people and injured another one thousand and seventy-eight. In causing some $7.5 million damage the airships had had a notable effect on Britain. In addition to having to deploy 12 RFC fighter squadrons with 110 crewed aircraft supported by 200 officers and

2000 enlisted men, over 12,000 artillerymen out of a total of 17,340 personnel were directly involved in Britain's air defence, effectively keeping them out of deployment to the front line. The British by the same token as the recipients of the bombing raids, recognised their strategic value and ensured that their future RAF policies were directed to this end. As to the Germans achieving their war ends through their bombing campaign it is clear that they did not achieve them. Ultimately the airships proved to be too vulnerable to the vagaries of the weather and the ever-increasing efficiency of the British air defences. Winston Churchill dubbed the raiders 'baby-killers' and the raids did little to damage British morale. If anything, they merely confirmed the popular image of the Germans as unscrupulous murderers of children and innocent people and who had to be fought and resisted at all costs.

Lyle goes Off to the British Army

Lyle had received another invitation to stay with the White's at Glasgow and so took the opportunity to explore some more of his English surroundings. He noted as he travelled by train that as they reached principal stations *en route* women would supply free cakes, coffee and tea to any serviceman. 'This is just one of the little things that the people are doing to help the Tommies. I have been received with open arms thanks to the boys at the Dardanelles, who have given Australia such a good name.'

The White family also proved to be awfully good to him and in addition to Mrs White insisting on being called Cousin Jessie, Mr White said that he was going to act 'in loco parentis' and was determined that Lyle should see Glasgow and that he would pay all his fares. Consequently, Lyle was able to visit such places as Renfrew, Paisley and its 11th century Abbey where Margaret the daughter of Robert the Bruce was buried. Returning through Parlick the home of the famous thread and cotton factories, Mr White also pointed out Glasgow University. The next day they took a steamer trip down the Clyde river past all the ship building yards at Greenock, Gourock and Kilcraigin. They observed that all of them were working as hard as they could and were most interested to see the Greenock works that were manufacturing 40 torpedoes a week, and others that were producing torpedo boat destroyers, submarines, as well as sea planes for the Royal Naval Air Service. Lyle noted that a lot of men were employed at these works, both paid and volunteers and that their work was so vital, that none of them could be spared for front line service. Indeed, he found it funny that in Glasgow and other large cities and towns including London, that women were fast taking the place of men in a range of occupations such as ticket collectors on trams and at railway stations.

The lack of money was a constant issue for him and more than once he had to cable to his father in Melbourne for an advance. He had not expected to be in England for such a long period of time and in particular to have so much leave, which meant more money was spent on train fares, hotel bills and food. Finding himself like everyone else, pretty hard up, he resorted to staying at the Central YMCA which wasn't a bad place, but had to sleep in dormitories with the British Tommies and found that it was not a pleasant experience. In the end, despite two further cables to his father, he took his father's advice and resorted to borrowing money from Dr Allan, who generously lent him a goodly sum which 'fixed me up beautifully.'

Lyle paid a visit to the War Office and he found that his application to gain a commission in the British Army had been successful, and that he had been gazetted to the 4th Battalion of the Notts and Derby Regiment, which was stationed at Tynemouth.

Whilst happy about the posting, he was philosophical about his financial state and future plans. 'While I am there, it will be pretty difficult to live on my pay, because nearly, if not all of it, will go in mess bills. However, when I get my transfer to the Flying Corps, it will be different as they are better paid. I am going up to London tomorrow to get my uniform and equipment for which I am allowed £50, but I don't think it will cover all I need including sword, pistol, binoculars, wrist watch, compass, wire-cutters for barbed wire entanglements and a lot of other things.'

In an interesting sidelight, he recorded that he played a cricket match against Hampshire's Eleven. Test and County cricket had been suspended during the war, but a number of games were played between representative teams and teams representing the various services and armed forces. 'We played a cricket match yesterday against the Hampshire Eleven. As several of Murray's heroes were playing, we had not much chance. In the opposing team were Jesse Hopkins (English XI), Haig (English XI), Meade (who plays in the English XI, but did not come to Australia) and Kennedy, the Hampshire crack fast bowler.'

Finally, after all his travels, financial concerns, sporting diversions, and visits with his family and friends, he collected his army uniform and accoutrements and travelled by train to Ipswich where he reported for duty in the British Army. He was surprised to find that he was not to live at the army base, but instead was to be billeted with a local family who had put their house at the disposal of the government. Putting on a civilian collar and tie for the first time in a quite a few months, he made his way to the house and was pleasantly surprised with the outcome. 'I am staying in a beautiful house, with their own hothouse for grapes and other fruit and who do you think it belongs to – Guess! You can't? Then to a Mr Grimwade – a cousin of the Grimwade of Felton, Grimwade & Co and also a cousin of Caulfield. He knows Charlie and Stan and a number of our other friends. Fancy meeting someone who knows our friends, and what a coincidence that I should be billeted on them. Isn't the world a small place? If the whole thing had been arranged it couldn't have been better.'

And so, a world away from home, but among friends, Lyle readied himself for the next part of his great adventure.

Chapter 5:
A Tourist in England

Settling In

On Sunday 26th September 1916 Lyle accompanied his British host, Mr Grimwade, a church elder to the 'Edward Grimwade Memorial Church.' The church had originally been named St Clement's Congregational Church after the suburb of Ipswich and the Church Hall was built in 1886 and named after the benefactor Edward Grimwade who had died the previous year. Lyle also enjoyed walks around the town of Ipswich and its lovely park; although he complained in a good-natured fashion that; 'The Park is a very fine one and this afternoon was quite full of people – mostly Tommies and their girls – and it quite made my arms ache answering salutes.' He observed the funny little sections of the town with their very narrow streets and the upper stories of the houses that leaned right out over the road. He did find the atmosphere at the Grimwades to be very nice indeed, and was reminded of his own home in Melbourne as they also held Family Worship every morning.

English Weather

Living in the southern part of the Australian continent and being used to warm summers, but mild winters, Lyle noted and recorded the difference in weather conditions in England and some of his preconceived notions were dispelled. 'I don't know whether it has been exceptional weather here or not, but my ideas of England have quite changed. It is almost into October and although I have been in England over a month now, I have only had one wet day and even then, it only rained lightly for about six hours up at Elie in Scotland. The weather is still quite warm and fine and I have been swimming up until last week. I don't know whether I remarked on the appearance of London at night which is horrible with every light out except those that are necessary. Here in Ipswich it is worse and walking along the streets at half past 8 seems as if it were after 12, they are so dark and silent.'

But by the very next day the weather had changed and the rains became more frequent and conditions suddenly turned bitter and cold, but with the enthusiasm of a newly arrived traveller, Lyle wrote home. 'We had an awfully sudden change today from beautiful weather to an icy cold day. It seems just like the middle of winter at home, but here the winter hasn't started. I'm looking forward to seeing an English Christmas while I am over here, with all the holly and the snow. It will be quite different from home.' A month later and on leave in London he again reported on the unusual weather conditions. 'I am at present in London and having my first experience of a London fog. The papers over here say that it is the worst for 2 or 3 years. It rolled up yesterday at about 3 o'clock, like a great thick yellow cloud and covered everything. Even during the day all the lamps had to be lit and the fog was so thick that, standing on one side of the road you couldn't see the lighted lamps on the other side. You will hardly credit this, but it is a fact. One of the other officers was with me and we got lost two or three times and found London policemen invaluable for putting us right again. While I am writing this, it is so beastly foggy, that I can hardly see the paper that I am writing on although it is midday.'

Finally, by the end of November 1915 he wrote home about a recent weather event and the much-anticipated events in the northern hemisphere. 'I wonder what sort of weather you are having in Melbourne? Probably the reverse of what we are having here. For the last week it has been freezing hard, not only at night, but during the day as well. About 5 days ago we had a fall of 4 inches of snow and it is still thick on the ground, so for the last week we have been drilling and marching in it. All the houses have a mantle of snow over them and the scenery is quite like the pictures we see of Christmas in England. We have no lakes or ponds near us, so we cannot have skating, but Cousin Mima has asked me to go and stay with her as soon as I can get leave and they have skating there.'

Although by the 3rd of January 1916, he observed that the days were becoming warmer, he was informed by the local people that even though they were through the worst part of winter, there would be more snow to come. As a keen amateur photographer Lyle was frustrated by the prevailing and then changeable conditions and ruefully lamented; 'I haven't sent any photos lately, but you can't take snaps during the winter; there is never enough light. On days when the sun is out, it is funny to see it at noon, only about 20 or 30 degrees above the horizon and of course South instead of North! We have had quite an exciting week as the weather has turned cold again, and it has been snowing steadily all day. You remember how at home we used to growl if we had to drill in the rain or when it was a bit cold. I'm beginning to find out what cold means now and to wish for a Melbourne

Summer's day and a North wind. However, it's all in a lifetime and as no ill effects have followed, I'm not going to growl.' Fortunately, by the beginning of March the elements worked in his favour and he was able to write about the beautiful scenery. 'When I woke this morning, I found that it had been snowing during the night and there was about 3 or 4 inches of snow on the ground. The sun was shining and as all the trees were all covered it was a perfect picture. I got some photos and will send them along when they are developed.'

Letters From Home

During the two-year period of his war service, Lyle was a prolific letter writer home, but it was not until late September 1915, four months after his departure from Australia, that he received his first news and contact from home, which came in the form of a cablegram from his father. Lyle remarked in a letter home a few days later that, 'I should get some letters in about a month or so and it will be jolly when they come. Don't forget to let me have plenty of news about everything.'

In the event it was not until late October and a chance visit to Jessie and Noelle Buntine, his South African cousins at school in England, that he received his first letter from his mother. 'I got your letter today posted on by Jessie, and it is funny that I had just decided to come down to Tunbridge Wells this weekend to see the girls at their school. You can imagine my excitement this morning on getting a letter from Jessie and opening it to find one in your handwriting. I believe they thought I had gone suddenly daft. But there was some excuse for me as this is the first letter I have received from home. It was lucky that you thought of sending this letter to Jessie for me and I was glad to get it. When you write, you can't say too much, as any news of home is acceptable. It's rotten being such a long way off and letters taking such a long time to get across.'

The frustration of being a long-distance correspondent, especially during a time of war showed through at times in his writings especially as the deliveries were somewhat intermittent. Thus, he could write home in October and November; 'I have just received your letters dated 19th September. You do not say whether you have received any of mine. I have written by every mail and sometimes more than one letter. I am writing this in the Club and have just finished sending off a lot of Christmas cards. I hope they get there in time. I have not had a letter for over two weeks and I don't know why.' But mail from home did arrive in December, his mood changed markedly as it had come in time for him to enjoy their contents before Christmas. 'Great excitement! My letters have arrived at last. Two from you dated Oct. 12th and 17th, so I must have got two weeks' mail at once. I also got very nice letters from Murray, Arnold and Bobbie. I received the school magazine and have had several newspapers and last week I got a pair of socks done up in a linen bag. I don't know who sent them, as there was no note attached. I stayed in and read all this morning and went over a lot of your letters again, in addition to some I got yesterday. I got two from you yesterday which were the postcards of your trip to Warrnambool and another letter. I do look forward every Saturday to the letters from home.' But the reminder of the circumstances of war was ever present in early February 1916, even in something as simple and common place as the delivery of mail as Lyle contemplated the effect on shipping of a German merchant raiding ship at large on the seas. 'The mails must have been delayed owing to the *Moewe* being about, because I got no letter last Saturday.'

Meeting People from Home Especially Caulfield Grammarians

For someone a long way from home and in age when communication was mainly by letter and the occasional cable (telegram), to meet up with a former school mate, acquaintance or friend of his father from home was especially significant and Lyle took joy in recording these occasions and reporting them to his family. 'You mention in your letter that Mrs Gardiner heard that her son Keith was deaf. You ought to have my letter by now telling you that I saw him at Southampton and he was quite recovered. I am very sorry to hear that Horace Harton (CGS 1905 – 12) has been killed. Who do you think I met last night? You'll never guess, so I had better tell you – Lloyd Reade (CGS 1905 – 09). I recognised him at once, but he didn't know who I was at first. He was looking well and happy and is a private in the South Australians, but has applied for a commission and is getting it this week. We swapped addresses and will try to keep in touch. He was wounded in two places, in the thigh and the shoulder, but is now right again. Here's another surprise. I was in one of the wards of the Harefield Park Hospital and ran across MacMillan from Metung, Gippsland. He said he met you and father and Murray, when you were up there for the first time. It was interesting to see him and yarn to him. He also is trying for a commission, but has to come back to Australia for a while first, so he says he will call on father when he gets there. I have spent all to-day down at the hospital as it is a real little bit of Australia and I enjoy going.'

Later in his British Army experience he noted that, 'The Captain in charge of our Training Company is Captain Davenport and he is a cousin of George Davenport, who was so ill at school. It is quite a coincidence that I should be under George's cousin.' And in wistful reminiscence of how his life had changed so rapidly, he noted to his mother in early February 1916, 'At this time last year I was up on Alec Langland's station at Medowra. It seems a long, long time ago.'

Friendships

Given his discharge from the AIF to pursue a career in the British Army, he had had little chance to make and enjoy enduring friendships, and although family and their friends welcomed him with open arms, he often found that his service life was a lonely one. His friendship with Sydney Davis, a fellow officer that he made as a result of his time at the British Army School of Instruction, certainly helped him to settle into the life of a serviceman, especially as both men were a long way from home. Davis had some family connections in England, so both men were able to enjoy some time of relief away from the Officer's Training School barracks and service life in general.

Sydney Davis was a Canadian, 'a colonial as well,' trainee officer and was also staying in the same house and together they both shared some experiences together during their training. 'The instructions finished about half past 4 and then I went on with Sydney Davis through some lovely woods and fields with coveys of pheasants and partridges in them. We also saw quite a lot of rabbits and I began to wish I had a gun. Grenville would have liked to be there. In places, the country was just like the road from Sale to Prospect and altogether we had a very enjoyable afternoon and went about 10 miles on our bikes. We only worked in the morning today, and much to my surprise I was told we could have the week-end off, so I went down to London with Davis. He asked me to go and stay at his Aunt's for the night, so I went with him. It was funny getting out there as he forgot the way and it was about half past 8 at night before we got there. They live out in Richmond, quite close to Hampton Court Palace. This evening Davis and I went over a munition factory and saw all the different stages in the making of shells and mines, of which there were plenty and it was most interesting. He also wants me to go down to his home in Cornwall with him.'

Events conspired to delay Davis on this journey in late October 1915, but eventually they were on their way and pleased to play the role of tourists. As usual Lyle's keen eye for detail painted a vivid picture of what they saw and experienced. 'I am now waiting at the hotel for Davis, who was to be here at one o'clock, but it is now half past so we have missed our train. I have just had a telegram from Davis and the train has been held up at Woolwich, so I'll have to wait another hour or so. A pea-soup fog has just rolled up like a wet blanket and gone off, so things are brighter now. Davis turned up at about half past 4 and we started for Minehead by the 6.30 train. If you look at the map of England, you will see Minehead on the south coast of the Bristol Channel. The train got into Taunton at half past 10 and we found that it didn't go to Minehead, (about 24 miles further on) so we hired a big Napier car with a closed in body and finished the journey in style at about forty miles an hour, arriving at our destination at about 12 o'clock. It was a beautiful drive and although it was showery, we were tucked in warmly and thoroughly enjoyed it. I went for a walk this morning and saw some very interesting places, one old church especially, built in the 16th century with most beautiful carvings in it and a 14th century font. Some of the fittings for candlesticks are of iron with brass tops and very old indeed. There are several very old houses about, built in the 14th century and some of them have a funny little flight of steps leading up to a stone about three or four feet just alongside the door. This is called the 'Hopping Stone,' and was used for mounting their horses. I'm afraid it doesn't say much for the 14th century horsemanship. There is part of an old cross here, with steps leading up to it built in the 14th century and called the Alcombe Cross. All the houses have stone walls and were built in the early times. There is an old place called Dunster Castle, that I must see before I leave. This month has been heralded in by some real English November weather and today is showery, with a bleak east wind and very cold, but as I have been going all morning, I have not felt cold. This morning I went up to Dunster Castle and was shown around by Mr Davis, who is the agent and bailiff of the estate. We passed through the village of Dunster, where I went through the Luttrell Arms Hotel and got some picture postcards which I am sending you. From there we went on through great iron gates and up a winding drive to the Castle, which loomed above us like some grim sentinel of the coast. Oh, what tales those walls could tell, if the powers of speech were vouchsafed them. Many of them are six and seven feet thick, with secret doorways and panels opening into them at the most unexpected places. What slaughter they have seen! What sieges they have stood! Until in the time of Cromwell they saw their last fight and afterwards the "Keep" was pulled down, and in the place where it stood the shock of many a fight, there now is — a bowling green! There is in the castle a most beautifully carved staircase with the date carved into it – 1681 – so it is not as old as the other parts of the castle and inside there are some beautiful examples of Chippendale furniture. The Luttrells were offered £2000 for one piece alone. In King Charles' bed-room, where he slept, there is a secret panel leading into the passage in the wall and, at the end of this, there is a room where Charles the Second hid while they searched for him. The church here is very interesting and in it is a most lovely screen carved from oak. In the old days of the church the dues used to be paid "in kind," i.e. in so many sheaves of corn, so many head of cattle etc. and all these were placed in a big barn in the churchyard called the "tythe barn." This is still standing, also an old dove-cote, where pigeons used to roost and could be got for the Vicar's table when needed. I wish father could see these relics as he would like them very much, so I am trying to give you a good description. One thing I forgot to mention is a desk full of valuable old documents.

One dated 1154 is the confirmation of a grant of land by Henry II to Reginald Fitzurze who was one of the murderers of Thomas A'Becket. I left Minehead at 10 o'clock this morning and was in the train nearly all day passing through Bristol and Bath and in the evening, I went around to see Meg White.'

Unfortunately, events conspired against the two men further cementing their friendship through more shared experiences as Davis was transferred from the Office's Training Course to take up his post in the Army, leaving Lyle to contemplate his own situation as the year drew to a close. 'I am sitting writing this in the Sunderland Club. It is really a very nice place indeed, and I am grateful for the use of it as we can't get any other place to write and read in quiet, and I have not made any friends in Sunderland. I am playing a lone hand here at present and my only relaxation is to get down to Harefield Park in Middlesex and see Dr and Mrs Allan. It is now about two months since I was there, so I am going down next Sunday.' A week later he wrote; 'I am pretty much by myself here, as there are no men I care to chum up with. I'll be glad to get out of this to the Front.' And finally, in mid-December, Lyle wrote ruefully, 'Syd Davis is now in the Royal Fusiliers and is down in Kent, so we have more or less lost touch with one another.'

Family Interludes and Other Visits

For most Australians of the time, and indeed for many other members of the Empire's forces stationed in England during their military service, it seemed like coming 'home' and seemed even more so if they were able to establish contact with members of their extended family. Fortunately, for Lyle this was the case as two of his younger female Buntine cousins, Jessie and Noelle the daughters of his Uncle Robert, were attending school in England during the war. In addition to holidaying with them and others in

Scotland, he took the opportunity to visit them at their school in Tunbridge Wells in late October; a visit he reported to Murray his next youngest brother. 'I felt like singing 'Put me on an island where the girls are few' today. I went down, as I told mother to see Jessie and Noelle at Tunbridge Wells. I saw them all right and then they took me round to have a look at the school and introduced me to a lot of the girls. You should have been there. You would probably have enjoyed it.'

Matthew and Jessie White and their adult daughters lived in Glasgow and Lyle was 'adopted' by the family very early on in his stay in England. A married son also named Matthew lived in another part of the city with his wife Dorothy and baby and Lyle was able to enjoy their hospitality and also take part in the normality of family life, especially when marking special occasions and events. Being his first time away from home and especially in late December, Lyle enjoyed celebrating all that the Christmas season had to offer, even if at the same time he found the occasion to keep in touch with his former medical studies. Amazingly he was able to carry out this unique visit to the University on Christmas Eve! 'I rolled out of bed about 10 o'clock and went to Princes Terrace, where Mr White asked me to stay for Christmas. He was at the office, so I went around there and we had lunch in town together and then went to Mr Young's place for dinner. Today is Christmas Eve and everyone is busy decorating the place with holly and mistletoe. In Scotland, however, they don't do much at Christmas, all the merrymaking is kept for New Year, which I am told is quite exciting. I went down to Glasgow University to have a look round. I found a couple of Med. students who took me round the Med. School and Chemical and Physical laboratories. In the Physical Lab. one of the students was doing vivisection on a couple of rabbits. They also took me round the Hospital and showed me the operating theatres, so I passed quite a pleasant morning. This afternoon I am going down to the station to meet Meg's sister Hetty, who has been away and is coming back for Christmas. Meg is coming today as well, but by a later train. Mrs White, who makes me call her Cousin Jessie, wishes to be remembered to you. Although I do feel lonely sometimes, I am all right now at Glasgow with the Whites, who are awfully good to me. I do hope that all at home are well and happy as I am, and having a good Christmas. I forgot to say, that I received a very nice letter from Uncle Bob. I sent him a photo when I posted those to you. Glasgow is awfully crowded now with people from the country and seems likely to continue so during the New Year week.'

During his stay with the White family he was able to give a daily report on the budding romance of one of the daughters. '5/1/1916 We got a telegram that Donald Patterson was coming and would be here this morning, so Hetty got up early and went to meet him. She didn't seem to want me around either – funny thing! 7/1/1916 Hetty and Donald are going stronger. 8/1/1916 The engagement announced. Well I wish them luck. They are a good pair.'

The engagement also precipitated other re-arrangements in the White household which would directly impact upon Lyle and his ability to further enjoy the hospitality of the White household, as he reported a few days later. 'Please excuse the paper, but even this seems hardly adequate to what I want to say. For a start, it's Murray's (Lyle's younger brother) birthday today and I am thinking of him, but I'm afraid I didn't remember in time to send him a birthday letter. Here goes for some news of the people over here. Mr and Mrs White are giving up the house in Prince's Terrace in Glasgow and going to live in Prestwick. Hetty became engaged about a week ago to a Canadian, named Donald Patterson. Meg is practically engaged to Captain Alexander – a very nice fellow and so you see Mr and Mrs White are quite alone now. Cousin Mima is still at the school in Melrose and (Miss) Murray Richardson is with her. Noelle and Jessie are at school at Hamilton House in Tunbridge Wells. I met another cousin of ours, a sister of Mrs White, called Mary Lyall and it's funny her son's name is Murray Lyall; she is the youngest sister of Mrs White. I also went around to see Walter Frame and he asked to be remembered to Father. So, I am now getting my letters addressed to Mr White's business address where they are then forwarded to me.'

Visits to his cousin Mima at Melrose also provided him with a chance to be with family and friends and to see some more of the countryside. His visit to her in mid-March 1916 was the weekend when he returned to Sunderland to find his immediate transfer to the RFC waiting for him. His letter home reveals no knowledge of this order at all at the time he wrote it. 'Today is Sunday and I am writing in the front room of Cousin Mima's. I got here last night and she met me at the station. It is quite a small visit, as I have to leave for Sunderland again at 11 o'clock tonight. This morning I went with Murray (Richardson) and Sheila R. to Melrose Abbey and had a walk along the banks of the Tweed. I did not stay out long, as it was snowing all the time and was quite damp.' The very next letter he wrote was the first one from his RFC Training School at Wantage Hall four days later.

Harefield Hospital

Other opportunities presented themselves for Lyle to meet up with friends from Australia in order to receive advice, support and hospitality and one such chance was with Dr Allan and his wife at Harefield Hospital. Dr Allan had sailed with Lyle from Melbourne on the *Orsova* earlier in the year. 'I got to bed early last night and was up fairly early this morning and then went into Paddington Station to catch a train for Denham, which is the station for Harefield, where the big Australian Hospital is and where Dr Allan is in charge. There are, as I think I told you, several University boys out there. It was quite like going back to Australia to get there. Everyone there is Australian – patients, nurses, doctors and orderlies. They are so much more friendlier and freer than the English. Dr and Mrs Allan asked me to dinner with them and there were two other doctors there who came over on the boat with us. They are all good fun and I spent the pleasantest day since I have arrived in England. Dr Allan was just about to write to me acknowledging the receipt of a letter from me and to let me know that father had cabled the money. I was rather hard up for a while and had to have it, but now am all right again and getting on famously. The boy, Sydney Davis, with me is very quiet and does not spend much money on anything, so I am being quite a miser too as while I am here, I am going to save as much as I can for, I don't know when I may need to spend again. At Harefield I dined on pheasant for the first time. Mrs Allan has a lovely little house, just a stone's throw from the hospital, so she and the doctor can see quite a lot of each other.'

Money Matters

The question of his finances always seemed to be a problem to Lyle and although he was not wasteful, a recurring theme through his correspondence was that of his financial circumstances and arrangements. 'I received a letter this morning from Mr White, in Glasgow, which was an agreeable surprise as he had re-addressed one from Cox's Bank, where I have my account at present. In the letter he enclosed a cable from father and one to himself as well. It is awfully good of father to send the money over and although perhaps I can't say quite what I want to get, I thoroughly appreciate his kindness as cash is getting rather short again after the Christmas vacation. I did a bit of travelling and spent most of what I had. My teeth are beginning to be ready for a trip to the dentist and I have to pay that myself.'

Inshaws at Gartcash

Lyle was by nature a curious person and 'technology' in all its forms had fascinated him even since his school days when he learned to tinker around with primitive radio contraptions. The chance to visit a large family of Scots who welcomed him with open arms was a most welcome event indeed and helped him to once again enjoy the simple pleasures of family life. What made this family most unusual however, was the inventive streak of the father and also that of the oldest sons. No ordinary family, they were actively using their inventions to enhance their life style as well as working to provide technological advancements for society at large. Lyle first spent time with the Inshaw family at their house at Gartcash on the outskirts of Glasgow in early June 1916 and then was invited back again the following weekend. 'You were asking whether I have warm clothing, yes, I have got a complete new stock of underclothing, and still have plenty of socks, so I am all right. In my last letter to father, I mentioned that I had been invited out to a place near Glasgow by Inshaw. I left on Saturday afternoon, and went out to a place called Gartcash by train and two of his sons met me there in a car and drove me home. Most of the way is along a private road through beautiful fields and woods. The house is a big one, standing in its own grounds and they have shooting and fishing rights for their estate.

When I got there, they made me welcome and were very good indeed. There is a private picture theatre and machine fitted up and we went and had a picture show in the evening. The machine is worked by a water motor, and so nobody needs to keep turning the handle. Altogether it was a most successful evening. After the show we came in and had supper and then some of the guests left and others, who were staying, went up to bed. On Sunday we went for a walk round the estate, as there is no church nearby. In fact, it is quite like Australia and felt quite like home. They wouldn't let me go on Monday, so I stayed and came away today. As I said, they are a family of engineers, and I found I was in a perfect hot bed of mechanics. Mr Inshaw has several inventions and patents to his credit, not the least being an electric clock over the house, and they are all connected up and run by electricity and no winding or attention of any kind is required. And where do you think the current comes from? The Earth! There are plates of zinc and copper buried in the ground and from these they get enough electricity to run the clocks, so there are no batteries to run out. Another thing (by the son this time). He has invented a marvellous motor engine. It is like nothing else on earth; but develops an amazing power for a very small weight. I think it is the coming engine of the century for aviation work and is the only really rotary engine in existence. He has two of them constructed and they travel at a tremendous rate. Next time I write I will probably be back in camp in Sunderland again. I have spent a very nice week-end and had a thorough good time. The Inshaws have been very kind to me indeed and the family are about my age. There are three girls and five boys, so they are a very jolly lot. Later that month he wrote, 'I went out and met a naval friend of mine, and had tea with him and a friend of his and also a game of billiards. Then in the evening I met John and Ralph Inshaw and they seemed anxious to have me next weekend as well. Very decent of them and I'm on, as it is a bonny place. I said goodbye to the Whites this morning, and went into town for lunch, then caught the train for Gartcash. Ralph met me with the car and took me back to Lockwood. In the afternoon we played a little billiards and then went to the private theatre and had the Cinema all the evening. We all lay in bed a bit this morning and then went for a quiet stroll through the woods and along the banks of a pretty little loch. Soon after dinner I had to leave and they took me back to the station in a car and I caught the train for Glasgow where I got the Newcastle train. It was late when I arrived so I stayed in the hotel overnight.' As Lyle's military life progressed, he was able to maintain contact and visit the Inshaws on a number of occasions, even up right until his final days in Scotland in 1917.

More Sightseeing

The life of a tourist in the mother country was one that Lyle took to with great enthusiasm and as a keen observer, related the scenes that he saw in a lively and interesting manner. In particular he was always keen to highlight something unusual for his readers. 'The rain cleared up in the afternoon and we were driven out in the Grimwade's car, which is a Ford, to see an English country farm. It belongs to Mrs Grimwade's son-in-law and is a very nice place indeed, quite a big one for England. They have about 150 acres. In addition to the farm they have a flour mill. What impressed me most was the greenness of everything and the number of pheasants and partridges about. In fact, the whole place round here is thick with game, but no one is allowed to shoot without a gun licence and even then, they must get permission from the man who owns the shooting rights.'

By contrast he also enjoyed relating about his travels in popular tourist spots and he wrote to his brother Murray. 'This old London is a fascinating place, especially the tubes. You come to a little place in the street and you go down about six steps, then into a lift which holds about 40 or 50 people and down in it about 200 feet and come to an underground city. At some of the stations they have moving staircases instead of the lift. I am, at present, in London. I went to Church this morning in Tunbridge Wells with Jessie and Noelle and tonight I am going off to Ipswich. I have been doing pretty well in the matter of leave lately and have managed to get from next Friday to Wednesday off. I went for a trip round through Newcastle and Shields yesterday on a motorbike. I went about 40 miles and enjoyed myself immensely. Whitley Bay is very pretty and I am sure you would like it. I intended to go to Melrose to see Cousin Mima next weekend, but find that I have to go to London on military business, so will have to put it off. Later I went with another boy to Durham which is a very interesting old town. The streets are about half as wide as the London streets and in some places, they are only six feet wide. We went and had a look at the Cathedral, which is a most beautiful piece of architecture and attended a service there. It took eleven parsons and about 100 of a choir including three old chappies all dressed up and carrying sceptres, to run the service. Coming back on the motorbike, the chap I was with, got a puncture and as he did not know much about it, I had to mend it for him. Then we found the water in the lamps was frozen and they wouldn't drip, so you can imagine the temperature, and we had to go to a house and get them thawed.'

Observations Of England

As a great supporter of the British Empire and feeling that he was 'home' in England, Lyle was also a keen observer of those things 'English' around him and as any traveller would do, was prepared to pass judgment on what he saw and experienced. Despite his opinions and some disconcerting experiences with some of his officer colleagues, he still found time to make note of some quaint English customs. 'We are just starting Lent and that is observed very much in England. The 1st March was St David's Day and as he is the patron saint of the Welsh, all the Welsh soldiers were celebrating and wearing leeks in their hats. The leek is the Welsh national symbol and is used a great deal on the table just about that time. Today is Shrove Tuesday and we all had pancakes for lunch; why I don't know, but it is the custom here. In one school in London they have a custom on Shrove Tuesday of tossing a pancake over a bar in the big assembly room and the boy who secures the largest piece gets £1. Rather queer custom.' He also found the ability to move around the country to be relatively easy, even given the restrictions of making journeys in war time. 'There is one thing about England, you can travel quickly. It is 110 miles from Ipswich and the journey can be done in 2 and a half hours; not counting time for changing in London.'

In particular, given his family background, that he was an Australian and that he might have been seen as an 'old man' of 20 years of age, he was somewhat scornful of his brother officers at the Officer Training School. 'I don't care too much for the (English) officers over here. Some are very decent, but some are the real 'Lah-di-dah,' 'Bai-Jove,' 'Don't cher know' brand.' He was able to pursue some sporting pursuits which he related to his parents. Morning. 'The officers here at the Sunderland training school are having a football match this afternoon and I had a chance of playing, but thought I might spoil the match as I don't know the game. They play "Soccer" and you can't touch the ball with your hands. Evening. Feeling very stiff! When I got down there, they were a man short so I played after all. For the first half I didn't do much as I was studying the different points of the game, but in the second half I got on better.' But his opinions of some of his fellow trainees were quite judgemental.

'Today has been much the same as usual with a little signalling in the morning, which wasn't too bad. In the evening a couple of the boys here got drunk and made a fuss. It seems rotten to think that boys of 17 and 18 can be officers and really the younger they are, the more they seem to drink. Probably they think it looks manly and they don't think about what the older ones say of them. There is a lot more ale and beer drunk than in Australia; where we have tea for dinner, they have ale. There is a dickens of a row here at present. The others are playing every sort of song from 'Sister Susie' to 'My Butterfly' and shouting at the top of their voices. It reminds me of the YMCA tent at Broadmeadows. The life here is usually pretty quiet; but we have our little excitements occasionally. Usually someone is drunk, which is one of the chief reasons why I want to get away somewhere else. For instance, as I am writing, there are a lot of the 'boy-officers' very merry just in the next room. One of them has a bad habit of firing a revolver round discriminately when he is drunk, which is rather disconcerting. I heard one old Captain say that there is more drinking among officers now than there has been since the old days in India.'

Opinions of Australia

As Lyle himself related, he was not averse to 'pulling the leg' of wide-eyed English people. 'I happened to mention to one of the officers here, who was a "farmer" before the war, about the 1400 acres of wheat on 'Meringa.' He didn't exactly call me a liar, but said he didn't believe me. The farmers over here with their 100 acres or so are a most narrow-minded lot. In fact, I got quite angry with this particular one when I mentioned the size of Langland's place at Medowra and he said it was quite impossible for anyone to manage it.' Not knowing the 'farmer' officer concerned, it is not possible to tell the source of his skepticism about the size of Australian farms, it is possible that he might have at some stage fallen prey to the well-known practice of Australians telling 'tall tales' to unsuspecting listeners. 'The people over here don't know much more about Australia than they did when father was over here. A chap asked me which part I came from the other day and I told him 'Victoria.' He said, 'That's in Melbourne isn't it?' I agreed with him. I usually think these sorts of people are too good game to lose and tell them thrilling yarns of hair-breadth escapes from angry kangaroos. One they seem to like is a tale of a fight for life I had with a wombat. Then they are always interested in a description of a Paddy-melon tree and that ferocious beast, The Sun-downer.'

Often events would conspire to provide reminders of home and the life that he missed whilst living so far away from family, friends and familiar surroundings. 'We had a little piece of the 'Back to Nature' business about 2 days ago. We were out on an Outpost scheme and I with two or three others was with a sentry group. We had nothing much to do, so one boy sprinted off to a shop a little way off and got some tea and sugar, and we lit a fire and boiled the billy, I mean the mess-tin and had tea. By the way, the people over here, don't know what a billy is or a swag either. While if you mention 'Matilda's' or 'Jumbucks' they ask you what language you are using and I have to reply with dignity 'English as spoken in Australia.' 'I received the papers, i.e. *Argus* and the *Speech Day Report*, also an *Australasian* and a *Punch* from R.R. I often think of the bush at home and experience what I think is known as 'The Call of the Wild,' and on these occasions I usually get a bike and go out of the town to somewhere I can sit and think of home with no-one to disturb me.'

At other times, however events went in his favour. 'I've just had a chat to an Australian doctor. I knew his face but didn't know his name. I went up and spoke to him and he said that his name was Meakin. He knows the school well, he says. It's funny, if I meet a Melbourne man and mention that W.M. Buntine of Caulfield Grammar is my dad, they are friends at once.'

War Happenings

Apart from meeting friends and new acquaintances, there were many reminders of the war all around people in the form of armed personnel and military units in the streets, recruiting drives and the constant activity by all sections of the population directed towards the war effort. One aspect of this conflict that marked it out from others, was the direct effect of battle visited upon the civilian population of England. Whilst some coastal areas underwent some shelling from German ships offshore, the most immediate and direct threat at this stage of the war in late 1916 and early 1917 came in the form of aerial bombing by Zeppelin airships. While stationed at Ipswich, Lyle experienced these machines first hand and later in his stay in England, also had the chance to see some of the destruction caused in London by their attacks.

'On another day I went down to the Coast and saw some of the guns for defence against both ships and Zeppelins. They are beauties! We had another Zep. raid last night (12/10/15) and they came right over Ipswich and dropped four bombs here. I suppose you will have heard of the effects at London. When you are a long way off you don't think much of them, but when they are overhead it is quite interesting speculating as to where the next bomb will drop. It was about half past eleven at night and I had just got off my clothes and was about to get into bed and had turned out the light and opened the window. Outside it was very foggy and I looked out and wondered if we should see anything of the Zeppelins. Suddenly I heard an explosion which seemed to shake all the windows, then another and another and then a fourth. By this time, I was out in the garden and we could hear the whirring of the propellers overhead quite plainly. Then the anti-aircraft guns started firing and driving them out to sea. After waiting awhile, we went into bed and went to sleep. About one o'clock in the morning, another Zeppelin came by, but I didn't hear it, as I was asleep.'

The raids continued into early 1916 and Lyle reported on their immediate result and by direct cause and effect to the British War effort. 'We want all the men we can get, if we are going to win this war. In England the Derby scheme seems to be working very well and several of the groups have been called up already. Then we had another Zeppelin raid last week and that always gives a big impetus to recruiting. Oh! By the way, I forgot to say that the Zeppelin season has started again. It opened on Thursday night (10/2/1916), when all the lights were suddenly put out. I was in the Club at the time and in company with several other officers, immediately hurried home. Orders were then given for no-one to leave camp until the raid was over, so we stayed in and had an impromptu concert that turned out very well.'

Lyle felt despair at all these events around him and even began to doubt himself, and in a rare insight painted a bleak picture of the war to his family at home. 'In your letter you seem to be worrying about me; you know a bad penny always turns up in the end and I'm sure to sometime, when this beastly war is over. I am beginning to wonder myself when it will be over. It is really much more serious than people in Australia think, and we seem to have come to a dead-end, with no chance of moving till after the winter. I am anxious to get out to the Front as I feel I have been in England long enough and I really want to get out and do my bit.'

But at home in Australia life went on despite the impositions caused by the war, but sadly the death toll of Caulfield Grammarians who had 'gone out and done their bit' continued to mount. For the boys at Caulfield Grammar School life continued in a relatively normal fashion, but a number of key changes entered their lives as a constant reminder of the terrible conflict being fought so far away. The School Magazine, avidly read by Lyle and other Grammarians on active service, reflected these events in a number of ways in both its direct reporting of events and in the general tone it adopted in describing the deaths of Old Boys and the mounting toll.

Life at CGS in 1915

In 1915 CGS competed in the SAAAV Swimming Sports at Brighton Baths and the undefeated 1st XVIII won the SAAAV football premiership for the third year in succession. The Victorian Football League (VFL) saw a number of teams withdraw from competition during the Great War, mainly because some people believed that fit, healthy, young men should be serving at the Front and not indulging themselves in sporting pursuits. Schoolboy football by contrast continued unabated throughout the duration of the conflict, as headmasters viewed it not only as a healthy pursuit, but as an excellent team sport designed to prepare young boys and men for military service. CGS was also engaged in the debate over whether sport should continue during the war and the following comments appeared in the School Magazine.

'Whether the semi-professional VFL should be relinquished during the war is an open question, and there are many who feel that it is unworthy of men to give any serious attention to games at the present time. But fortunately, no such objections can be taken to school football, and as the season proceeds and boys at first a little awkward and undeveloped are gradually changing into fine young athletes with perfect control of wind and limb, one comes to the conclusion that there can hardly be a better pastime for the boys of a nation at war. Though the school was devoted to football, the boys are this year keener than ever.'

Once the Great War began the reporting of the doings of the CGS Cadet Unit became much less in content and the impression is gained that although all CGS boys were fully involved in their Junior or Senior Cadet training, that the magazine had far more important and weighty military matters to report on during this time. Ongoing mention was made of the Cadet Unit, but the fulsome reports of the pre-war period were much scaled down and often written in a perfunctory manner. It is clear that the Cadet Unit continued to train throughout the war, with many of its former members being reported as enlisting as soon as they were of eligible age.

In 1915 most classrooms were decorated in red, yellow and black, the colours of the Belgian flag with total collections for the Belgian Fund for the year being £217. A number of senior boys worked for the "Harvest Help League" by volunteering their services to help Victorian farmers to bring in the harvest. The school magazine noted, 'The Minister of Public Works, Mr F Hagelthorn spoke in terms of the highest commendation of the patriotic spirit being shown by the boys who have volunteered to take the place, so far as they can, of men who have gone or are going, to the Front to fight the Empire's battles.'[63] A branch depot of the Red Cross Workers was established at CGS and numerous boys gave up their Saturdays to manufacture much needed supplies such as crutches, deck chairs, bed rests and stools for wounded soldiers. The Debating Society staged a Model Parliament in the Assembly Room and £23 was raised to support missionaries in the field.

The Anzac Campaign had begun on 25th April 1915 and the service and deaths of four Grammarians killed at the landing on the first day was widely reported in the June edition of the CGS magazine. Many former CGS students, including a number who had fought for the Empire in the Boer War, left no doubt as to where their loyalties and actions lay as they farewelled other former scholars who had volunteered for service at the front. The school already had a war history as its records show that at least twenty Old Boys served in the Boer War, of whom six died. Tom Stock became the first Grammarian to be killed in action and to perpetuate his memory, some of his contemporaries paid for a fine marble tablet to be placed at CGS and which read as follows. 'Tom Stock was a member of the First Victorian contingent and was killed in battle while fighting for Queen and Country near Rensburg, South Africa, on February 9, AD 1900.' Hence the CGS Old Boys off to the Great War were following in the tradition of the school's military service and sacrifice to the Empire.

By the end of Gallipoli campaign in December 1915 the lives of seventeen Grammarians had been claimed, with four lost at the landing and five on the one day at the Battle of the Nek, where it was recalled that the men knew they were going to certain death, but still charged regardless of the consequences. The June 1915 issue of the School magazine is the first in which battles and their subsequent casualties are first mentioned. Under the banner heading 'Old Caulfield Grammarians and the War,' contained a list of the forty Old Boys who had been accepted for service in Europe. A special emphasis was given to six members of the Army Medical Corps and those who were 'already at the Front, having gone from England.' Accompanying this list was the CGS Roll of Honour with 114 names of 'CGS men accepted for service in the various branches of His Majesty's Military Forces.' On a more sombre note and edged in black, were the names of the five Old Boys who had 'Died for the Empire,' followed by the list of the eleven wounded or missing Old Caulfield Grammarians. Lengthy obituaries outlined the dead men's lives and were accompanied by their photographs. Also reproduced was a letter from an Old Boy who was in Germany at the outbreak of war and another outlining the 'Thrilling experience of Lt. Noel Fethers at the Dardanelles.' There was a letter from a soldier in hospital that mentions his wounding and the death of his cousin. 'I got drilled through from the left hip joint to the groin in front. It was not painful, but bled copiously. Fortunately, it missed the femoral artery by about half an inch. I believe that a few minutes after I was wounded Erle (his cousin) was hit and died very heroically.' The letter extract ends with the following words. 'It was hell on those hills on Sunday. Australia has paid a heavy price, but has reaped a name which will ring true all the world over. The cost was heavy, but the pearl was of great price.'[64] Noel Fethers was one of five brothers and four cousins from Caulfield and Malvern Grammar Schools who saw active service in the AIF during the Great War. Two were killed in action.

The message in these articles was that pluck, cheerfulness and the ability to stay true to a higher code of conduct and belief was the hallmark of a Caulfield Grammarian and were attributes to be emulated by all in these times of trial. The school's general reaction to the involvement of its Old Boys in the Dardanelles campaign was in the first instance to eulogise and pay tribute to their lives and heroic or noble deaths. By including reference to the cheerful endurance of suffering and pain, the school was making it plain to its young school boys that these were virtuous characteristics and to be exemplified by all Caulfield Grammarians. Indeed, these were just the sort of qualities that Old Boy soldiers needed to carry with them to help them endure at the Front.

The first reunion of Old Boys during war time took place on 22 October 1915 in conjunction with the school athletics sports at the school and included some older former students from the 1880's. At this event the wider school family was reminded of the nature and seriousness of the war. The reunion was attended by the Headmaster W.M. Buntine who outlined the part played by CGS boys, past and present in the Great War. Buntine was followed by the Mayor of Caulfield, Cr. Noel Murray, an Old Boy who asserted his determination to organise the men of the district to make the best of their resources of time, money and strength.

Murray then expressed his pride in the patriotism shown by men from his old School, and proposed a motion embodying a patriotic message to those at the front.

Two Old Boy speakers were of supreme interest at this reunion as they had returned to Australia after passing through the first days of the Gallipoli campaign. At Buntine's request they related something of their experiences. As the school magazine noted, Gunner W deG Gill who had been wounded in action, stood pale and serious, and in a matter of fact way, described the landing of the first Australian gun. As noted, 'opposite him there hung on the wall a roll of honour inscribed with the names of two hundred men, some of whom, khaki-clad, with all their active service before them.' The School magazines published a Roll of Honour of Old Boys killed in the war as well as listing those who had enlisted. By the end of 1915 eighteen Caulfield Grammarians had lost their lives on active service, either in combat or illness, including four at the Landing at Gallipoli and another six who died at the Battle of Lone Pine.

Lyle Buntine was an avid reader of the School Magazine and requested copies of them as often as possible not only to read but to pass on to fellow Grammarians that he encountered. No doubt he read the names on the Honour Roll and recognized many names of men that he had known personally and reflected upon the dangers and chance of death that a soldier encountered during his military service. Lyle was now embarking upon the more serious aspect of his military training in his quest to eventually become a pilot in the Royal Flying Corps. But first he had to undertake the rigorous officer training in the British Army and be successful in this work before he would be permitted to apply for the RFC.

Chapter 6:
Officer Training in the British Army

Military Training

Upon joining the British Army, Lyle was first posted to the School of Instruction at Ipswich where he noted that, such was the pressure on the Army to replace junior officers being lost at the Front, that the military authorities were trying to crowd a six-month course into five weeks. He noted that they had a very strict officer in charge, 'who was a bit too strict for my liking,' but he was getting through the course very slickly indeed. On his first week at the course, Lyle found himself busily undertaking squad and platoon drill as well as lectures on musketry. In fact, although he had completed similar activities before in his school cadet days and his initial AIF training at Seymour, he found the intensity of training in this short period of time as like nothing he had had to do before in his life. Unusually, along with all of the other officer cadets, he had to hire a bicycle for a month in order to be able to complete a number of tactical schemes. He confessed that he had undertaken an unsuccessful exercise on night navigation, as he had been confused by the unfamiliar northern hemisphere stars and having the sun in the south at midday instead of the north as he was accustomed to in Australia. After a while he noted that a four-hour parade with another two hours to complete in the afternoon would have been cause for much complaint at home, but here he didn't even notice their length. A variety of activities designed to simulate the conditions they would face at the Front were undertaken. He cheerfully reported that he had spent a whole morning digging trenches in the rain and then the troops engaged in exciting night attacks on the trenches, where the trenches were captured and converted and attacks of the 'enemy' were beaten off successfully. In passing he commented that these exercises were invariably undertaken in the rain, which increasingly became part of their usual weather pattern. Practical use of the 'Stoke's Mortar,' '… an awfully brainy arrangement and well used in the trenches,' was Lyle's comment following a lecture and training session.

He also informed his family that although he had received his commission into the Notts and Derby Regiment, he ruefully acknowledged that to take it up would be expensive and that in addition he would be expected to travel First Class when taking the train. In due course he travelled to London to undertake his purchases as befitting an officer. 'I have had quite a busy time this afternoon shopping. I bought about £15.00 worth of clothing and equipment in addition to what I have already, but will need it all for winter. Then I had to get a good sword and revolver and they cost quite a bit – and a sleeping bag. However, I think I am pretty well set up now.'

Towards the end of October, he was able to report that he had received his certificate from General McGregor who presented them to successful course candidates. Lyle had been exempted from the examination and commented that only about 60% of those who sat the exam passed the course. Following some leave in London, he journeyed to Newcastle to rejoin his Battalion, only to find that they had moved some twelve miles way to Sunderland. After staying in a 'fourth rate' hotel, he was eventually quartered with another officer in an empty house which they then had to furnish with tables, carpets and a few pictures to make it look home like from scratch. In addition to his fellow officer having a gramophone, '.... so, we are not without music – of a type,' and a servant to cater to his every want and clean his buttons and belt for him, he thought that he was installed in state. He was the proud possessor of a 3-ply woollen sleeping bag and supplemented by three army issue blankets, was now able to combat the increasing cold. The messing arrangements were well served with good meals and waiters and in addition there was the occasional concert for wounded soldiers in the town, to break the monotony of training. Lyle's first 6-mile route march with a full pack broke that spell and ensured that he was 'pretty tired' when he completed the march.

 He also noted that his battalion should be about 1000 strong, but owing to continual drafts being sent away to the front, it was now down to the size of one company of about 100 men and most of those were officer's servants, signallers or machine gunners. His performances had made him stand out and the outcome was that he received orders to join a 'Young Officer's Company,' a unit made up entirely of officers who had to go completely through the military work from the beginning, have exams, pass them at intervals and those who qualified in this manner, were sent to the Front.

 This particular company was housed in the Chester Road Schools in Sunderland and was where Lyle and the rest of the men were now billeted. From the comforts of a shared house, Lyle now joined about another 100 officers who now had to resort to eating and sleeping in a big draughty room. Five shillings a day for expenses in the Officer's Mess was also seen to be quite expensive living expenses and did not provide much of an opportunity for the men, over half of whom were under the age of twenty and in some cases only 17 years of age, to save much money at all. In mid-October 1915 Lyle's intensive training at this facility began in earnest. A typical day began with parade at 8.30am followed by section drill, an hour of physical drill and then some musketry training. The day continued and only came to a conclusion with a lecture that began at 9.00pm and finished an hour later, with no one allowed out of the school to go to the town after that time. In this way it was quite natural for the men to be quite tired and go straight to bed.

Lyle, whilst not enjoying the cold weather, wrote to his family with delight about an unusual event. 'I really must add this bit before I go to bed. We went to the lecture and on coming out, I thought someone had been sprinkling sawdust on the ground as the whole surface was covered with a beautiful white mantle. It was snow – so I had my first experience of it and it is very pretty too.'

A few days later, he wrote that all the men had been up at 6.00am for a parade at 8.00am before undertaking a training exercise which involved marching out to the coast to take a position, as a small unit of an army supposed to be attempting to land and capture Sunderland. Soaked by the rain and lying on the damp ground, the men's only relief was when they stood to fire volleys of blanks at the 'enemy.' Lyle's fitness seemed to be improving as he noted that after this exercise, he was none the worse for wear and did not even have a cold. In fact, he reported that he had been involved in some strenuous physical exercises, including completing some long distance running as well. As a result of these ten mile runs and the associated ten weeks of strenuous training, he and his fellow officers were well and truly ready for active service. In addition to the continued round of drill and physical exercise, skirmishing and attack drills, the training diversified to include bayonet fighting, lectures on bombs and grenades, which to some extent were seen as even more important than just relying on rifles alone. Lyle made the unsubstantiated statement that, 'in fact whole attacks are made and positions defended at the Front without a single shot being fired.' Leaving this statement to one side, he expressed some pleasure in being able to undertake the lectures on signalling as they involved putting to good use the 'wireless' practice he had already undertaken at CGS in his boyhood.

After nearly two months of the training regime, Lyle observed that the physical drill was getting better all the time and all of the soldiers were improving because their muscles were getting into trim again. One afternoon they had signalling and bayonet fighting and, on this occasion, he revealed that they had been trained to stamp on their opponent's instep and to, 'kick him and do quite a lot of un-British things; but as they say now, 'There's only one good German and that's a dead one.'

The Training Company was arranged into four platoons and newcomers were assigned to platoon number four. Each fortnight the recruits underwent an examination and had to achieve a minimum score of 60% to progress to the next platoon; a fact that Lyle duly noted in late November as he moved out of the 'recruits company' into Number 3 platoon. Early December saw the men continuing their work at some pace with most mornings taken up with physical drills, the afternoons with bayonet practise, interspersed with the occasional twelve-mile route march with full pack and rifle, a journey that usually took in the order of four hours solid marching. In mid-January 1916 Lyle reported that he was still at the same old grind of drill and trench digging with some improvements in his living conditions. To his delight the usual round of evening lectures from 9.00 – 10.00pm had been dispensed with, giving the men a little more free time. In addition, it appeared that a number of the 'bad eggs' in the company had been weeded out and sent to their battalions which resulted in a great improvement in the general atmosphere of the company. By the same token, some interesting characters still remained and Lyle reported on one young officer, who when drunk would indiscriminately fire off his revolver. Worse still, during the course of a practical lecture on 'Bombs' on a third-floor room, the fuse of one of them was 'accidentally' lit, which resulted in a mass exodus from the room, with men kangaroo hopping over desks and tables to escape with one man jumping out the window and hanging on to the ledge by his fingers! Lyle did not report on the aftermath of the resultant explosion.

Each man took his turn as Orderly Officer and Lyle was no exception, although the task of ensuring that the office work carried on correctly was by its nature generally a mundane one, as the Officer on Duty was not permitted to leave the barracks. The weather turned cold as mid-December approached, and soldiers like Lyle from a warmer climate began to think that the coldest experience of their lives was to stand still on a parade ground and undertake rifle exercises, when there was plenty of snow on the ground and the butt of the rifle was like ice. However, this was not the case, as the men discovered when they marched out of the town to complete a field sketching exercise in the snow! They were spared another twenty-mile route march with full pack and rifle, only to march ten miles in the snow to undertake a mock attack on a position with a bayonet charge up a steep hill at the end of the exercise. Field exercises now replaced a good deal of the parade ground drill and as February progressed the soldiers were engaged in engineering activities, practical bridging, trench-revetting and topographical studies. Lyle passed comment that the English soldiers he worked with proved to be most unpractical as he observed that whilst they showed that they knew the theoretical side of the work, in practical matters such as knotting and lashing with wire, '...they were nowhere.' At this point in their training the men were visited by an officer who had just returned from a tour of inspection of the Front in France. He was able to provide them with a realistic description of what conditions they were likely to face when they took up their duties across the Channel. 'Today we had the usual work and in the afternoon an excursion into the fields for instruction in map setting etc. One of the Captains who instructed us was in the retreat from Mons and can illustrate all his points from practical experience and it is very interesting indeed to hear him.'

The weather continued to be bitterly cold with frequent snow falls and blizzards and it was welcome relief when they could retreat inside and get warm by a cosy fire. Lyle especially welcomed the arrival of a fur vest in the mail from Australia. It was certainly appreciated as he recorded that six inches of snow fell one day in early March, a precursor to more falling during the day, unfortunately just before they had to undertake a drill exam. At the same time, he was eagerly waiting for news concerning his application to join the Royal Flying Corps and each letter home reflected his growing impatience and frustration at the delay in hearing any further from the War Office.

The time was drawing near for Lyle to complete his course and undertake his final examinations. On Saturday 26th February he sat and passed the first of a series of exams, with another due to be taken the following Saturday and then the final on the following Wednesday. This last one was the qualifying test to be promoted to Captain, although there was no certainty of that happening as his battalion was a reserve unit and promotion was much slower than in a service battalion. Preliminary testing of the men was carried out to determine which would be allowed to undertake the examinations. The first two days were involved with drill, physical exercises and bayonet fighting. The third day saw much activity in the form of field engineering, and here the men were involved in making sniper's posts, loopholes, single-lock bridges, bridges of boats, rafts, trenches, defences for a house and machine gun pits. In addition, they were involved with live fire exercises with bomb-throwing from trench positions, including the excitement of having one man dropping his bomb just over the front of the trench instead of throwing it the required distance! Despite the concussion nearly blowing them down, they escaped the shrapnel blast. Other practical exams were held in musketry and raft-making having to construct one that was able to hold 80 men at a time. In the second last week of the course the entire company of 300 from 2nd Lieutenants to Major Generals were assembled to hear a lecture on strategy by the eminent Irish military thinker, Dr T Miller Maguire. The General who introduced him said that although the speaker was not a soldier by profession, he had taught the general all he knew about strategy. Lyle along with the rest of the audience found that with Maguire's inborn Irish humour bubbling out the lecture was both interesting and instructive.

Posting to RFC

After about six weeks at the training company Lyle went to the Adjutant, Major Wyberg to inquire about transferring to the RFC and after a day or two returned to undertake his Medical examination which he passed. Then his journey through bureaucratic red tape began in earnest. The Adjutant informed him that no application could be forwarded to the War Office for consideration without having the medical certificate attached. But although Lyle had passed the medical, he was informed that he could not have the papers without War Office authority. He could not obtain War Office authority without the medical papers, '... so what the dickens is a man to do?' In late October he wrote to his parents, it seems to be a 'washout' about the RFC for a long while anyway.'

However, the Adjutant was sympathetic to his plight and hoped to correct the situation. Lyle wrote to his father that he might just have to complete his infantry training, be posted to the Front and then take up his RFC position when his papers arrived. Finally, on 8th December 1915 came word that he had definitely been accepted for the Flying Corps and he was advised that his orders would arrive by the end of the month. 'It seems like a long time, but there is so much 'red tape' in England. By Jingo! I can't get over my luck. Fancy me an aviator.'

However, by the end of January 1916 his papers had still not arrived and Lyle expressed his impatience and thought that he might have to go down to London and shake the War Office up a bit. Eventually in mid-February and having waited six weeks past the date for his orders to arrive, he wrote a letter to the War Office, describing it as 'kill or cure' but he was really desperate for news about his RFC transfer. With only a few days left of the course to go, Lyle only had one exam left to complete and was to sit for that on Tuesday 14th March 1916. But fate was to take a hand and he finally received word from the War Office to report to the Royal Flying Corps. By great misfortune he had to report for duty there on Monday 13th March and so missed out on completing his final exam by just one day.

Chapter 7:
Training in the Royal Flying Corps

School of Military Aeronautics

Once accepted by the RFC, transfer recruits such as Lyle, were posted to the School of Military Aeronautics at either Oxford University or its extension college at Reading. Lyle arrived at Wantage Hall, Reading on 16th March 1916 and was overjoyed to have finally achieved his dream of joining the Royal Flying Corps. 'Ground School' as it was known, was very much like a concentrated university course where for 3 or 4 weeks cadets lived in the University Colleges like students, but were under parade ground discipline at all times. Later on, in the war the courses became longer, but at this stage instruction was necessarily curtailed by the increasing demands from the frontline squadrons for replacements. All cadets were considered probationary until they had finished the course and consequently badges of rank could not be worn. Practical courses in aerial observation and wireless telegraphy were seen as vital, but others such as knowing the workings of the aneroid barometer seemed pointless to these potential 'knights of the air.'

Shortly after his arrival, Lyle remarked to his father in a letter on the ever-changing group of friends that he made as his service life continued. 'Here I am at last, where I have been wanting to get for quite a long time. Think of it! Actually in the RFC. Isn't it great luck? About the time you get this I should be ready to leave this preliminary school and go to actual flying. We have a tremendous lot to do here first, as we have to know several engines and wireless and bomb dropping, rigging a plane and several other things, in addition to the theory of flight and how to fly. So, it looks like a busy time for the next five weeks. It seems a pity that the exam for which I was working should be lost and only by one day too. It was to take place on Tuesday last and on the Monday, I had to leave and come down here. I regret it more as I was certain of passing. Another thing is that just as I had made several friends at Sunderland among the officers I had to leave and so I am more or less alone again. Well I hope that I'll be able to make some nice friends here and stick with them for longer this time.'

Daily life for the cadets usually started at 6.00am for breakfast, parade and then inspection. Classroom work followed with two lectures, two practical work periods and two 15-minute recesses with the day ending at 4.00pm. Cadets were then free until the following morning. Occasionally the Commanding Officer would call a Study Parade and all cadets would be confined to their rooms to study. Weekend leave was given freely and it would appear that there was some real pressure on cadets to learn, with exams usually being a repetition of material learned by rote. As a 2nd Lieutenant, Lyle earned 7 shillings and 6 pence per day, but once he had graduated from ground school and was posted to a training squadron his pay increased to 11/6 with the extra 4/- being flying pay.

Training Begins

He observed that this stage of his service life was reminiscent of his former days as a medical student at Ormond Hall at the University of Melbourne and as he studied for his RFC exams, he found it hard to realise that he was doing 'War Work,' the daily reminder being that everyone was dressed in khaki. As with all pilots in training, work with the Gnome and Beardmore engines was important and the recruits had to run them on stands and then be able to dismantle and reassemble them and be thoroughly conversant with their operation. Coupled with frequent lectures and the dread of 'make or break' exams looming, study was constant. The pace of exams, lectures, training and practical work was relentless, with students finding little time to themselves during the day. 'I am in the thick of exams at present and we have just had four today. I found them fairly easy and think I passed them all right, however, we have twelve more to do before we are finished, so I still have a lot of work ahead of me. You would hardly know me if you saw me here, working till 11 o'clock at night and up at 6 o'clock again in the morning. You will never realise the amount of work we had to do in three short weeks and had to pass the exams or go back to the regiments and leave the Flying Corps. The nervous strain was telling on everyone and for the last three days I have had only about 10 minutes a day to myself.'

Apart from the recent advent of the aeroplane itself, other technical marvels were increasingly being incorporated into the war effort and consequently pilots had to be able to operate such inventions as the Morse code buzzer and the wireless, the latter being used for telegraphy from aeroplanes. Lyle found that he was working much harder than he had done at Sunderland and as he warmed to the tasks, he also found that was able to explain the workings of the wireless to others and to reinforce his own knowledge about mechanical matters at the same time.

'Yesterday we took an engine to pieces and built it up again and we have to do this with all the engines. I won't ever be out of a job after the war because if the worst comes to the worst, I'll get a job of chauffeur to somebody.'

The RFC was only in its formative years and was composed of an eclectic group of young men. Upon joining the course at Reading, Lyle noted that his comrades on the RFC course were different to others he had encountered in his military career. 'It will give you some idea of the class of men in the RFC when I tell you that nearly all of them have seen active service and about a dozen of them have the Military Cross or DSO. They are a grand lot of chaps and one thing that surprised me more than anything is the total absence of drinking in the mess. I told you about the last place I was in and you will see that it was a different place altogether. Amongst the hundred or so officers here, there are hardly ten who drink and even then, they only just take perhaps a glass of wine with their dinner. It's great being in this Corps as most of the fellows are very wealthy and sons of, or connections of peers and best of all they are gentlemen.' The realities of war however, were never far away and from time to time the recruits were advised that their course was to be cut short, as the RFC wanted men to go and *'strafe the Huns.'* Naturally the young airmen were anxious to be away from their ground duties and take up their flying duties, but although some men left early to join the flying squadrons, the inevitability of the relentless grind of training prevailed for most of the recruits, broken only by the arrival of news from home mixed with sparse amounts of leave.

Life Apart from RFC Training

As with all servicemen far from home, Lyle longed for news from his family and friends. On a number of occasions, he found that there might be a gap of three or four or even five weeks before mail from Australia was received. Apart from resorting to cabling home, at times like this he lamented his situation and surmised that his mail had gone to bottom of the Atlantic when mail boats were torpedoed by such ships as the German raider *SMS Moewe*. This auxiliary cruiser was used for mine laying operations in the North Sea and then directed to raids in the North Atlantic where she sank, mined or captured some 45 Allied ships making her the most successful surface raider of WWI. When mail did arrive, he was very pleased to receive such delights from Melbourne as the YMCA paper, as well as personal letters where he learned of the death of his Uncle Martin and the engagement of his cousin Mac Gibbs. Due to his accommodation at the University he was then, when time permitted, able to retire to his, 'nice little study of my own to write where I have all my photos round the wall, so it is quite homelike.'

His letters home noted the vagaries of the weather and in particular the unusual amounts of snow they were receiving in that part of England at that time of year, but fortunately the War Office had made provision for the recruits to receive plenty of coal for their fires. A week later he commented that the weather had now become quite hot with a damp moist kind of heat that was most oppressive. Life for a young Australian in the motherland was full of new adventures and travel was high on the list of their priorities. Lyle was no exception and when in London he took his father's advice and found that one of the best ways to explore it was from the top of a motor-bus. In addition, the London Underground proved fascinating to him and he observed that the trains hustled and when they pulled up at a station, waited for about 10 seconds before taking off again, and leaving him uncertain that they had actually stopped at all!

After time spent in action or barracks or camp, all servicemen far away from home and hearth relished the opportunity to visit a family in their home and spend some time in the normal world far away from the dangers and privations of service life. Lyle had a number of chances to do this, either through family connections or friends or acquaintances made through his service life. Thus, it was that he often visited Dr and Mrs Allan at Harefield Hospital. At the end of his RFC exams he took the chance to travel to Dumferline in Scotland, where apart from visiting the local abbey where the legendary Scottish king Robert the Bruce was buried, he enjoyed finding a beautiful glen that he found was just like an Australian fern gully. He continued on to Glasgow where he met up with Mr and Mrs White and then went out to the nearby village of Gartcash to spend the weekend again with the Inshaw family at their estate. Having already stayed with them the previous January he was greeted as a welcome guest. He recorded that with his new-found knowledge of all matters mechanical, he spent much of his time discussing engines with George Inshaw and became so wrapped up in the topic, that the twenty or so other young people in the house party, gave them up as hopeless cases. Finally, they managed to tear themselves away from their discussions to join the others and enjoyed themselves participating in the rabbit shooting, billiards and evening entertainment. Lyle had obtained a copy of 'The Man from Snowy River' and had learnt a few of the pieces and this was his contribution to the evening concert. 'They went down very well as they were quite different to any poems you get over here.' Returning to his quarters at Reading, he finally heard on 20th April that he had passed all his RFC exams and was overjoyed four days later to be posted to a Flying Training Squadron based at Thetford in Norfolk.

Training Squadron

Arriving at his posting to the 12th Reserve Squadron at RFC Thetford at about 5.00pm on 26th April 1916, Lyle found that he was being accommodated in a tent as the billets were already full. This situation did not last long as the next day his servant found him lodgings in a hut just a few hours before a rain storm arrived. 'I came on here last night from Reading. This is where we do actual flying and then go to an Active Service Squadron. If the weather continues fine then I shall probably get my Royal Aero Club Certificate in about a month and then my wings in about another month after that and then may go out any time.' The Royal Aero Club was founded in 1901 as a club for balloonists, and its members included and trained most of the military pilots up to 1915 or so when military training schools took over the task. By the end of the war some 6,300 military pilots had gained the RAC's Aviator's Certificate. 'The hours here are pretty long. We start in the morning at about 5.00am and continue until it is too hot and then start again about 4.30pm and go on till dark. This, of course, is when weather permits. In the middle of the day we do lectures and work on engines and machines. We were up at 5 o'clock this morning for early morning flying. It seems a pity to get up so early on a Sunday, but I suppose it's got to be done, so as to take advantage of the weather, for there is never any flying done between 9.00am and 5.00pm as it is usually too windy.'

Located south east of Norwich in the East Anglian countryside, RFC Thetford's surroundings greatly appealed to Lyle due to the fact that he was able to indulge in his passion of walking. 'Today is Sunday and I've just come in from a ramble through the woods and coverts here. The other fellows seem to prefer to sit inside and smoke, but give me the woods very time. Just at present everything is very beautiful and the trees are all carrying young leaves of a lovely green colour. There's no doubt about it, the English Spring is as fine as anyone wants to see. The woods around here are thick with rabbits and all kind of game and if I had taken a gun with me, I could have had some lovely sport as there are rabbits all over the place and pheasants, partridges and pigeons overhead.'

In these modern times of the twenty first century it is easy to take flight for granted, but in 1916 it was still a great novelty and many people had not seen an aeroplane, let alone take a flight in one. 'Our aerodrome is situated on a small hill and at the bottom there is a very pretty creek with all the woods on the other side. As I was walking back this afternoon, I passed crowds of people in cars or bikes or on foot, who were all lined up outside waiting to see the flying. I'm afraid they'll be somewhat disappointed as it is too windy today. The day itself is just like a Melbourne spring day with a south wind and blowing like it does along Brighton Road.'

Flying Training

These training squadrons were spread throughout southern Britain and once trainees had completed enough solo flights, they were often transferred to a specialist unit or squadron for further training. However, in the war demands of mid 1916 the needs of the front line usually curtailed further lengthy periods of training. A trainee began flying as a passenger as soon as possible after arrival at the squadron and then soon after began their period of dual instruction. Lyle recorded that on the 26th April details about his experience with this event. 'Tonight, I had my first fly with an instructor and enjoyed it immensely as I was allowed to do some of the piloting by means of dual controls. It seems great to me that I am actually flying.'

As in Lyle's case the most common type of aircraft used for this purpose was the Maurice Farman S.11 or 'Shorthorn.' This 1912 version was built by the Farman brothers in France and equipped with a 70hp Renault engine could fly at nearly 70mph, although it usually only achieved something approaching 60mph. Made with wooden struts, wire bracing and fabric covering, the instructor sat behind the pupil in the nacelle mounted on the lower wing. The Shorthorn was called 'Rumpety' by student pilots for the rattling sound its air-cooled engine made, as the tolerance between the cylinder and piston were larger than normal to allow for heat expansion of the metal. Pilots claimed that it was well named because just like its bovine namesake, it flew like a cow! The Shorthorn was not a good choice for primary training as it was underpowered and had a very high drag factor, being a pusher with a high profusion of bracing wires. As a result, its stall speed was only about 5mph under its top speed. Some said that the Shorthorn looked like a Victorian bathtub caught in a baling wire explosion. The Shorthorn at least had the virtue of dual controls, but verbal instruction in the air was impossible. Sometimes notes were passed, sometimes the instructor would kick the seat of the trainee and occasionally a trainee who had 'frozen' at the controls would be hit repeatedly to induce the correct action. The pupil sat in front of the instructor and learned to fly by resting their hands gently on the joystick and feet lightly on the rudder while the instructor took it through its paces. In this way they could feel the impulses of the instructor's movement as he guided the machine through the sky. The famous Canadian ace Billy Bishop recalled his training on the Shorthorn as something like the first time you started downhill on an old-fashioned bicycle.[65]

These dual flights were of a short duration, usually at low altitudes under 1000 feet and within the sight of the airfield so that other pupils could watch. Lyle recorded, 'I had rather bad luck today. It was awfully hot, quite like an Australian day. I got up at 5.00am and went out, but our instructor didn't come, so we didn't fly this morning. In the afternoon he had to go away on business, so again we had to just watch the others.' In addition, because of the plane's deficiencies, training flights were little more than a series of landings and take-offs and could only be carried out in perfect weather which meant wind no stronger than 5mph. Early morning and early evening when the air was calm tended to be the most active flying time. Because of this factor it could take a trainee some weeks to amass just a few hours of flight time. One recruit has left us with a vivid description of his first flight in a Shorthorn;

'The nacelle was halfway up the interplane struts and a shallow side panel hinged down to simplify the gymnastic feat of entering it. When seated I lifted the panel and secured it with ordinary door bolts, I was in the nose, well ahead of the wings. The instructor sat behind, perching between the upper and lower wings' front edges. Wooden bearers, running aft from the nacelle's structure, supported part of the engine between the wings and part behind them where the pusher propeller could revolve. A mechanic stood within the booms and wires behind the propeller. It was his unenviable task to help start the engine from his encaged position. Before doing anything he first assured himself by question and answer that the pilot's ignition was switched off and the gasoline turned on. Then he primed the engine from the carburettor and he did this by manually rotating the two-blade propeller as if he himself were the starter motor. It was hard work and when he thought he had done enough he paused and called to the pilot: 'Contact, sir.' After the pilot had responded by switching on his ignition and then announcing 'Contact,' the mechanic hopefully and lustily heaved the propeller a quarter-turn round, while the pilot twirled a hand starter magneto to boost the spark at the plugs. Usually the Renault rattled into life after one or two heaves and the mechanic could emerge from his cage. The air-cooled V8's pistons had ample clearances and one could always hear them slapping against the cylinder walls, loudest when the engine was cold. With no device to compensate for cylinder expansion and contraction, its valves and tappets chattered incessantly. Its propeller revolved on an extension of the camshaft at half engine-speed and the reduction gear was noisy. The fuel tank, between the rear seat and the engine, was in a nasty place should a crash occur. The hot engine could break away from its mounting, rupture the gasoline tank, ignite its contents and the burning mass might fall on the aircrew. Fortunately for their peace of mind, few, if any pilots or pupils thought about the several features of the Shorthorn that lowered its safety level below par. Enough that they were flying! For what more could they ask?'[66]

Most of the flight instructors seem to have been good men, and it must be remembered that many of them had already endured the rigours of war and for one reason or another were no longer capable of serving as front line pilots. The RFC command thought that a spell as an instructor would be just the tonic to restore them to good health. Lyle commented, 'Today there has been a very strong wind which of course kept us from flying. However, the instructors don't mind winds much and during the afternoon one of them was up and doing loops and tail-slides in spite of the fact that there was a 40 mile an hour tail wind blowing. It was very pretty to watch him and the trail of smoke showed how perfect were the circles he flew. Just as I write the last line, I heard a machine, so all of us went to the window and there was one of our instructors up in the most unstable machine we have got here and the wind blowing about 50 miles an hour. It's the chap who did the loops last Sunday. He is a jolly fine pilot and the only one game to go up today.' These experienced pilots having survived six months or so at the Front did not want to be killed at the hands of an inexperienced pupil, and so they adopted an approach whereby they rarely relaxed their grip on the dual controls and encouraged their charges to solo as soon as possible. The student therefore had to master the use of the rudder pedal as soon as possible during their first few moments of solo flight. Because the knowledge of aerodynamics was limited at this stage of the war, students were also discouraged from 'stunting' and began to develop an inbred resistance to attempting certain kinds of aerobatics. Most bad accidents were caused by stalling and although by 1916 the Royal Aircraft Factory at Farnborough had conducted research into the aerodynamics of spinning out of control and recovering from the spin, most instructors were still completely ignorant on the matter. As a novice pilot Lyle had learnt enough already to understand some of the forces and inherent dangers involved in flying. 'Today is Sunday and we didn't get up early this morning as there was a very strong wind blowing, so it was too bumpy. These bumps are the worst part of flying as the air seems to be solid and quite jars the machine. Sometimes you get a straight bump which lifts you about 20 or 30 feet and at other times bump you down. The worst is, when a bump catches you under one wing tip and tilts the machine, that's the time you want to be awake.' Not that the realities of his situation and confidence in his own abilities were in short supply! 'They are starting to push us on now very fast as the pilots in France are getting used up and they want others to take their places. The weather has been rather bad lately for instructional purposes, so I haven't had much flying, but I hope for some more tomorrow. I was up tonight and the instructor told me I was good for such a short time in the air. It is a recognised fact that Canadians and Australians make the best pilots as the Englishmen are too careful and that doesn't pay. It is safer to be a little venturesome.' A letter to his brother reveals his sense of ironic airman's humour as he relates the words of 'Our Hymn' set to the tune of 'Tarpaulin Jacket.'

'A young aviator lay dying
And as in the debris he lay, he lay
To the swearing mechanics around him
These last dying words he did say.
Take the connecting cylinders out of my kidneys
The connecting rods out of my brain
From the small of my back take the thrust-box
And assemble the engine again
And it was so.'

Flying Solo

Finally, on 7th May 1916, Lyle's great day arrived and all his diligence and patience during his training came to fruition. 'I was informed by my instructor that in about another 10 – 15 minutes I will be able to take up a machine myself. What price me a giddy bird! I did my first solo flight! It turned out a lovely evening and the CO came up and asked if anyone wanted to go up. I made a dash for him and he took me up for a while. Then he asked me I felt all right to go up alone and of course I said, 'Yes,' and he said 'Righto,' and so up I went. It's all right flying with an instructor in the machine when you know, that, if you make a mistake, he will correct it. Just as I was leaving the ground alone, I thought, well now, I'm for it, so if I don't fly the machine right no one else will. However, I got on all right and came down soon to try to make a landing. Then off I went again and got up to 2600 feet. It was great up there. Then I tried a couple of banks and sharp turns and did a volplane down. When I got down the CO came up and said, 'That's the best show for a beginner I've seen in a long time.' It's lovely flying up at a height, because when you are up there you don't get any bumps and can just rest your elbows on the sides of the machine and lean back and look around the country.'

Most cadets had only received a few hours dual instruction before they soloed with the first flight usually fulfilling the criteria of 15 - 20 minutes duration, low altitude and within sight of the airfield. Before the autumn of 1917 it was generally agreed tacitly by RFC instructors that a pupil stood a better chance of improvement if they taught themselves. Therefore, students usually spent much more time soloing than under dual instruction. As they grew in confidence and skill they were encouraged to fly further and higher and for longer with flight times increasing to 45 minutes to an hour. Accidents were a common occurrence with upwards of two dozen crashes a day at most training airfields when training was in full swing and the RFC averaging one death per day amongst student pilots training in the UK. These training airfields would be littered with the remains of crashed machines and often ambulances would keep their engines running constantly in anticipation of the next crash. The constant need for pilots at the front in 1916 by necessity further curtailed the amount, consistency and quality of training made available to the trainee. 'One chap had a bit of a bust a couple of days ago; smashed the machine, but not much hurt.'

Lyle wrote to his brother Murray to describe his progress as a flier and some of the conditions he had to face as a solo pilot. 'Every kind of machine has a totally different method of flying and sundry little things peculiar to itself. I was out this morning in a Maurice Farman and was up about 2500 feet. None of the other chaps in my squadron were up, as they all considered it was too bumpy and they really never want to be up in worse bumps. They were of the type called cloud-bumps and are the worst of the lot. This morning the clouds were only about 3000 feet, as they were quite low. I would have gone right through them if had not been so windy, but as it was, I was only too glad to get down to 'Mother Earth' again. On one occasion I was doing a rather steep bank and a left-hand turn, when suddenly I got a bump under my left wing which put the opposite bank on. The machine started to slip slide for about 200 feet and I only got out of it by hard work with the aileron and by putting the rudder over and making a right hand turn instead of a left hand. Another time I got a straight bump that lifted my machine 200 feet and followed by a bump that sent us down again about 50 feet. In fact, on the whole it was about the most exciting morning I have spent yet. I have got in about 5 hours solo flying now, which is not so bad. I did a spiral from 3000 feet in a machine yesterday, which some of the fellows said wasn't too bad. The part that worries me at present is the landing. I can land as well as most of the chaps here, but a perfect landing is a very hard thing to do. It is quite a new sensation to be flying in a cloud. It is like a London fog and nothing can be seen. You don't know whether you are flying level or up or down, or with one wing low, so the only thing to do is to get your head right into the machine and keep your eyes glued to the instruments and they will tell you how you are going. It is useless trying to go by feel. It was rather funny this morning and quite disconcerting for a time when I found that I had lost the aerodrome. It was quite hidden by a thick carpet of clouds beneath me. Fortunately, I had noticed my bearing on leaving, so flying on a compass course I broke through the clouds when I judged I was somewhere near and by a stroke of luck, was only a mile off and being about 1500 feet up I glided down quite nicely. I had another experience today – this time it was air pockets. It was blowing about 20 miles an hour, but the CO wanted me to put in some flying time so as to be ready to leave for higher instruction. One of the instructors came up and asked me if I'd like to go up and try. Of course, I said 'Yes' and up I went. The bumps were much worse than any I had yet experienced, still I went up to about 2000 feet and flew around a bit. On my way down I go into an air pocket. I was about 500 feet above the ground and fighting the bumps hard, when suddenly a giant hand seemed to take the machine and fling it towards the ground. I didn't recover until I was 200 feet lower and then it was with a sudden jerk. I seemed to leave the seat altogether and was only kept in the machine by the belt and the strenuous grip I had on the control levers. In making a landing the wind picked up the machine and threw it on to one wing and the wing was crashed, but fortunately it didn't go over so no damage was done. And all's well that ends well, so why worry? I was up this morning early and left the ground at 5.00am sharp to have an hour's flight. I got up and climbed as hard as I could and got to 8000 feet in about 40 minutes. It was so cold up there that the carburettor froze and so as the engine stopped, I had to descend. I think this is higher than any other men under instruction here have been up to at present.' During the final stages of this training Lyle underwent the tests for his Royal Aero Club Pilot's Certificate which he passed and as was the then practise, was announced in The Times newspaper.

Meeting up with Old Friends

Lyle took the chance whenever he could to catch up with family and friends whilst he was in England and took particular pleasure in meeting up with other CGS Old Boys. One such person was Captain Marcus Southey who was in charge of the Australian section of the Convalescent Hospital at Epsom, near London. Southey was just about to leave for a cricket match when Lyle arrived at about 2.00pm and looked well and told Lyle that the exercise he was getting was keeping him as sharp as a fiddle. Lyle remarked that Southey had a lovely job which involved all work being finished by lunchtime and the afternoons being spent in cricket or golf, whilst every evening there was a concert in a nearby large hall! The Camp also contained a cinema, shooting gallery and skittle alley, which Lyle greatly appreciated making full use of after the privations of his RFC camp. Southey brought news of a number of other Caulfield Grammarians; Bob Fowler, Zumstein, Le Souef, B Croker, H Southey and J Robinson.

At the conclusion of his course at 12th Reserve Squadron in May 1916, Lyle was granted a week's leave and called in to some of his old friends at the Regiment in Sunderland on the rail journey north. 'I travelled up in a Pullman Observation Car, so was able to enjoy the scenery all the way. Near Berwick and the Tweed, the railway runs along the top of the cliffs within a dozen yards of the sea. It is late spring now in Scotland and everything here and in England is a beautiful green. Even smoky old London has on her spring costume.' He stayed with the Whites in Glasgow and went to visit the Inshaws at Gartcash who chided him for not visiting for a longer period of time. A cousin of his old friend Whitworth also lamented the fact that he was unable to visit him at Cardross. Whilst Lyle greatly appreciated the offers of hospitality he received, he was also conscious that for a serviceman with limited periods of leave and restricted finances, trips to Scotland could not be indulged in too often. Upon his return to Thetford he was delighted to discover that he had been selected from his squadron to attend a machine-gun course at Hythe near Dover. 'This is a splendid course and one that all the boys wanted to get. So, I am very lucky in being the one to go. Hythe is a very pretty place and only about 5 miles from Folkestone and about 15 miles from Dover, both of which were well known watering holes in pre-war time.'

Active Service Squadron

Once a student pilot had completed between 10 – 20 hours in the air his elementary training was considered to be finished. Usually transferred to an Active Service Squadron for Higher Training the pilot learnt to fly on a variety of machines, was encouraged to fly every day and was often sent on cross-country flights. Here they were expected to fly above 8000 feet and to study and improve their aerial navigation, banking and turning, interpretation of signals from the ground, especially important before the wide spread use of wireless, and observation. Gunnery practice was also emphasised and in Lyle's case this was why he was sent to the RFC Machine Gun School at Hythe for further training. During this three-week intensive course at Hythe, Lyle was put through his paces as learnt more about the theory and practise of aerial machine-gunnery. 'Today we spent a lot of time at the shooting range and had quite a lot of practise during which I discovered that firing from a machine gun is much harder than it looks! This morning I got in a fair amount of aerial practice shooting at a target on the ground and this afternoon I was up again. One of the pilots who takes you up is quite a stunt man and does some banks. You fly over the target and directly you have finished firing you feel the bank. Down goes the wing and round you come then over the target again. It's quite good sport.'

By early June his time at Hythe was up and so he packed his kit once more to take up his posting at RFC Norwich awaiting further orders. He was genuinely sorry to be leaving as he had enjoyed seeing a different part of England and also enjoyed the work of training, although he recognised that there was still much to learn. He thought that he might be stationed there for about another three weeks or so until his orders to join an active squadron in France arrived. In the meantime, two recent events in the war occupied his thoughts as they did for many people of the British Empire. He wrote, 'We have had news today of the death of Lord Kitchener who was drowned on the 'Hampshire' on a trip to Russia. It is one of the worst blows since the commencement of the war and it is very sad that he should have gone and especially just at the time when we were rejoicing over the naval victory at

Jutland.' Horatio Herbert Kitchener, the Earl of Khartoum (1850 – 1916) had been appointed British War Minister on the outbreak of hostilities and was responsible for the formation of Britain's New Army. The Battle of Jutland took place in the North Sea on 31 May 1916 between the British Home Fleet and the German High Seas Fleet. The British lost three battle-cruisers, three cruisers, eight destroyers and 6,100 men. The Germans lost one battleship, one battle-cruiser, four cruisers, and five destroyers with 2,550 casualties. The battle was a success for the Germans in terms of ships sunk and men lost and it contributed to Russia's exit from the war. The British were disappointed by the inconclusive nature of the result, but it became an important strategic victory for them as the German fleet remained in port for the rest of the war. Lyle commented that, 'The first news we got of this fight seemed to make it out to be a defeat (for Britain) or a draw. But later news showed up the fact that it was a brilliant victory and ended by the Germans scuttling home with Jellicoe after them.'

Lyle often saw the Royal Navy torpedo boats and destroyers at Hythe and Dover and every now and then saw an aeroplane passing overhead on its way to France, 'Flying far up in the air like some great bird of prey. I don't think there is much doubt now, but that we have obtained the mastery of the air and I think we are going to keep it. The Germans are yielding more every day to the superiority of our machines and to British pluck and endurance.'

Lyle, to the best of our knowledge had no face to face contact with Germans, but was happy to share stories about them in his correspondence and his reflections provide an insight into some British attitudes towards their foes. 'There is an amusing little tale told here about a destroyer engaged in guarding a certain port in England. There were 3 German submarines that used to hang round this port and they got so well known to the crew of the destroyer that they gave them names. They called them Fritz,

Hans and Karl. After some time, they succeeded in sinking Karl and sometime later they sank Fritz and so only Hans was left; but the crew of the destroyer refused to sink Hans as he was such a rotten bad shot, having already had several shots at them and missed by yards. They said that if they sank Hans the Germans might send another submarine which was a better shot and so it would be worse than if they left Hans.'

He also expressed his opinion of his German foes. 'There are some curious incidents in connection with the RFC. For instance, Immelmann the great German pilot, first learnt to fly at Bristol and one of my friends was there with him. His best friend was a man whose name I forget for the moment. When the war broke out Immelmann and his friend met in an aerial battle and the Englishman was killed. During the battle neither recognised the other. Immelmann had him buried decently and later on took a photo of his grave and sent it to his family, which shows that all Germans aren't brutes. It is funny to hear the fellows talk of Immelmann, the German pilot, as an old friend. Many of them have had fights with him and have usually come off worst. The friend of his that I couldn't remember, was an Englishman called Le Bas which sounds French but he was English.' Lt Owen Vincent Le Bas was originally a member of the West Surrey Regiment before joining the RFC where he was posted to France to serve with 10 Squadron. On the morning of November 7th 1915, and flying as an observer in a BE2C plane piloted by Captain T D Adams, he was shot down by Max Immelmann in an action near Arras, becoming the sixth of Immelman's victims. Oberleutnant Max Immelmann (1883 – 1916) was Germany's first air ace of WWI scoring seventeen victories until his death in 1916. As a successful fighter pilot flying the Fokker "Eindecker" monoplanes with forward firing machine guns, he was dubbed the "Eagle of Lille" and was responsible for developing a dogfight manoeuvre whose name – the Immelmann

Turn – remains to this day, comprised of a simultaneous loop and roll design to allow him to dive back at pursuing airmen. Awarded the Pour le Merite (Blue Max) in January 1916 he was shot down near Lens by British pilot George McCubbin on 18 June 1916.

Letters to Home

Throughout Lyle's time in England the issue of receiving his pay in a timely manner was a cause of frustration for Lyle and on more than one occasion he had to rely on the generosity of friends. He wrote home, 'I'm afraid however that I'll have to curtail my leave very much as the wretched government hasn't been paying up any too well lately so I've had to get another loan from Dr Allan until they do. There's no doubt he has been good to me.' Later when he arrived at RFC Norwich, he reported the changed conditions and his ongoing financial concerns. 'The messing is better here than at Thetford though quite as expensive. At least we do get good plain food and don't have margarine with finger marks on it in place of butter. However, we have our little trials in other ways. For instance, I arrived this morning and when I reported was requested to plonk down £10 in advance for Mess bills. Only having about £7 in the bank I have not yet decided what to do. When down at Harefield Dr Allan tells me that they pay about 2/- a week as against our 7/- a day. The wretched government owe me about £20 now which I may get.'

As always news from home was often foremost in his mind and his correspondence to his younger brothers, little sister and mother contain such things as birthday wishes, comments on new dogs in the family, requests for copies of the School magazine, weather reports from his various bases and news of his travels, such as a pamphlet outlining the account of the crypt and bones at Hythe Church! News of Caulfield Grammarians and in particular those were serving in the military feature in his correspondence and in reply his father, W.M. Buntine, the Principal of CGS, kept Lyle informed not only of the doings of the school but the progress of the lives and military service of former students. He wrote to his father, 'I just posted a letter to you yesterday, but I am sending this as I got a letter from Arnold Young this morning. I am sending it on and it will explain itself and I think some parts of it will go well in the (School) Magazine. He asks for a list of Old Boys. Will you send some of the names with their units? I will forward them to him. Lloyd Reade has got his commission in the 15th Battalion, Royal Fusiliers and is at present in a training camp at Kilworth, County Cork, Ireland. The school seems to be doing well. How many are there on the roll now?'

Only two of his father's letters have survived and in this reply he says, 'My dear Lyle, your cousin Jack Gibbs is in London with the Pay Corps and George Little is the Colour Sergeant with the machine-gun section and is on his way to Aldershot. I shall send you a few of the Roll of Honour sheets so that you may distribute them to any who may ask for them. Eric Staughton is with the artillery on the Western Front in France. George Sproule is in Salonika. Murray Buntine (NSW) left two weeks ago.'

It is in a birthday letter to his father at this time, when Lyle is aware that he will soon be fighting at Front in a war for which he has been training, that he expresses some of his innermost feelings in a rare show of emotion and fortunately his father's letter in reply has survived.

'12/6/1916 at RFC Norwich. Dear Father, this should reach you about the 1st August, allowing for the present delays on the postal service, so I want to make it a birthday letter. Very many happy returns of the day. I shall be thinking of you on that day and of all at home so many thousands of miles away. It will be the second birthday that we have spent apart since this terrible war began and I do hope that August 1st 1917 will see the war at an end and

I shall be able to give you my best wishes personally instead of through the medium of a letter. I know Father, that in the past I have often worried you, and given you cause for sorrow; but when we meet again as I feel sure we shall do soon, I shall strive to make some amends with all my power. I am your affectionate son, Lyle.' His father's reply expresses pride in Lyle's achievements as concern as to his war work.

'25/6/1916 at Caulfield Grammar School, East St Kilda. My dear Lyle, let me congratulate you too on getting your Pilot's Certificate. You do not know how much we appreciate your regular letters. You have been very good to us to keep us in touch with you so much. We never forget you for a single day and we are sure you are in God's hands. I sometimes shudder to think of you being called upon to take part in aerial conflicts; but you undoubtedly have a gift for the flying work and perhaps this is your duty. At any rate I know you will play the man. Your affectionate father, W.M. Buntine.'

Adventures whilst training and preparing for war duties provided some relief from the tedium of the seemingly endless waiting to be posted to the front as Lyle described in a letter to his mother from a small village in Cambridge. 'Hildersham Rectory, Cambridge. (c/- Mrs De Gay, 24 Durham Terrace, Bayswater London) Dear Mother, I'll bet you are rather surprised to see this address. So was I at the time. I have had some exciting times since I last wrote to you; but we're always having those in the RFC. Well I'll proceed to explain. I think I told you about having a forced landing near Norwich and going to a gentleman's house in a car for the night while the engine was repaired. I returned from there on Friday and on Saturday two of the officers set out to fly to London to take aeroplanes down from Norwich. One of them got through all right; but the other came down and we got a wire from him on Sunday. The CO then told me to go down and stay with the machine until it was repaired and then take it to London while the pilot who brought it here went home. So, I came down here on Monday morning to this pretty little village between Hamerhill and Cambridge. I found that the other pilot, Britton had smashed some of the struts in landing, so had to wire for them to be sent. They came down here yesterday and we got the machine repaired and I intended to start this morning; but it came on to rain and as I could hardly see the ground from 1000 feet I could not get away. The Rector here, The Rev. Mr Phillips, won't let me go to a hotel and is keeping me at the Rectory which is very nice. They have a beautiful big garden something like Rippon Lea and about half the size. Since I came here, I have divided my time between trying to repair the plane and agricultural pursuits. Yesterday I was out haymaking and feeding the poultry and the donkey and today I have been mowing a lawn and gathering strawberries; and beauties they are too, just like those in Hobart. Last night I went up to try the engine and as quite a crowd had collected, I threw the machine about a bit to test it. When I came down, they wanted to make a collection in aid of the 'poor airman.' I am writing this now so that it will catch the post. Best wishes and love to all from your loving son, Lyle'.

Although his mind and actions were firmly in the present, his thoughts also turned to the great adventure that lay before him as he outlined in a post script to the letter. 'P.S. There is a splendid model of Loos battlefield here at Norwich made by one of the men and about 10ft square. Dotted all over it are little electric globes too small to be seen at first, but on moving a lever over a lot of points they all light up in quick succession just exactly like shell bursts. It is still very windy and cloudy so we aren't doing much at the present. I hope it will clear as I am anxious to get into the air again. I am going to work up my French a bit in preparation for the other side.'

Once a pilot had flown some 25 hours or more, he was awarded with his Wings, although at this early stage of the war there appears to have been little consistency in criteria and method of their presentation. As before the needs of the front line dictated the amount of time available for training in-depth. One writer claimed, 'Fourteen hours! It's absolutely disgraceful to send pilots overseas with so little flying. My God. It's murder.' [67]

So, having gained his Wings and with his training completed, there was little else for Lyle to do but ready himself for the telegram from the RFC posting him to operational flying at a fighting squadron on the Western Front.

Chapter 8:
Life at the Front

Lyle Arrives at the Front

The writer Ralph Barker noted by comparison with their army comrades that the RFC lived a civilized life, still to some extent officers and gentlemen, comfortably housed in farms and sometimes chateaux. If squadron life at first was dominated by the public-school element, it was beginning, by 1916, to be democratized as casualties increased and men from all walks of life, not to mention 'colonials' as they were still apt to be called, contributed their own distinctive aura to the mixture. RFC Commander Trenchard's dictum, for reasons of morale, was 'no empty chairs at the breakfast table', and sure enough another raw newcomer would arrive the same day.[68]

Thus, it was that another raw newcomer, an 'Australian colonial' from East St Kilda, 2nd Lt Lyle Buntine wrote to his parents from the Hotel Cecil in London on 3rd July 1916 about his impending departure for the Front. 'I am writing this at one o'clock in the morning on the day of my departure for France. It is just almost a year (except a few days) since I left Australia and now, I am off for serious business. I have had a year in England

and on the whole enjoyed it fairly well and it is only right that now I should be up and doing, as my training is completed. I got my wings on July 1st the same date as that of my first commission in the CGS cadets in 1913. By the time you get this I shall be in the thick of the work in France. It does seem a long time since I first arrived in England. When I recall the different phases of the work, I can hardly imagine that it is only a year. There was the camp at Southampton, then the School at Ipswich, then the Sherwood Foresters Battalion and the training at Sunderland and afterwards the Reading school; then Thetford, Hythe and Norwich and now – well the serious business is starting. After living for almost a year in England I have been suddenly sent out to the front on 20 hours' notice. All today I have been collecting kit and equipment together and buying things that I needed before going out. It has been quite an interesting day and it came as rather a sudden surprise as I expected about another fortnight at least in England. But as I think I said once before a lot of us are being sent out now. I did not cable home as I did not think it was any use worrying Mother any sooner than necessary.'

It was not long before he had arrived in France and was writing to his mother once more. 'Just a line from Boulogne while waiting for a train to take me to my destination 'somewhere in France,' although I think it is somewhere near Amiens. We left Charing Cross this morning at about 11.30 and then got a boat from Folkestone and arrived here about 3.30. I have to wait until 9 o'clock before my train goes and quite a little party came over with me and as we knew each other it was very nice. On arriving here, we were split up into twos and threes and sent to different places, at least we were told where to go and are now waiting for trains. It was very funny on arriving here as none of our party could speak French very much, but with a great effort we managed by dint of putting our heads together to get a 'commissionaire' to take our baggage off the train to the cloak room and then got tickets for it and here we are waiting now to complete our journey. There are a lot of English soldiers about here; but mixed up with them are the blue coats of the French poilus. It's a funny world I have dropped into this time. Everyone jabbers and gesticulates terribly. It's enough to drive one crazy. Well I will stop now and go and see a Charlie Chaplin film somewhere, at least I can understand him.'

Later in his stay in France he tried to overcome his lack of language by reading French with the aid of a dictionary and trying to converse with some of the local inhabitants. He must have made some progress because by mid-August he was able write part of a letter to his mother in French and noted, 'I hope you will be able to read this. I'm glad to say that my French is improving a lot although not anywhere perfect yet; but I can usually understand the people now and I read the French papers.'

'*Tu me fis savoir dans to derniere letter que tu asrais revise savoir de la langue francaise ainsi je renferme un petit chapiter francais dans cette letter. Depuis peu nous avions eu une grande quantite de travail mais hier il pleuvait ainsi nous ne volions pas. Il y a quatre jous j' ai vale pendant plus de huit heures. A cela je valais de bonne heure le matin et le soir tres tard. Je trouve a ma bonne joie que nous vaons des chevaux, ainsi je vais a cheval tous les jous. C'est tres amusant. Je termine ma petit letter francaise en t'envoyant mes meilleurs baisers de France.*'

(In your last letter you had advised of your knowledge of the French language so I am reaffirming a little French chapter in this letter. Since we have had a great deal of work but it has rained so we have not flown. Four days ago I flew for more than 8 hours – I arrived on time in the morning and in the evening very late. I found to my great delight that we have horses so I go by horse every day – it's good fun. I finish my little French letter and send you my best wishes from France.)'

Lyle did make the observation early in his time in France that, 'These French people are funny and the people who live in our farm seem never to talk to each other except at the top of their voices and they are always having rows with one another or seeming to do so.'

No 11 Squadron

Lyle continued his journey to his posting the next day and described it in some detail, although under wartime censorship restrictions he was unable to disclose his location. 'Well here we are at last, as they say 'somewhere in France,' although my real address at present is 11th Squadron RFC, BEF France. You will have to guess at the date by the time this takes to reach you. I have had some very funny experiences on my way here especially in my attempts to speak French. Then again the trains over here are rather peculiar and remind me very forcibly of the Gembrook railway as you can walk alongside the train most of the time. I spent all last night in the train and it took 9 hours to do a journey which can be done in a car on the road in 1 hour comfortably. The last part of the journey here I did by car. The roads were fearfully dusty so when we got here, we looked like we had had a flour bag sprinkled over us.'

And so, it was that Lyle joined the 3rd Army's IIIrd Brigade's Royal Flying Corp's No. 11 Squadron as a replacement pilot only a few short days after the commencement of the Battle of the Somme. This squadron had originally been formed at Netheravon in England in 1915 and had arrived in France at the St Omer airfield on 25th July 1915. By the time Lyle joined them they had been based at Vert Galand, Villiers-Bretonneux and Bertangles, but had eventually settled in January 1916 at Savy, an airfield they also shared with No. 60 Squadron. 11 Squadron had been the first in the RFC to be equipped with the two-seater Vickers FB5 Gunbus in December 1915 and had consequently been seen as the first 'fighter squadron' in the RFC. In this 'pusher' type of plane the observer sat in front of the pilot, who in turn sat in front of the engine, and consequently the observer had an unobstructed field of fire. A 60 Squadron pilot thought very highly of the crews of the FB5's and FE2b crews of 11 Squadron and noted especially of the observers; 'They were not strapped in, and they had to move around their roomy little cockpits, oblivious of their safety, standing up on their little boxes, firing now forwards, now rearwards over the top plane, wielding their Lewis guns in the icy blast as though they weighed no more than rapiers. They also operated the bombsight and released the bombs. Although sluggish and difficult to manoeuvre, the machine was sometimes thrown about in combat, and then the observer sat on the floor with both legs from the knees down hanging over the outside of the cockpit, gripping the edge with the back of the knees and at the same time gripping the gun with both hands to hold on. At the best of times they had little more than a strong grip and a Lewis gun to hold on to, yet they claimed to have no fear of falling out. The airstream held them in.'[69]

 The FE2b was the make of aeroplane that Lyle would pilot in a number of operations and these craft had been delivered to the squadron in June 1916. Powered by a 160 hp engine positioned behind the pilot, it was a 'pusher' type of plane, its top speed was 91mph, and with a ceiling height of 11,000ft saw combat service longer than any other machine in World War 1. The plane was a two-seater, with a gunner in the nose, a position giving him a very wide field of fire for his free Lewis gun or guns, for sometimes two were fitted. In the latter case the second gun was a on a telescopic pillar mounting, enabling the gunner, by a considerable feat of gymnastics to stand and fire to the rear above the pilot's head. The craft proved a true fighter, especially during the Battle of the Somme, in the summer of 1916.[70]

No. 11 Squadron boasted a VC winner already in the form of Lt. G.S.M. Insall and amongst its pilots when Lyle arrived, was Lt Albert Ball who had joined the squadron on 7th May 1916 and who by the end of September that year would have claimed 31 German machines. Ball was somewhat of an eccentric character and preferred to live by himself in a hut at the aerodrome. During Lyle's time with the squadron Ball would fly many combat missions, but also spend some time away on leave and then be transferred to 8 Squadron for 'rest' duties. Ball would later transfer to No. 60 and No 54 Squadron and at the time of his death on 7th May 1917, had downed 44 enemy aircraft and had been awarded the VC, DSO and two bars, the Legion of Honour and the MC. Another notable squadron member during Lyle's time there was Frederick Libby, an American who became the first of his countrymen to down five enemy planes; but as an observer his scores did not qualify him to be recognised as such. During his time with both 11 and 23 Squadrons Libby was accorded ten aerial victories and on 26th September 1916 was awarded the Military Cross.

Life with the Squadron

Although it had been contended that the officers of the RFC lived a 'civilized life,' Lyle's letters paint a life of some contrast as concerns his accommodation and living conditions, although it could in no way be compared to the life of the soldiers in the trenches. 'Well we are staying at a farm at present, quite comfortable, but quite dirty. The house is built in the form of a square with living rooms on one side and stables on the other three. In the yard is a great pool of stagnant water in one corner and the sweepings from the stables all come out to the yard in which are a lot of ducks and fowls. These French farmers seem to be a very dirty lot. It has been raining today so not much doing in our line. All day we have heard the big guns though we are far away from the reach of the shells here. By a bit of luck, I discovered that we have some horses here, so managed to bag one for a ride this morning and this is the first ride I have had since leaving home. All the rain has cleared off and the weather is lovely so I can appreciate camp life. Of course, we have our meals in the farm, but have to live in tents. It's funny sort of weather here. If it's wet the roads are very muddy and within a few hours the rain stops they are all dust again. We get leave here about once in every 3 months which isn't bad, so by the time I get your reply to this it should be just about my turn. We have a splendid lot of fellows in the mess and get on well together in spite of the cockroaches – beasts. My tent is pitched in a very pretty orchard under a beautiful green chestnut tree, like the blacksmith and all-round the grass is beautifully thick and green though quite short like a lawn.'

A fortnight later his situation had changed and as the son of a school headmaster he wrote, 'It is rather a funny coincidence that my billet now is in a boys' school or 'Ecole des garcons' and as I am writing I can hear the little chaps at lessons in another room. I have just been furnishing the room a little with mats for the floor (which is brick) and a small spirit lamp etc.' But it was not long before he moved yet again. 'I have shifted my residence again. This time it is a tent in a very pretty little wood. Right in the centre all hidden by trees. This part of France is awfully pretty. No wonder the Frenchmen call it 'La Belle France.' And then he moved again five days later, 'What do you think? I have shifted again. This time to another farmhouse. Quite a comfortable place too. I think we shall be staying a little longer this time. I hope so anyway.' But these accommodation arrangements did not prove to be as comfortable as he had hoped. 'I told you in my last letter that I was living in a farmhouse. If I ever have my doubts about it, they were quite dispelled last night. This place reminds me very much of the Eastern Market at home. There are about a dozen fowls here and just before going to bed last night they all seemed to think the war was over and started cheering frantically – the roosters leading. Then about 11.30pm a wretched cow started to give us some music which lasted for some time. The next item was rendered by a fox-terrier which started at 2.30 and woke me up. He kept going for a solid half hour. The next interruption to my beauty sleep came in the form of my servant at 3.00am and I had to get up in a hurry to be ready to fly with the first signs of dawn. Finally, as I was going out of the gate, I was chased by half a dozen excited geese and had to fly for my life. I'm beginning to think that war is nearly as trying to the nerves as civilian life. I only hope tonight will be a little quieter.' His nerves were further tried by the advent of an insect infestation. 'For the last three weeks or so there have been a lot of mosquitos about. I've only got to open my windows at night with a light on and I can imagine I'm home – there I've just killed another. That makes ten.' But eventually things settled down and he was able to write to his father, 'I wish you could see the little room I have here. It is splendid and I've got it furnished nicely and pictures on the walls. It is nice to have some place where you can read and write quietly without being disturbed by anyone. It's much better than a tent, especially in this weather.'

He did however greatly enjoy being able to ride some horses on a regular basis and wrote, 'I was out for a ride this morning with my friend the Irishman and had a good gallop. There is some very fine country round here and we are getting some jumps put up. One of the horses here is a very fine jumper. He does about 5ft which is not too bad.' The Irishman, 2nd Lt Archibald James Cathie was his observer and had done a lot of work with another squadron before joining Lyle at 11 Squadron. Lyle wrote that, 'We have already had several hours flying together and we suit each other well.' He also noted his own brother Murray's improvement at billiards and noted that his own standard had gone down sadly due to playing French billiards on a table with no pockets. He was also pleased that the squadron had 'managed to import a set of cricket materials into our squadron so as this afternoon was very bad for flying, we managed to get in a good game.'

He also wrote of some entertainment and the beauty of the countryside, despite the hostile environment of war. 'It is just after 10.00pm and a glorious evening and a real Australian night with not a breath of wind. The air is quite warm and all is still except for the distant rumble of guns and the sound of the dynamo supplying light for the work-shops. I have just come from a concert which we got up. There was quite a lot of very good talent there too. After the concert I went for a stroll and watched the continual flicker of the star shells all along the line turning night into day and it is a wonderful sight like a gigantic fire-work display.'

His concern for the parlous state of his financial affairs continued into his life at the Front, although once again his parents came to his rescue, even if he did not always condone their methods. 'I have just received your letter containing a £5 bank note and yesterday I got one from mother containing a £5 draft. So, this makes £10 I got. You ask me if I received all your cables and letters. Yes, I have received each one you mention and have had altogether £60 from home. I don't know how to thank you for sending so much; but I don't think I shall need to ask for any more now as my pay, when I get it, completely covers expenses of mess bills etc and leaves some over. As I am now at the Front, I only need to spend about £10 a month and so I am saving quite a lot. This is certainly one advantage to being in France as you can't spend much money and your banking account goes up proportionately.

Don't you think it is rather risky sending money by post now that it is so irregular? Thank you very much for sending it. It was very good of you indeed and came just at an opportune time for me. In my last letter to Father I think I told him I had an account at Messrs Cox and Co's bank at 16 Charing Cross SW London and their Melbourne agent is the Bank of Australasia.' But he complained about the slowness of the military bureaucracy in recognising his changed in status now he was at the Front. 'They have a queer way of getting into the RFC over here. You must go into an Infantry regiment first and then go to Flying School and when you have finished your work there you are gazetted as a Flying Officer and after that you are sent out. You don't get your extra flying pay till you are gazetted and are not supposed to go out until you are. However, I have been out here for nearly three weeks; but have not been gazetted a Flying Officer yet owing to some delay or other. It's the usual way they do things and a lot of other chaps have the same bother. I wish they would hurry up though of course it makes no difference in the long run.'

Sharing News from Home and France

Contact with home and family and friends was always a high priority, which perhaps explains why Lyle was such a prolific letter writer, but at the same time he was eager to hear news from home as he noted a few weeks after his arrival in France. 'The event of the day out here is the arrival of the mail bag and I must say the postal service does very well indeed and we get our letters most regularly.' He noted the passing of the school year at CGS and wrote, 'By the time you get this letter I suppose the 3rd term will be well started and everyone in training for the sports. Please tell the boys to let me know the results and ask them to send me a program. They sent one last year and I can hardly imagine that it is a year ago as the time seems to be passing very quickly.'

To his younger brothers Murray, Arnold and Bobbie, he wrote in a very affectionate vein and was always interested in how their lives were progressing and was keen for their news, even if he sometimes adopted a light-hearted vein.

On the occasion of their father's birthday on 1st August 1916, he wrote to his medical student brother Murray, who was also studying at The University of Melbourne, 'Best wishes for your bones and prosectors exams. I see you are already ahead of where I stopped in Med. Thanks for paying my sub to the Medical Students' Society. Their magazine, the 'Spec' hasn't come yet, but it will probably roll along next mail. Things are getting fast and furious here now. I was up at 3 o'clock this morning and have been doing that about every second day since I came here. Another chap went up in my machine this morning and the damn fool came down and made a rotten landing and busted it up. I was pleased, I don't think! It kept me from going on a lovely stunt against the Huns, (can't tell you what it was.) Archie (German anti-aircraft fire) was makin' an awful ass of himself yesterday and the day before. I let him have a few pots at me and tried to see where he was shootin' from, so's we could lay some eggs on him but I couldn't spot it. There are a couple of wild Australians with me in this squadron. One from Wangaratta and one from Queensland, so we have a pretty good time. I have got a new observer now a 'wild Irishman' and quite a good sport. He wants me to go over and have some shooting on his place in Ireland when I get leave and I will if I can get off. We had an awful accident here the other day. A chap went up and stayed for a long time. In fact, so long that all his petrol ran out and he couldn't get down and I believe he is still up in the air and has starved to death. Rotten luck ain't it. I say, have you got a censor out home now? You seem to be suppressing the news and your letters aren't so breezy as they used to be. How did you get on at the billiards? Did you get into the final? I say 'scuse the writin' please but I have got a rickety old table. The Australians seem to be doing very well in France and the papers have quite a lot in about them. Well toor-a-loo as I must buzz off now. Best of luck in your exams from your affectionate brother, Lyle. P.S. Talk about heat, I've been in my shirt sleeves all day and sweating like the deuce. It's a horrible damp heat. Only about 70° or 80° but you feel it very much. P.P.S. I've just got to go and see if I can raise a "Hun" for a scrap so cheero.'

On the occasion of his own 21st birthday on 10th August 1916, he wrote to his brother Arnold and included a recent photo of himself, 'How are you getting along? Remember me to any of the lads who are about that I used to know and if any of my friends are coming over ask them to write to me c/- The Royal Aero Club, 166 Piccadilly, London. As you know I am out in France now and have had some pretty lively times. I have got quite used to Archie now, though I can't say I'm altogether in love with him. It's not nice to know that you are sitting up there and are the target for all the guns the Huns can bring to bear on you. I had a scrap with a Fokker a while ago which was quite exciting while it lasted, however he came off second best. It's rather rotten luck that I can't tell you anything about our doings here, but of course regulations must be obeyed. By Jove! the guns are kicking up an awful row now. It is a very calm night and sound carries a long way. It will be quite strange to live somewhere where you can't hear the guns. I've been flapping about a good deal lately, but it wasn't all enjoyable as I had rather a rotten jaw-ache yesterday. Today has been wet and rainy so I have only been up for an hour or so. Do you know I can hardly realise that it is my twenty-first birthday? Well ta-ta old chap. Write soon and let's hear the news. What do you think of the photo? I am your affectionate brother, Lyle.'

In a later reply to Arnold he wrote, 'It's great to know that the old school has got the premiership in footy again. When will you be playing again yourself?' But given the novelty of flight at that time he also included a letter he had written whilst in the air. 'I thought this might interest you as it is written in an aeroplane. I've just left the ground and I am up 1000 feet and just starting off for work. All the country is spread out underneath. Now we are passing a motor car on a road. Now a church. Now over a big wood. Now up 3000 ft and going for the lines. I can see them now. Wonder if I'll see any Huns tonight? Bump, I went through a big cloud just then. Up a bit higher now and very cold too. Quite a nice trip. I'm down again now. Plenty of Archie but no Huns this time. They've rung their tails. Ta-ta Lyle.'

On the subject of the growth of the oldest of his brothers he commented to his mother that, 'I'm beginning to think it's a good thing I started flying as from your accounts I may need it when home. Either that or a step ladder when speaking to Arnold and Murray. Aren't they ever going to stop growing? I'm sure I stopped long ago.'

He commented to his Mother on receiving a letter from his much younger brother Robert (Bob or Bobbie) that 'the last letter of Bobbie's is some letter and he has improved wonderfully.' To his youngest brother he wrote, 'Dear Little Bob, you did write me a nice long letter last time and I was very glad indeed to get it. How well you have been getting on! I wonder if you have been away for the August holidays? A little bird told me that the school is divided up into Houses now. Which one are you in? Don't forget to let me know how you get on in the Sports. I wonder how long it will be before we are all together again? Not long, I hope. The Germans are funny people. Especially their Flying Corps. They always try and run when they see us coming. But we have some good fights all the same. We have had quite a nice warm summer and it is getting on in to Winter now when we can't do very much flying. I am rather sorry that I've got to give up my nice little room and live in a tent for a while. Well Bob I'm afraid I haven't much more news so I will just say goodnight and best wishes from your loving brother, Lyle. PS. Write to me again soon.'

Personal Matters

But to his mother on the day of reaching his official adulthood, he wrote and sent a photo, 'I feel that I must write a few lines to you this evening, the evening of my twenty-first birthday. This is the second birthday I have spent away from you now, but I do hope that I'll be able to spend the next one with you and father, back home in Melbourne. Do you remember the funny little party I told you about, this time last year? I was on the *Orsova* then, this time it's France. I know you've been thinking of me and my thoughts have been with you and Father today. I haven't done very much work today as it's been rather wet so I've had a day off, except for an hour or so of flying. I am sending you a couple of copies of a photo I had taken a short while ago. The man standing up is my observer – an Irishman who has just got his commission. He is a very nice chap and we have often been out riding together on the horses. I'm jolly glad we've got the horses as we can get a little exercise on them and it's what we need here. I have got hold of some mementos out here and will try to send them home when I get back on leave. It is quite the fashion to collect pieces of shell etc. out here. I made quite a welcome discovery today. I have been wandering around for several days looking more or less like a third-rater or a caricature of Paderewski. But today I discovered that one of the men here used to be a barber so I looked him up and now I'm a little more like your son again. Well Mother, I'll stop now and write again later on. I'm expecting to get a letter from you tomorrow so au revoir and the very best love from your loving son. Lyle.'

Lyle also wrote that at the nearby hospital, Sunday was reserved for Officers and so after visiting the local bath-house for his bi-weekly clean up, he kept an appointment with the dentist. 'I am not doing very much today (compared with the usual) so am going to see the dentist – my usual trouble. I don't think my teeth will ever be any good.' He also noted that 'while I am on the ground now, I get a sort of perpetual ringing in my ears which is from the noise of the engine and changes of atmospheric pressure.'

He also wrote that he was awfully pleased to get their cable on the day of his birthday. This had been forwarded on to him in France by Miss Sylvia de Gay who had also sent him a birthday letter as well. Sylvia de Gay was a young violinist from Melbourne who had been viewed as such a child prodigy that in 1911 a public subscription and fundraising events were held by Melbourne 'society' to help swell the 'Sylvia de Gay Fund' to pay for a scholarship for her to further her studies in Vienna. She had performed at the Melbourne Town Hall and before the Governor of Victoria and in due course, accompanied by her mother and sister, duly proceeded overseas to pursue her studies. However, after the outbreak of war and being stranded in Austria, a hostile country, fortunately in April 1915 they were involved in an exchange between 'English' and German women and they were able to return to London.[71] In England Miss de Gay had been performing in concerts with Ada Crossley, the renowned Australian singer and Lyle had obtained the latter's autograph which he had forwarded to some friends at home. Lyle seems to have formed quite a strong friendship with Sylvia as she is often mentioned in his letters and Lyle used her mother's address in London as a place to where his letters could be forwarded. As the war progressed, Sylvia gave numerous performances in England and eventually joined a travelling concert party, Lena Ashwell's Modern

Troubadours, and spent time performing to troops in Egypt and the Middle East. Whether a romance had existed between Lyle and Sylvia may never be known, however she remained in Egypt with the concert party only leaving it when she married a British army officer in May 1918.

Other family members were not far from his thoughts and in various letters he mentions such people as Murray Richardson, a young girl who was a friend of her Buntine cousins and who had stayed at Scotland with them and who had taken to sending him cigarettes on a regular basis. His mother inquired about their South African Buntine cousins and Lyle replied that, 'I have just got your last letter written on July 5th. In it you ask about Uncle Bob's girls and Mrs Pinson. I haven't heard of her for a long while and do not know if she is still alive or not; but I think she is. I had a letter from Jessie a few days ago. She and Noelle are with Cousin Mima and the Richardson girls up at Elie for their holidays. I think Jessie is anxious to leave school and go back to Africa or come to Australia.'

To help him settle into life far away from home, his Aunt Sara and another woman had sent him 'letters of introduction' to their English friends and family; 'It was very nice indeed of them to send them over and I shall use them at the first opportunity I get, although it will be some time before I back to England.' He related that he had received a letter from his soldier cousin Jack (John) Gibbs who, 'seems to be fairly well and having a pretty fair time of it in London.'

But his thoughts were firmly planted at home when he wrote to his father on the August night of Walter's birthday. 'I was up at 3 o'clock this morning, long before dawn. When we are working here, we work pretty hard I can assure you. It is just 9.45am (summer time) so it will be 7.25pm with you and I have been trying to think what you and Father will be doing. You will probably be in the dining room writing and Father will be in his study or with you. I wish I could wish Father 'Many Happy returns' personally. But I'm thinking it all the same. Ta-ta to Mother and best love to yourself and Father from Lyle.'

To his younger sister her wrote a month later, 'Thank you so much for your birthday letter. I got it a bit late but that didn't matter at all. It was kind of you to think of me. I am always thinking of the folks at home and wondering how long it will be before I see you all again. I shall be very glad when that day comes. We have been very busy all summer and now the wet weather has come when everything gets slowed down. I have moved from my room and had to take a tent. But it's not too bad and I'm fairly comfortable. I had a letter from Jack Gibbs this morning. He seems to be fairly well and having a good time. It's rather rotten luck that all my friends are over in England now I have come out to France. Well Girlie, I'm afraid I'll have to leave off now as I haven't much news.' But as always with a serviceman in wartime, some matters could not be written about at all as Lyle ruefully commented, 'I'm afraid I've not much news as all the interesting bits are 'taboo.' The life out here is so full of incident; but so much bound up with our work that of course we can't say much about it.'

But matters of accommodation, money and domesticity were secondary to the fact that Lyle was there to undertake important military work and so he soon took up his duties as a pilot in the Royal Flying Corp's No. 11 fighter squadron.

Chapter 9:
Aerial Combat at the Battle of the Somme

The Battle of the Somme (July – November 1916)

'During the period of preparation before the Battle of the Somme, the RFC had been successful in securing both a numerical and qualitative superiority over the disputed battlefields. The RFC had struggled in the early stages of the aerial preparations, but the arrival of the new generation of aircraft, coupled with the determination to follow a cold blooded aggressive air strategy, had left them ready to reap the fruits of aerial supremacy at the very moment it most mattered, when the offensive was finally launched.[72] At the end of the day of July 1st, and victorious on the ground, it was apparent that the Germans had been roundly defeated in the air. Over the battlefield it was estimated that some 100 pilots were in the air for some 108 hours and there were only nine combats. The British had truly harvested the fruits of the RFC aerial supremacy.[73] The artillery observation aircraft were almost immune from the attentions of the German scouts pinned back miles behind their own lines by the British offensive patrols.⁷⁴ British Commander Haig realized his dreams of a breakthrough were unlikely to be realised in the short term, and he came to see the fighting in July and August as an attritional period whereby the strength of the German Army would be worn down ready for another major offensive in mid-September. ⁷⁵ By late July, there were serious battles in the air as the reinforced German scout formations fought hard to prevent successful raids on their vital rail junctions.⁷⁶ In all this fighting the RFC continued to play its part. It was absolutely central to the detailed planning of the attacks for the contact patrols to determine where the troops had got to, while the aerial photography exposed the exact location of hitherto unseen trench lines, machine gun posts and trench mortars.⁷⁷ The raison d'etre of the scouts was to protect the Corps' machines. The pilot's reward was made manifest only in the continuation of the routine reconnaissance and artillery observation flights. The Corps' aircraft operated behind the invisible screen provided by the offensive patrols of the scouts. But the cost to the scout squadrons was a constant drip, drip of casualties which slowly raked backwards and forwards through the ranks until few of their original personnel remained. Pilots became experienced veterans in just a few weeks, if they survived.⁷⁸ Many pilots however, did not understand that the whole principle of Trenchard's air offensive relied on the scouts not being tied to the Corps' machines. They often were there, but their prime job was to seek out and destroy the German aircraft, wherever they may be and preferably well behind the German lines. They were not to play policemen patrolling a beat. ⁷⁹

The Official History of the War in the Air emphasised that it became possible at this time for the RFC to do its work for the army without effective opposition from the Germans, due to two main contributing factors. 'It must now be told how it was possible for the RFC to do its work for the army little hindered by the German air service. This was brought about in two ways – by seeking out and fighting the enemy's aeroplanes far over his own lines and by creating such a threat to the vitals of his communications, through incessant bombing, that he was compelled to use up much of his fighting strength in defence.[80] Perhaps the most important work of the Flying Corps during these days was the methodical location and registration of the new (gun) emplacements, an essential preliminary to counter-battery work.[81]

This work by the RFC was so effective in the stage of the Battle of the Somme from July until early September that the German General von Below later complained of three areas of dominance by the RFC in these early weeks. 'First: The enemy's aerodromes enjoyed complete freedom in carrying out distant reconnaissance. Second: With the aid of aeroplane observation the hostile artillery neutralized our guns and was able to range with most extreme accuracy on our trenches. Third: By means of bombing and machine gunning from a low height against infantry, battery positions and marching columns, the enemy's aircraft inspired our troops with a feeling of defencelessness.'[82] German records subsequently described July and August 1916 as the blackest days in the history of the German Air Force.

The first phase of the Battle of the Somme in the first two weeks of July 1916, saw the British, at enormous cost, gain a six-thousand-yard footing on the main or Bazentin ridge, despite stubborn German resistance that lasted about a fortnight. During that time, and beyond, Trenchard's declared objective of keeping the German Air Force too preoccupied in defence either to interfere significantly with the work of the corps squadrons, or to intrude effectively over the British lines, was achieved.[83] The second phase of the battle, which lasted for two months, until mid-September, settled into a tense and debilitating struggle for possession of the main ridge. Most significant for the RFC was that the German Air Force began to show signs of a recrudescence.[84] But for most of that summer, however, the RFC enjoyed an air superiority they were never to know again, and life in the better equipped squadrons seemed ideal, so far as soldiering could be ideal in wartime.[85]

Given that RFC No. 11 Squadron was equipped with fighting machines it was no surprise to find that they had largely been employed on escorting bombing raids on the allotted IIIrd Brigade northern section of the Somme battlefield. The brigade also found time to make numerous attacks on the major town of Bapaume and on the occupied villages to the west and south of the town and the Official War History noted, 'The raids were made chiefly by B.E.2c's of No's 8 and 12 Squadrons and to a less extent, of No. 13 Squadron. Escorts were provided, up to the end of August by No's 11 and 23 Squadrons, after which date No. 60 Squadron, on 1st September on their return to the front from a temporary rest, took on the duties of No. 23. Each bombing pilot carried usually two 112lb bombs and the escorting pilots often dropped, in addition, a small number of 20 pounders.'[86]

The Royal Flying Corps Communiques[87] were weekly communiques produced for internal RFC consumption in the air arm from June 1915 until the end of 1916. Whilst not covering every single combat, casualty or event in the RFC, they do provide an excellent source of day-day operational detail during this period of time. This is especially important as 11 Squadron does not have a published history of its service in the Great War. On some days the communiques outline specific combats of interest and also special acts of heroism, but also record the daily weather conditions, especially when flying was not possible. The first few days of the Battle of the Somme, naturally enough, saw heavy activity on all fronts and it was recorded that on July 2nd although the weather was fine, there was a great deal of cloud during the morning, successful reconnaissance was carried out on all fronts. On the same day there were 11 combats on the fronts of the IIIrd and the adjoining IVth Armies, with four enemy aircraft being brought down, sadly at the loss of two of 11 Squadron's pilots. In a world first feat on the 3rd July, just the day before Lyle joined the squadron, it was recorded that Capt. Crooks of 11 Squadron brought down an enemy kite balloon using Le Prieur aerial torpedoes. These weapons had been designed by an officer of the French Naval Air Service and were mounted on the wing struts of the Nieuport planes, were fired electronically and were primarily intended as an anti-balloon weapon.

Lyle in Combat

Lyle's baptism into his flying duties must have been arduous and to some extent frustrating as the communiques' daily reports indicated fickle and inclement weather in the first few weeks of July. Notes in the official records such as, 'Low clouds, rain and thunder, a very unfavourable day for flying; low clouds all day until evening; weather unfavourable; weather again unfavourable; a thick cloud bank east of the line made observation difficult; clouds and mist, no flying until evening; very misty in the morning; clouds, mist and rain – unfavourable weather for any successful flying,' were very common. In fact, even in the last two weeks of July, although the weather seemed to improve, the daily reports were still indicating difficult conditions. 'The weather almost entirely prevented work before evening; on the IIIrd Army front there was no activity; fine, but low clouds all day, so little artillery co-operation was possible; clouds were again low throughout the day making artillery work difficult; weather continued unfavourable for observation until evening; and finally, although the weather cleared in the afternoon there was still a considerable amount of ground haze, which made observation difficult.'

Lyle often commented on the weather and given the nature of his work and the dangers involved he wrote in various letters, 'I am really wishing for bad weather now to give us a bit of a rest.' 'Yesterday was Sunday and as it was wet it was a quiet day for us.' 'Today again is wet and the clouds are very low so though I have been warned for duty, I don't expect I will go up.' 'It has been wet and raining today which is rather good luck for us as we have an easy time. Of course, the wet days are very bad for the men in the trenches, but it's an ill wind that blows no one any good.' On some days conditions were deemed satisfactory for flying, but once in the air the situation could be a very different one to that on the ground as Lyle related. 'Today has again been wet and frightfully windy. As you rise higher so the strength of the wind increases proportionately and this morning, I climbed pretty high and at one time had the experience of being blown backwards. I seemed to be moving slowly over the ground tail-first. The worst of it was that I was too close to the trenches for comfort. You may be sure that I quickly got down to a lower level where the winds weren't so strong. In the end I had to come down altogether as a rain storm came up.' 'Today we have had more rain. It looks as though it has set in for a real wet week, so I suppose we'll have all this time to make up when it is fine next.' 'Today we have been more or less moping round in hourly hopes of the weather clearing. But it only grew worse. During the afternoon we had a terrific thunderstorm and bigger hailstones than I have ever seen anywhere. I fact you couldn't call them hailstones. They were just pieces of ice, some nearly as big as your fist. I invested in some rubber boots a while ago. They cost 50 francs but were well worth it. I have been able to walk where I wanted lately and down some of the roads which are nearly knee-deep in water and mud while other people have a bad time of it.'

Despite these weather conditions, the squadron's work had to continue and the communiques noted a number of bombing raids on an ammunition dump at Croiselles, Bapaume Station, St Leger, the railway sidings at Moyenville and on the railway line itself between the towns of Vitry and Douai. Other raids were carried out on Aichet-le-Grand and Henecourt. But all this activity came at a cost and Communique No. 42 which reported on the period from 4th – 12th July recorded that, although there was no significant challenge to RFC superiority, the scale of their operations inevitably resulted in a continuing high casualty rate. Since the start of the battle some twenty-four RFC aeroplanes had been lost with thirty-nine aircrew personnel killed or missing.

But at times flying duties just had to take priority and the advent of finer and more consistent weather meant that Lyle was able to report about his life in the air. He set the scene for his parents in one of his early letters when he wrote, 'Somebody the other day said that the life of an officer in the RFC was one of hours of idleness punctuated by moments of intense fright. Well, he didn't go so very far wrong. Of course, he means that on lots of days it is impossible to fly and we just spend them looking over the machines and keeping them in good condition. Then perhaps we may have a patrol of say 3 or 4 hours and during the whole of that time Archie is popping off at you and you hear the little pops all round and see the clouds of smoke and then realize that you are certainly unpopular with someone down below and you get angry and want to throw things at them; (so you throw bombs). You know the maps in the papers showing the position of the line from time to time. It is very interesting to have a look at those and then go up and fly over the places mentioned and compare the maps with the actual thing as we see it outlined beneath us.' Even at this early stage of his combat career he was well aware of the dangers involved and wrote, 'I have arranged as you have asked for you to be cabled should any necessity arise; but I hope it won't though I'd be awfully glad to see you over here mother. By the way in case of accidents all my belongings will be sent to Cox and Co, 16 Charing Cross London SW and are kept there until claimed.'

When he came to writing about his actual combat flying, he was at times somewhat guarded and tried to use humour to convey his experiences to his family, even if the humour was a little bleak. In response to a letter from his younger brother Murray who described a run-away motor bicycle, Lyle described an incident between an RFC pilot and a French farmer. 'What do you think? An aeroplane did the same thing the other day with one of the fellows. He had a forced landing and when he got things fired up, he got a 'yokel' to help him start it. He turned the propeller and told the 'yokel' when to switch on. The silly owl did so too soon with the result that the 'bus' went off at top speed and sailed away by itself into the air. The 'yokel' and pilot jumped clear so they were all right, but the machine went on up to 300 or 400 feet and then got its nose up too far and slid gently onto the ground, tail first completely finishing it.' The same letter described another 'humorous' incident. 'A funny thing happened a short time ago. One of our machines was chased by a Fokker and dived steeply to get away. Another of ours suddenly appeared and chased the Fokker. Then another Fokker came along and if you please another British machine, so the people on the ground saw five machines all in a line diving steeply to the ground and firing hard at one another all the time.'

But Lyle could also laugh at himself and described another humorous incident, which was in reality a very close call for all concerned. 'A rather funny incident happened last time I was flying. You have heard of the 'sausage' or kite-balloon employed for observation and anchored behind our lines. Well, last time

I was up it was very cloudy with the clouds about 4000 feet, so I got well up above them and after working for two or three hours up there I started to come down again. All the time we could only see the ground in patches but still enough to steer by. When I came down, we had to go right through the clouds and when we got through them, I suddenly saw that we were just on the same level as a 'sausage' and going straight for him and only about 100 yards away. When you are travelling about 70 miles per hour it doesn't take long to do 100 yards. I banked quickly and so turned out of the way. But imagine the feelings of the people in the 'sausage' when they saw me coming straight for them out of a cloud. I bet they weren't particularly pleased.'

As always Lyle was a keen observer of life and events around him and wrote to a number of people about his day and sights from the air. 'We do, however get magnificent views of the fighting and often see the yellow clouds of gas moving across from one set of trenches to the other. Occasionally we see a mine blow up and all the time there is continual bursting of shells. Then there are the fights in the air and during a fight you live quicker than you would ever have thought possible before. However sometimes it rains and then we can't go up at all so just sit about smoking. But we have not had very many slack days lately.'

Although he tended to dismiss the annoyance and dangers of German anti-aircraft fire, Lyle also expressed a general wariness about being hit, even though he tried to laugh off the incessant 'Archie' (Flying Corps slang for anti-aircraft fire) he encountered almost every time he flew. In his first letters home he wrote, 'We get plenty of flying here and a fair amount of fun. Of course, 'Archie' is a bit of a nuisance, but it is quite pretty to see the little clouds of smoke left by the bursting shells. Sometimes they come rather close and then are unpleasant.' Later that month he wrote, "Archie' was very amusing today and made an absolute fool of himself. He wasted dozens of shots on machines that he should have known he couldn't hit.'

But he also wrote to Mrs Allan at Harefield Hospital at about the same time when trying to give a general description of his flying experiences. 'I have had some interesting experiences since I came out here. It's the usual thing to go up and see the air full of puffs of smoke from bursting shells all around you. Some of them come jolly close too. A couple of days ago I came down with the plane riddled with holes; but fortunately, I wasn't hurt. 'Archie' has developed a bad habit of throwing up a lot at a time now and you have to move pretty quickly to dodge him.' But as he moved into August, he was a little more reflective in a letter to his mother. 'Another pretty strenuous day and I had some pretty close shaves. 'Archie' was better than I have ever seen him in quite a long while. It makes you think a lot when a shell bursts about 10 feet away and pieces go through the machine as some did this afternoon. This morning I was playing target for 'Archie' who got a couple of inners, but no bullseyes; so, I got back all right. But I always remember that you are praying for me and it gives me courage.' But to his younger brother Murray he took a more cavalier approach as he described his work as an artillery spotter. 'Archie' was makin' an awful ass of himself yesterday and the day before. I let him have a few pots at me and tried to see where he was shootin' from, so's we could lay some eggs on him but I couldn't spot it.' Eventually he confided to his father, 'The life out here is full of incident; but so much bound up with our work that of course we can't say much about it. I have had some pretty narrow shaves since I got out here in all sorts of ways. It's not nice to be over in Hun territory and get the contents of a shrapnel shell into your machine as happened once, well more than once, and just get back. I think I told you in my last letter that I have broken my duck with regards to aerial scraps.'

But eventually Lyle's luck with 'Archie' ran out as he described in a letter in late August to his father. 'Well I've had an exciting time of it lately. My engine was hit by 'Archie' and I just got back over the lines where I had another forced landing in view of the German trenches. I landed near a Brigade Headquarters where a Brigade Major found me and I ended up having dinner with the General and a lot of Staff Officers and had a good time. While I was there during the evening, the Huns started shelling the machine and one shell dropped 8 yards away, but did no great damage. We could hear the shell coming about 6 seconds before it got to us. I got the nose-cap of the shell that came so close and some of the men got the caps from the other shells that dropped all round. After dark I moved the machine behind some trees and no more shells dropped, as they thought we had gone. I got the engine fixed up and returned safely the next morning. The Germans must have been very annoyed when I took off.'

But danger also lurked in the sky from enemy aeroplanes and Lyle shared some memories of his first combat experience as well as one that could have cost him his life. 'As the events happened some time ago, I don't think there can be any harm in telling you about a couple of the aerial combats that I have had. The first time I ever saw a German machine was on the second occasion of going across the lines and was only a short trip above the clouds. I was flying along with some other machines, but I had got rather far behind. Suddenly the shelling stopped, and I saw just above me and slightly behind, a small grey monoplane diving straight at us. There was no need to turn field-glasses on to him to see whether he was German or not, for almost immediately came the pop-pop-pop-of his gun. Quickly we replied, but he was past in a flash and manoeuvring underneath. He came at us three times again and then we got into a position where we could fire at him without him being able to reply. However, just then our gun had a temporary stoppage and he dived straight to earth. I think we hit him all right, but he was under control. This chap was the much-talked-of Fokker. The only damage we got in this scrap was a couple of bullet holes in the wings which didn't matter. I shall never forget my feelings in this first scrap. When I first saw him coming, my first thought was, what a pretty machine and how well he flies. Then came the sound of his gun and I realised that he was doing his best to bring me down and if I didn't get busy mighty sharp, he would succeed. Another time I tackled a big two-seater German. He was a good way above me to start with and we were both firing hard, when I felt something hit my hand and almost at once the engine stopped. He had got a bullet in my petrol-tank and also on the way in it had smashed one of the instruments and cut an electric wire and two of the control wires. It was a splinter of wood that hit my hand. I thought for a moment or two that it was all up; but luckily another of our machines turned up and so allowed me to get safely across the lines which were not far away. We were not out of the wood, however, when the other machine turned up. We had to cross the line rather low and the Germans turned field guns on to us and I could hear the whistle of rifle bullets fired from the trenches at us. It was quite an exciting experience and I thanked God when I was safely down. On another occasion, I saw a machine in the distance behind me, so just went on pretending not to see him and this gave him courage and up he came. I let him get fairly close and then whipped round suddenly and let him have it hot and strong. I never saw a more surprised German and he disappeared in a wild dive. Directly after he had gone, I saw another, so I went after him full tilt, but he didn't wait to say 'How do you do?' to us and I could only get in some long-range shooting. I don't think I ever told you of my visit to the 'Big Push.' Well on one occasion I had to land there, only about a thousand or two thousand yards from the front-line trenches. Then I realised what trench fighting was like as shells were bursting all round and some within 30 yards of where I was. At one place the Germans had laid their guns onto a road and kept up a continual fire on it. All the time there was a stream of men and horses going along it and the noise was terrific. It surprised me to see how well the horses stood it. The sound of a shell on the ground is totally different from the sound in the air. When a shell bursts near you in the air, you hear one loud bang and that is all. On the ground, however, after the burst you can hear the reverberations and echoes, which seem to magnify the sound. On the whole though, I don't think I should mind the shells much on the ground because you can always comfort yourself with the reflection that you haven't got far to fall if you do get hit.'

After only a few weeks of first-hand experience over the Somme battlefield, he was able to give a definite opinion about the characteristics needed by a pilot to survive and in response to the death of a former Brighton Grammar schoolboy RFC pilot. 'You mention about the Brighton Grammar School old boy who was killed while learning. It seems to me now that I look back on it that the most dangerous time is while learning. The first few times a man goes up he is tempted to try and out-do the others and you do awfully silly and dangerous things. However, one thing I noticed particularly is that you can nearly always recognise the type of man who is going to have accidents. A man who is slow and even sure on the ground and in everyday life is no good in the air. You've simply got to do things quickly. And especially out here in France where you have anti-aircraft guns of all kinds and enemy aeroplanes carrying machine guns to contend with.'

But as August came the bombing raids of the 3rd Brigade continued mainly on the railway stations at Bapaume and Bihacourt, whilst attacks were made on the aerodrome at Brayelles. Other raids were carried out on Oppy, Grevillers and Boyelles. The aerodrome at Douia which housed some Fokker detachments was also regularly bombed, sometimes three times on the one day. The inclement weather during mid-August also saw little or no flying and it was not until 19th August that 3rd Brigade was able to resume bombing missions against hostile trenches near Gommecourt and in the valley between Warlencourt and Courcellette. But a few days later on 22nd August the squadron was involved in a major aerial battle with a large formation of German planes consisting of LVG's and Rolands. The enemy force was routed and with two of their planes destroyed and one sent down, 11 Squadron reported that the description of aircraft flying in all directions suggested a near state of panic amongst the Germans.[88]

For the remainder of the month 11 Squadron and the Third Wing maintained its escort role to bombing and reconnaissance missions with notable actions on 2nd September when a patrol encountered five enemy aeroplanes and fought a battle which resulted in the loss of three squadron members either killed or missing and one wounded.

Lyle tried at times to make light of his situation in a variety of ways. 'I wish I could tell you all the things that have happened lately. All I can do is to assure you that we have been very busy and the Huns haven't been particularly pleased at the form our work has taken.' Lyle's daily routine was naturally determined by operational matters, the weather and enemy activity, amongst other things. He tried to paint an idea of his day during various parts of his correspondence and it should be remembered that he was no doubt trying to paint any events in the best and safest possible light. After just three weeks he gave the first indication of his work load. 'It is now 12 o'clock and I've had a pretty hard day. In addition to several hours flying I have had a lot of work while on the ground as I was the orderly officer today. I am writing in my room and have just walked down from the aerodrome about 1 mile away. It is not a very easy road to find at night either, as the path goes along a winding railway embankment, over a bridge and through a small wood.' A few days later he wrote to Mrs Allen, 'I suppose you are wondering what has become of me. Well, I have been absolutely as full as I can stick of work and when the evening comes, we are usually too tired to write letters. I got up at 3 o'clock this morning and have been on the go ever since. We do this about every second day and the other days we get up late, i.e. at 6 o'clock. It's usually past eleven before we can get to bed so you can understand that I'll be ready for leave when I get it.' To his mother a few days later, 'I posted you a letter today so this is just a note before I go to bed. I'm so tired I can hardly write. I've been up since 3 o'clock this morning and have had a lot of work,' whilst a day later he told her, 'I had quite a late morning this morning. I didn't have to get up till 5.30am, but since then have been going hard. It is only lunchtime and I have already been up for 4 hours in the air.'

A week later and there was still no let-up in his day. 'Well I had rather a record day yesterday. I seemed to live in the air and only come down for meals. I think I'll have to agitate for an eight hours day for poor aviators, when I get into parliament. Again, today I have done plenty of work though not so much as yesterday.' But sometimes the long day turned out alright for him. 'Yesterday was Sunday; but there's no rest for the wicked. I had to get up at 6 o'clock and be on duty all day until dark. Today has been wet again so up to the present I have just been 'standing by' on the aerodrome. I wrote the last bit at lunchtime and during the afternoon it cleared up and so we went over and strafed some Huns and as usual got plenty of 'Archie.'

But for Lyle each day brought action and danger although he was able to write about them in a light-hearted manner and at the same time offer his own insights into his experiences. After six weeks with the Squadron he wrote home, 'We had a most interesting little scrap a short time ago. It would have made you laugh to see the Huns all sprinting for home with us after them. The funny part was that they were far more at the time than we were and also over their own land. The air was thick with bullets and shells and we could hardly see for the smoke and a haze that came up as well. They didn't want to get bitten. Their only thought was to get home as soon as possible. Sorry I can't tell you more about it or when it happened. Often when we have seen some Huns, their first action is to put their nose down and make for home at top speed. I often wonder what they tell their commanding officers to account for their precipitate retreat. I must mention that fur waistcoat that you sent to me. It has been doing very good service indeed. I have not used it much until this month. But lately the weather has been getting quite cool and I can assure you that the temperature is considerably cooler above ten thousand ft than at sea-level and I can always manage to feel cold if I want to. Of course, the great cure for cold is 'find a Hun' and in the ensuing excitement you get quite warmed up. It often amuses me to think of how we used to make heroes of Harry Hawker and Gilbieaux at home and really their flights were such easy things to do. Harry H has got a nice easy and highly paid job in England and I don't think he has done very much fighting at all.'

The very next day he wrote again, 'Well I had another pretty fair scrap today and the Hun did some pretty good shooting. One bullet hit my petrol tank and so put me rather out of it. Only another half inch and I would have had some sick leave. Today has been rather an eventful one for me and I've had some interesting experiences apart from the little scrap. I wish that I could tell you some of the things that happen. I seem to be talking an awful lot about myself and you must be getting rather bored with it all. Well I'll shut off steam for a while and get to bed. I am ever your loving son, Lyle.'

To further explain his own experiences and to try to give a view of his life from another perspective, Lyle sent home a clipping from the English Daily Mail newspaper where a war correspondent described the role of the Royal Flying Corps in battle. Lyle commented to his father about the article that, 'The writer is of course a layman with regard to the air. It's all very nice to talk the way he does, but he doesn't mention 'Archie.' I have been out here now nearly two months and have had four fights with varying results.'

LATE WAR NEWS
Our All-Seeing Airmen. Every Enemy Gun Marked.
Increasing Value of the Bomb.

From W. Beach Thomas – With the British Army in the Field – Wednesday

'In watching the British attack up-hill towards Thiepval and among trenches as tangled as a pattern of quick hedge in winter I saw, but nearly missed, a spectacular detail full both of beauty and meaning. Lifting my eyes a moment from the battle among the ditches I caught sight of one of our aeroplanes. It served as a pointer to another and then another, until the sky seemed full of them, all quite inaudible through the noise of the guns. Some were high, some comparatively low. No German gun could shout without drawing their eagle eye to it, and no German plane came near to return the compliment to spy upon our fire. I believe that our artillery hit over a score of enemy emplacements this day, but I know that not from the information of my own eyes. What happened in the air above me was this. These circling eagles of ours saw one German plane, greatly daring, though skied inconceivably high, making towards our line. In a moment their dilettante circling ceased and the flock steered a straight course for the enemy. 'Up and at 'em' is at least as true of a British airman as of the British soldier. 'Down and away' was the only possible answer of the German and he took this alternative with admirable celerity.

Spacious Vision

Our airmen always thus gather to a battle. They have a strange experience. Again and again when the storm breaks they see the thunderbolt. Our great howitzer shells at the top of their flight are perfectly visible, and even give the impression of not travelling at any immediate speed. As the war goes on many airmen find that they see scores of things previously invisible. They know what to look for and perhaps become attuned to what they work in, gaining a technical as well as a spacious vision. How much their universal presences, their eyes as well as their missiles, have affected the enemy's emotions, we know from many letters and other evidence. So even in close and local attacks on trenches our airmen play their part and make beneficent journeys over the infantry. But one hardly heeds them. It is difficult to attend to any part of the field, except where the infantry is engaged, especially in a fight of this nature. One forgets the artillery itself if a single fighting soldier is visible. And the men are more visible in every attack than was the case in the early trench fighting with bombs.

Success Every Time

The value of the bomb increases daily. Even in such a frontal attack as I saw and described yesterday the bomb took the first place. It is yet more prominent in the smaller fights which are now succeeding. I will try and explain how and why. On both ends of the line now converging on Thiepval we are moving up and not across trench lines – though of course they are zig-zagged and criss-crossing interminably. On the left of our advance up the steady slope to that little fringe of trees which is Thiepval the dominant object is the trench. The parapets are singularly distinct in spite of the shells and their mosaic is still unbroken. On the right, where we move slanting-wise out of the old German second line, the shell hole predominates. In both spheres we have continued to make way by bombing and in spite of violent counter attacks the German has failed. Give our men enough bombs and they now win every time. If their bomb is a good a missile and does not fail in quantity none of these stiff local attacks fails and such struggles are almost continuous in this part of the field.'[89]

Although the German planes may have been described as 'down and away' by the journalist, danger still lurked for many Allied pilots especially in the area of the Front where the German aces Max Immelmann and Oswald Boelcke. Boelcke was among the first of the successful German air fighters of the Great War and by mid-June 1916 had scored 19 victories against Allied aircraft. The first biography written about him stated that Boelcke's skill and diplomacy now came to the fore in producing a scheme for the new concept of fighting air units. The new units would be called Jagdstaffeln (Jastas) and in the summer of 1916 with the Battle of the Somme about to begin, Boelcke was recalled from leave to take up his duties.[90] Oswald Boelcke was given command of Jasta 2 on 30th August 1916 and on 2nd September Boelcke downed his twentieth victim. This was Captain Robert Wilson flying a DH2 from 32 Squadron who was forced to land when his plane caught fire and came down near Thiepval with Wilson surviving to become a POW. Boelcke later visited Wilson and invited him to visit his aerodrome and then entertained him in the mess. The first batch of new Fokker biplanes was delivered on 6th September and Boelcke claimed other victories on 8th and 9th September over Flers and Bapaume respectively. The War Diary for his Jasta records just nine individual 'hunting expeditions' in the period up to 14th September, but Boelcke's still managed to achieve five victories during the week of September 8th – 15th. His first combat mission with the new Jasta was flown on 17th September, two days after Haig renewed the assault in what became the third and final phase of the Battle of the Somme.[91] Lyle was indeed fortunate not to have encountered Jasta 2 in action as when 11 Squadron encountered them in aerial combat on 17th September, four of the Squadrons' planes were downed, including one claimed by Boelcke himself. A further two 11 Squadron planes were downed by Boelcke in October 1916.

After being based at Savy since January in 1916, 11 Squadron moved to a new base at Izel-Le-Hameau on 31st August with all the associated work of relocation of an entire squadron, whilst at the same time trying to maintain an involvement in flying operations. Lyle was not one to reveal his true feelings about his life and circumstances, but in one letter to his father written in early September he wrote not only of his experiences, but of his sense of foreboding each time he took to the air. He also mentioned the circumstances surrounding the relocation of the squadron and took the chance to contrast it with his move from Broadmeadows to Seymour in the early days of his enlistment.

'I have just received your letter written on the 9th July. I have been writing you a long letter containing a fair account of our work – as much as I am allowed to say. I will not post it just yet; but send this instead. I must thank all at home for their long letters and I do enjoy them very much. After being in nice billets for the summer we have moved into tents now for the winter. It's rather a funny arrangement but we have got to make the best of it. The guns are making a big noise this morning. It sounds louder because the wind is that way. At present we are in rather a muddle and working hard to get things straightened out. It is no joke for a whole squadron to move. But the organisation here is very good. The Australians could well take a lesson from it. Do you remember the time we moved from Broadmeadows to Seymour and what a time of it we had up there? And that time you drove up in the car and we had an impromptu picnic. I wrote the last part of this letter during the morning; but left in a hurry as I got word that we had to go up at once. However, clouds came up too low to let us do our work. We started again to try this afternoon but this time a thunderstorm came and we had to go back again. The guns have rather increased in shelling during the day. It is now raining hard and I am writing by candle-light. The candles are kept in a continual flicker by the concussion of the guns. I don't envy any poor fellows in the trenches on a day like this. I have managed to make my tent very comfortable now with the aid of my servant who is not too bad. You know they say in the army that the man who makes the best officer's servant is a burglar. By Jove! It's true. You don't get things given to you. You have to take what you can get. I wish these guns would stop for a while. Well I'll stop now Father. Thank you again for your very nice letter. I will try and live up to your standard. It makes one think very hard – when you get into a machine, a mechanic swings the prop. and you are off to be fired on by anti-aircraft guns and perhaps tackle a Fokker or two. I'm not ashamed to say that I always offer up a silent prayer before I start. Good-night Father and may we meet again soon. Your affectionate son, Lyle.'

Wounded and Shot Down

On the day of 9th September 11 Squadron as part of larger formations, was involved in a great number of actions as reported by the RFC Communiques. A formation of about 20 hostile machines was engaged by machines of the 3rd Brigade near Miramount and in the course of the combat two hostile machines were engaged by 11 Squadron members and were driven down damaged. Two other 11 Squadron members drove down another enemy machines, apparently out of control and one hostile machine was seen to make a forced landing near Bapaume.[92]

Of even more interest is the reference in the Communiques to the 3rd Brigade attack on the same day on a dump at a railway station between Achiet-Le-Grand and Miramount where a great number of bombs fell on the dump and railway and a considerable damage was caused. The RFC Communique then reported amongst the list of casualties for that day; *11 Squadron. 2*[nd] *Lt. WHC Buntine, wounded.*[93]

Lyle had been piloting aircraft no. 6988 a two-seater FE2b, and the official account and citation for the action recommending him for the award of the Military Cross detailed what had happened. 'For Skill and Gallantry. On the 9th September 1916 2nd Lt Buntine with Sgt Godfrey Julian Morton as observer was escorting a bomber raid. At about 4.30pm near Bucquoy, three hostile machines were seen. The escort leader gave the signal to attack. 2nd Lt Buntine attacked the nearest hostile machine which at once made off. 2nd Lt Buntine followed for a short way and then saw two more hostile machines near the Bois De Logeast. These were attacked and one made a vertical spinning nose dive into a field north of Achiet Le Petit, striking the ground nose first. This is confirmed by another pilot. 2nd Lt Buntine then turned west to rejoin the rest of the escort and was attacked by three hostile machines who dived from behind. The observer fired half a drum from the rear gun, but 2nd Lt Buntine's machine was now hit in many places and control temporarily lost. 2nd Lt Buntine was severely wounded in the right arm. The machine dived so suddenly that the observer nearly fell out, but the pilot leant forward and pulled him back. 2nd Lt Buntine managed to land the machine without accident in our lines. Most of the propeller was shot away, the radiator and engine hit in several places and all the controls cut except the left-hand elevator and the rudder control.'[94]

But it was not until 13th September, some four days after his wounding that his family had any inkling of his situation when a cable arrived at the Buntine household from the War Office in London.

> *Regret to inform you 2nd Lt WHC Buntine, RFC 11 Squadron was wounded September Ninth. Details sent when received. Secretary War Office.*

The next information they received was another cable from Lyle five days later on 18th September.

> *Fractured arm. Hospital Forty-eight Bryanston Square London. Nothing serious. Lyle Buntine.*

Coincidentally a cable from the War Office arrived at the Buntine home the same day.

> *2nd Lt WHC Buntine RFC was admitted to 2nd General Hospital Havre September 13th with gun-shot wound right arm. Not serious. Further news sent when received. Secretary War Office.*

His first letter of explanation home was written on 14th September to his brother Murray and was written with his left hand. 'Please excuse the writing. My right arm got a couple of bullets in it during a fight I had with five German aeroplanes. It was a gorgeous scrap while it lasted. I managed to bag one German completely and another I'm not certain about. We drove the rest off looking pretty sick. I am at present in a hospital ship at a port in England. Will write again later, your affectionate brother, Lyle.'

Lyle's letter from Lady Carnarvon's Hospital for Officers in Paddington, three days later to his mother described in greater detail what had happened to him. 'I must warn you first of all that this is going to be a funny old letter as I am not yet much good at writing with my left hand. You will by this time have got a cable from the War Office and also one which I sent you. You will probably be wondering what happened to me, I will try and tell you. I was flying well over German Territory at a height of about 10,000 - 11,000 ft with some others of our machines when I observed three German aeroplanes below us flying at about 6000ft. Our leader turned to dive and as I wanted to get in early, I turned my machine on one wing-tip and just simply fell down until I was in range of the Germans. Just then I noticed that the other machines had disappeared after some other Huns so I had three to attend to myself. Then the fun began. I had no time to worry about anyone else. For about ten minutes we were living at lightning speed. The one German to whom we had devoted considerable attention suddenly crumpled up and fell to the earth a complete wreck. The other two machines then made off and I found myself victorious; but several miles across the lines at a height of only 4,000 ft. 'Archie' then started shooting and as I was so low he fairly had a field day. You may be sure that I did quite a lot of dodging for a while, at the same time climbing and making for the lines. Soon the shells suddenly stopped. Then there came a whistle of bullets from behind and I felt as if somebody had hit my right arm with a hammer and it fell to my side useless. I grabbed the joystick with my left hand and swung around to see what was there. I saw two German aeroplanes diving at me, firing as they came. We went for one and drove him off. Then we went for the other; but before he went, he fired several shots at us which cut all the control wires. The engine was also hit and stopped. Somehow or other I managed to cross the lines and land safely. Then I sent a man for a doctor and lay down on the ground as my arm was pretty painful and I was feeling faint. Since then I have been in hospital. Love to all from Lyle.'

It can only be imagined what the feelings of the family were at this stage, especially those of his parents on learning of Lyle's serious wounding. Despite his nonchalant attitude, the wound to his right humerus bone had been serious enough for him to be evacuated to England for recuperation. But an even greater shock, albeit a pleasant one, was in store when a cable arrived at Lyle's hospital from the Squadron's Commanding Officer, Major T. O'B Hubbard.

> *King has awarded you Military Cross. General Higgins sends you congratulations. Accept mine also. Hubbard.*
>
> The accompanying Military Cross citation read; 'For *conspicuous gallantry and skill. As escort to a bombing raid he attacked several enemy machines, one of which fell to the ground nose first. Later he was attacked by three enemy machines, his own machine being severely damaged and himself severely wounded. With great skill he managed to land in our lines, though most of his propeller was shot away and his machine otherwise much damaged.'*

Lyle related to his father in a letter of 20th September of how he had received the great news in person.

'I told Mother what happened to up till I went into the first hospital. I stayed there for a couple of days and while there I received a visit from my Major Hubbard and 3 other boys from my squadron nearly twenty miles away. It was very good of them to come. As the Major was going, he said, Buntine you've done well. I wouldn't mind going through it all again to have him say that. After that I left that hospital and spent a day and a night in a hospital train, but writing with the left hand is too tedious to admit of long descriptions. The end of the train journey was Le Havre at the mouth of the Seine river. From there we went to Southampton and thence to London. For the last couple of days, the doctor has been alternately putting my arm under the x-rays and pulling it about. It is quite straight now. I got a tremendous surprise yesterday in the shape of a telegram from our Major which said – 'King has awarded you Military Cross. General Higgins sends congratulations. Accept mine.' When I got it, I was too overcome for words. I think there must be a mistake for I've certainly done nothing to deserve it. I'm waiting now to see if it is confirmed. Will stop now, Au revoir, Lyle.'

But the award was confirmed in due course and one can only imagine the pride that the Buntine family felt in Lyle being a recipient of such a significant award. Poignantly, his cousin Mac Gibbs had received a posthumous Military Cross following his gallant actions at Fromelles just a few months earlier.

His observer Sgt Godfrey Julian Morton who had been saved by Lyle's quick thinking and using his unwounded left arm to retrieve the observer, survived the action unscathed, but just eight days later was not so fortunate. On 17th September as an escort to a bombing raid on the Marcoing Station, 11 Squadron planes were engaged against 20 hostile aircraft and four 11 Squadron machines were shot down. Morton was initially listed as one of the eight missing airmen, but was later reported as Wounded in Action, having received gun-shot wounds to the foot and thigh. Having been forced to land, he became a Prisoner of War, however a month later his bravery in his final action was recognised with the award of a Military Medal. Lyle's former observer friend 2nd Lt Archibald Cathie had also been slightly wounded in the same action.

Convalescing

During his convalescence Lyle was able to catch up on some letter reading and also wrote home of a number of family, friends and acquaintances he had come across in London. 'Do you remember Austin Laughlin and a boy named Nolan who were both scholarship boys? Nolan is in France with the Australians and Laughlin has a commission in an English Regiment and was recently awarded the Military Cross. Yesterday I was allowed to get up and went to Horseferry Road. Just as I was going in the door, I met Val Blogg who is with the Australian Dental Corps. While there I met a man called Cowan who used to go to Queen's College in St Kilda.'

He also had a visit from his younger cousin Jack Gibbs who was then stationed in London and they recalled the death in action of Jack's older brother as Lyle wrote home, 'Isn't it sad about Mac?'

But he managed to also enjoy some of his time whilst recovering as he wrote on 26th September to his mother expressing birthday wishes to her. 'Today I went to an "at home" given by The Hon. Mrs Edwards to Australian Officers. Madame Ada Crossley was singing there and Miss de Gay was playing. There were also several other well-known artists so I enjoyed it immensely. I met a couple of men I knew there. Doyle from the University and Rigby from Caulfield. So, on the whole I'm not sorry to be wounded. My arm will probably be healed up soon so I will get some leave and will be off to Scotland.'

Despite his wounding Lyle had planned to enjoy some rabbit shooting on the hill ground of the Island of Arran in Scotland and had answered a newspaper inserted by Lord Graham to seek his permission for this venture. His gamekeeper had replied to Lyle and pointed out that he would be liable to find his own accommodation and ammunition, but would receive 1/6d for every rabbit he shot and delivered. In addition, the gamekeeper would try and find a boy and pony for Lyle to work with and informed him that he was writing to another 'Colonial' and offering him the same terms and suggested that they share the use of the boy and pony between them.

In the event these plans did not come to fruition as Lyle was summoned by cable on 6th October to 'Report to Room 8 at Australia House tomorrow morning 7th inst.' As a result of this meeting he was able to cable his parents two days later and inform them that he was, 'Progressing splendidly. Awarded Military Cross. Endeavouring obtain leave Australia.' In fact, Lyle had been ordered home to Australia to recuperate and was to leave England on 13th October 1916.

Chapter 10:
A Wounded Hero Returns Home

Return Home on the Kaiser I Hind

Lyle was invalided home to begin the recovery process from his severe wound and embarked upon the P&O ship the *Kaiser-I-Hind* (Empress of India) which sailed for Sydney with 309 passengers from London on 13th October 1916. Amongst the passengers were business people bound for Gibraltar, Colombo and Singapore, but also a large number of Christian missionaries who disembarked in India at Bombay, now called Mumbai. Lyle reached Melbourne on Monday 21st November and according to the ARGUS was given a hearty reception by the pupils of the school.[95]

The CGS school magazine under the heading *Aviator Welcomed Back* recorded Lyle's visit in the following way. 'About seven years ago a lecture was given in the School Hall by a former member of the staff, now Professor of Physics at Adelaide. The subject was 'Modern Kites and Aeroplanes.' On a screen were shown pictures of machines which could actually fly several hundred yards before wrecking themselves; and the lecturer assured his interested audience that without a doubt men would eventually solve the problem of flying with a machine heavier than air. The other day, in the same School Hall, some who heard that lecture listened to another lesson about aeroplanes, monsters weighing a ton, capable of staying in the air several hours and able to fly hundreds of miles at a height greater than that of any Australasian mountain. Other Old Boys back from the war have given vivid accounts of fighting on the land; but Lt WHC Buntine, with his arm in a sling from a wound received in an aerial battle against heavy odds, was able to describe warfare from a novel point of view. Needless to say, Lt Buntine received a tumultuous welcome and on his entrance into the assembly C. Campbell the School Captain, voiced the congratulations of the school to the first Old Boy aviator to return with a military distinction. Lt Buntine's reply took the form of an interesting talk about flying in general and the construction of aeroplanes. As the boys looked at the little purple and white ribbon, emblem of the Military Cross won by the speaker, they felt that only the speaker's modesty prevented them from hearing some stirring tales. Among the many interesting facts related was the difficulty the airman has of judging his height when there are mists. The speaker said that sometimes, after descending thousands of feet, he would at last see the shadow of the aeroplane as a tiny speck on the clouds below. Though the boys would gladly have remained all afternoon listening to similar stories, they greeted with enthusiastic applause the announcement that there would be no more school that afternoon.'[96]

In addition to the praise from his former school, Lyle's father W.M. Buntine, the Principal of CGS, had written to him and expressed the view that, 'You have done wonders since you left Australia, and will, I think, be the first Royal Flying Corps man to return from the battle front to Australia. Of your brave deeds and your wonderful gifts of mechanical skill and self-reliance, all our friends are never tired of speaking. We all feel that you have done your family, your school and your country honour.'

Newspaper Interviews

Lyle's experiences were indeed unique and he gave a newspaper interview which reported on some of his time at The Front.[97] 'I was tackling some machines ahead, when some others came up behind and let me have two bullets in the arm. I had been shot down no less than six times, but this was the first time I had been wounded. On one occasion I had to land, as the result of a bullet penetrating my petrol tank. It happened that I had landed at Pozieres just after it had been taken by the Australians. The Germans commenced shelling me, but I managed to get clear all right.' He also reported on some of the combat conditions he underwent especially with the improvement in German anti-aircraft fire. 'At one time we had supreme contempt for the anti-aircraft guns, but we treat them with more respect now. On one occasion, I was fired at by a battery of six guns, the shells exploding around me in a circle. The beggars then commenced firing inside the circle and for a time they had me thinking hard. It is no joke when high explosives are bursting near one's machine. Sometimes they turn the machine upside down. It is not very difficult to right matters, but the guns give an uncomfortable feeling.'

He also took the opportunity to pass comment on his foe. 'German aviators never come over the British lines now and one has to travel well over their territory before one can get an opponent. Then they accept battle only when compelled to. I believe I am right in saying that during the past six months no aerial fighting has taken place over the British lines and that on average about 15 machines, British and German are brought down every day. While the deeds of German and French aviators are faithfully recorded in the press of their countries, practically nothing is published in the English press concerning the doings of British aviators.'

In the aerial world of these 'Knights of the Sky' Lyle paid a high tribute under the heading 'Boelke was Great Sport' to the sportsmanship and chivalry of Captain Boelke, the German aviator, who had been killed in action on 28th October 1916. 'I happened to engage him on one occasion and found him a splendid opponent. It was about the time he had brought down his twentieth machine and I was out with a squadron of fighting machines and went away on my own. Boelke singled me out and for some time we manoeuvred for the advantage, all the time peppering away with our machine guns. Finally, Boelke passed me at an angle from which neither of us could fire. His machine was quite close to me and as he passed he grinned up at me and waved his hand. He was a great sport and I was sorry to hear of his death.'

The report concluded by seeking to praise Lyle's flying achievements and to note his relationship with one of the most famous members of 11 Squadron, Captain Albert Ball. 'Lt Buntine has a number of enemy machines to his credit, but, being extremely modest, he refused to say how many. One of his particular aviator chums, Captain Ball has brought down about 30 machines. Captain Ball is not yet 20 years of age and Lt Buntine describes him as the most daring aviator on any front.'

First Medical Board

Lyle's daring behavior had come at a price however, in the form of his wounded arm and on 5th December he appeared before a Medical Board, namely Col. G.W. Cascader and Col. G.A. Syme of the Australian Army Medical Corps, at Victoria Barracks in

Melbourne. Col. Syme found that as a result of being wounded by machine gun fire from an enemy aeroplane at Gommecourt, France on 9th September, Lyle's right humerus bone had suffered a compound fracture. The doctor also reported that the wounds had healed and that the fracture was now united, but that Lyle suffered from stiffness of the elbow joint and that further treatment by massage was recommended. But for the first time another medical condition was noted by the examining doctors and they observed that Lyle was suffering from marked traumatic neurasthenia.

Traumatic Neurasthenia

This term was often used in World War 1 to describe 'shell-shock,' but is now seen as an obsolete term for post-traumatic syndrome or combat related stress. A Medical Textbook published by Sir William Osler in 1916 provided the following definition; 'A morbid condition following shock which presents the symptoms of neurasthenia or hysteria or of both. The condition is known as 'railway brain' or 'railway spine.'[98] The book continued, 'The condition follows an accident, often in a railway train, in which injury has been sustained, or succeeds a shock or concussion, from which the patient may apparently not have suffered in his body. A man may appear perfectly well for several days, or even a week or more, and then develop the symptoms of the neurosis. Bodily shock or concussion is not necessary. The affection may follow a profound mental impression; thus, an engine-driver ran over a child, and received thereby a very severe shock, subsequent to which symptoms of neurasthenia developed. Severe mental strain combined with bodily exposure may cause it, as in a case of a naval officer who was wrecked in a violent storm and exposed for more than a day in the rigging before he was rescued. A slight blow, a fall from a carriage or on the stairs may suffice.' Osler wrote that, 'the first symptoms usually developed a few weeks after the accident, which may or may not have been associated with an actual trauma. The patient complains of headache and tired feelings. He is sleepless and finds himself unable to concentrate his attention properly upon his work. A condition of nervous irritability develops which may have a host of trivial manifestations, and the entire mental attitude of the person may for a time be changed. He dwells constantly upon his condition, gets very despondent and low-spirited, and in extreme cases melancholia may develop.'

Noting similar symptoms in their patient, the Board ruled that Lyle was not fit to serve at home or abroad and that his neurasthenia disability would be likely to continue for at least three months. So, he was sent away to continue his leave with his family at home in East St Kilda, but ordered to appear before another Medical Board in early February 1917.

Family Times

A letter from his father to Lyle upon his return expressed the delight and depth of feelings that his family had upon him being home once more. 'How glad we all are to get you back for a little while alive and in some degree of health after all you have gone through. Your letters have been intensely interesting one need scarcely say and every item is always read several times. We offer you our heartiest congratulations and offer up to God our deepest feelings of thankfulness for his having answered our prayers and spared you. We shall have, 'oh such a time,' when we meet you again and trust you may be able to spend Christmas at home. In the meantime, goodbye until we really see you for ourselves. We shall want to just sit still and listen to you for a whole day. Then the boys of the school will want to have a look at you.'

The number of the battle deaths experienced amongst CGS Old Boys had now reached thirty-four and his father also commented upon those in this letter. They had particular poignancy in marking the death of Lyle's cousin Lt Richard (Mac) Gibbs who had been killed at the Battle of Fromelles on July 19th 1916. He had been posthumously awarded a Military Cross for his actions in leading his men of the 59th Battalion against the German lines. 'Poor old Mac Gibbs was killed, also Henry Tyrer, Gilbert Evans, Frederick Holst, Charles Murrell and Roy Dimant about the same time. What a time our poor Anzacs have had and what a magnificent standard they have set! I hope you managed to see Alec. Langlands before you left England. Your Affectionate father. W.M. Buntine.'

A Holiday

No doubt Lyle enjoyed the time home with his family and quite certainly the Christmas of 1916 would have been heartily celebrated. Extra celebrations were certainly in order when in January 1917 Lyle's exploits received special press coverage. For in a major publication entitled 'Deeds that Thrill the Empire – True stories of the most glorious acts of heroism of the Empire's soldiers and sailors during the Great War,' page 835 outlined the action in which he had won his MC under the heading 'Second Lieutenant WHC Buntine attacking hostile aeroplanes, one of which falls to the ground nose first.' The brief article outlined the details of the action and concluded that he was awarded the MC for his conspicuous gallantry and skill. The article was also accompanied by a professionally hand drawn illustration of the action. High praise indeed as the magazine was circulated throughout the Empire for consumption by an audience eager for news of their heroes at the Front.

But he also wanted to enjoy some rest and relaxation during his time in Australia and so with his many family connections in Gippsland travelled by train to Sale. From there he journeyed to the small town of Heyfield prior to staying with the Langlands family at their property at nearby Medowra. Four of the Langlands boys had attended CGS and Robert had been killed at Gallipoli, whilst his brother Alec had taught for a year at CGS before enlisting. Lyle wrote to his younger brother Murray at this time and invited him to join Lyle at the Criterion Hotel in Sale. He apologized for taking Murray's gun, but also asked him to send some lines and spinners to the Sale Railway Station for him to collect before he left for Medowra as he was then going to the Gippsland Lakes for some fishing.

Second Medical Board

On his return from this vacation, Lyle was examined once again by the same Medical Board at Victoria Barracks on 5th February 1917, which noted that since his last examination in early December his arm had greatly improved and that the bone was quite firm and all the joint movements were quite satisfactory. However, they also noted that he reported sleeping quite badly, that he was still neurasthenic and that he appeared very nervy and 'funky.' They concluded that they did not think he was yet fit for active service in the Flying Corps and that his neurasthenic condition was likely to last at least another three months. Given the battle conditions that Lyle had faced on the Western Front, including surviving being shot down six times, being subjected to increasingly accurate anti-aircraft fire, the stress and strains of life and combat in the air and then being wounded in battle and surviving a crash landing, it was no wonder that the symptoms of neurasthenia manifested themselves during his convalescence. But as his leave at home drew to an end, the time had come for him to return to England and to his military life. But at least he knew that the Medical Board had declared that he could not resume his active duty with his squadron at the Western Front and face the perils and uncertainty of deadly combat. In fact, another type of military life awaited him.

Return to England

In early March 1917 Lyle took leave of his family and travelled by train from Melbourne to Adelaide and enjoyed some overnight hospitality with Mr Reade, the father of an Old Boy acquaintance. In London Lyle had run into William Lloyd Reade, a Gallipoli veteran but now a 2nd Lt in the 12th Fusiliers of the British Army. Lyle's wound must have recovered quite well because in the evening, he took a small boat for a row on the Torrens River and remarked that it was just perfect, restful and so very quiet. He noted that it was beautifully warm right up to midnight and that it was the first real Australian evening he had seen for quite a while. He visited the Adelaide Naval and Military Club and was surprised to discover that Cedric Hayward, a South Australian he had trained with in the RFC was home on leave. They had both trained at Reading and learned to fly together and had quite a competition to see who would get to France first. Lyle recollected that he had beaten Cedric to the Western Front by just three days, but noted that Cedric had been brought down by German anti-aircraft fire on the Somme just a week after Lyle was wounded. Hayward had also been sent home on leave and coincidentally was travelling back to England on the *RMS Medina*, the same boat as Lyle.

Sometimes chartered steamships were employed as troop transports and these carried troops of the 1st AIF. The *Medina* was the last of the ten ships in P&O's M-Class delivered from Caird & Co of Greenock in 1911. She was 12,358 tonnes, was 184 metres in length and 21 metres broad with 1164hp quadruple-expansion engines. During construction it was decided that RMS *Medina* would convey King George V and Queen Mary to India for the Delhi Durbar and so she was initially commissioned into the Royal

Navy and her crew was mainly naval personnel. She was provided with an extra mast, necessary to maintain royal flag etiquette, and she was finished with a white hull with bands of royal blue and gold and buff funnels. Various large rooms intended for public use were redecorated as royal apartments. *Medina* left Portsmouth for India in November 1911, returning in February 1912 where she then returned to Caird & Co. for refitting and was delivered to P&O in June 1912 before commencing work as a troop transport.

Leaving his home and family in Melbourne must have been very difficult for Lyle and he wrote ruefully to his mother on 11th March once he was on board the *RMS Medina* that he knew that she would be thinking of him. To some extent he may have regretted returning to Australia because he had found that the parting had been so very hard. But he added a cheerful note to his letter and said that he looked forward to meeting again as soon as the war was over. He also asked his mother to forward the X-rays of his wounded arm as he had left them behind in his bedroom. In the same letter he expressed gratitude for all of the unexpected parcels from her he had just discovered amongst his luggage.

The ship sailed from Adelaide to Fremantle and although there was a big swell in the Great Australian Bight, Lyle had not succumbed to seasickness as yet. In fact, he related that a number of the young men had played a number of cricket matches on the decks and that although one of the chaps tried to run a dance, it was a failure. But the cricket at least provided some exercise for the young passengers.

Upon landing in Fremantle, Lyle travelled to Perth to attempt to catch up with an old family friend Col. Courtney, but he was unavailable, so instead Lyle was driven back to Fremantle by a family friend. Lyle remarked that it was a lovely day with no clouds and quite warm but with a cool breeze. On his last day on Australian soil, he described driving along the top of a ridge with the most beautiful blue of the river below and with green lawns, palm trees, beautiful bushes and a beautifully kept red gravel road, Lyle wrote to his mother that he didn't think that the drive from Perth to Fremantle could be equalled anywhere.

Rejoining the *Medina*, he poignantly began his letter with the observation that the ship was now past Fremantle and that they had all had the last sight of Australia some of them would have for a long time. For the first time in a letter to his younger medical student brother Murray empathising with his return to University studies, Lyle expressed the hope that he soon might be doing the same thing. It became apparent that during his time at home Lyle had sought permission to return to his own medical studies at the University of Melbourne. But he also made it clear that he wouldn't know anything about a possible recall until he returned to England.

In the meantime, he settled down to shipboard life and involved himself in many more cricket matches relating to his brother that he only bowled 'horribly deceptive underarms,' but still managed to get the bowling average and six wickets in one match. Lyle however, praised his younger brother as the only cricketer in the family and was eager to hear about his wicket tally and his general progress at school.

By the 22nd of March the *Medina* had reached Colombo in Ceylon, now Sri Lanka, and Lyle disembarked and ventured inland for three days to the city of Kandy. He described it as 'a more beautiful place I have never seen.' The window of his bedroom looked out over a beautiful little lake only about 10 or 12 yards from the hotel porch with tropical vegetation all around and a native bazaar on one hand and a temple on the other. Lyle had arrived in the evening by train from Colombo and took a ride in a 'ricksha,' before he went to bed. This was the first time he had seen life in Asia and he was quite fascinated with all he saw and experienced. He described the night as being wonderful and as still as could be with fire-flies flitting everywhere. He went to see a Buddhist temple in a big courtyard with other smaller shrines in it and several sacred bo-trees on which were hanging offerings of all sorts. Lyle found it to be a most eerie and weird place as girls were dancing around beating big drums with priests blowing a kind of trumpet and there were large crowds of pilgrims and worshippers. For the staunch Anglican from St Mary's in Caulfield he commented that he was rather glad to get out of the temple as he wondered what would happen if the worshippers should resent the presence of an unbeliever.

Lyle received a letter from a family friend, Billy Gordon who had invited him to visit his tea plantation in the inland hills and so accompanied by a Captain Church he drove in a car to Neuralia about 50 miles inland from Kandy and to a height of 6000 feet. This drive he described as a wonderful experience as the road climbed 4000ft in 35 miles with the last part being particularly steep. All along the way he passed numerous very pretty waterfalls with some of them having a sheer drop of nearly 300 ft and the road itself being very narrow with a high bank on one side and a drop of a thousand feet on the other side. He noted that down in Colombo it had been very hot, but up at this altitude it was distinctly cold. After Lyle had travelled some 155 miles inland, Mr and Mrs Gordon met him in their car and took him another 25 miles inland to their tea plantation property 'Rappahaunock,' where they arrived at 10.00pm, had dinner and went straight to bed. The next morning, they toured the property and factory and Lyle found it quite interesting to see the tea being withered, rolled, dried, graded and packed. Mr Gordon tried to present him with a chest of tea, but after amicable negotiations, Lyle left with three pounds of tea instead; a much easier amount to carry in his baggage. He also had his photograph taken with some of the tea-picker women and then Mr Gordon drove him to a station, so he could catch a train back to Colombo. Lyle passed on to his parents the suggestion from Mr Gordon for them to spend some time at his plantation and he added his own endorsement, 'And believe me Mother, you could not find a better place anywhere in which to spend a fortnight or three weeks.' Perhaps it was at the Gordon's that he also tried his first mango and recalled the words of his father who said that the fruit was very nice, but very sticky and should really be eaten in a bath.

By the 28th of March he had left Colombo, 'What a glorious place it was, and stopped briefly at Bombay now Mumbai, in India. Lyle disembarked and took a four-hour tour and enjoyed himself thoroughly indeed. But the realities of life were never far away and he commented that they had passed his former ship 'Kaiser-I-Hind' on its return voyage to Australia and he wistfully noted that he wished he could have waited long enough to go back home on her. He also took the chance to bare his soul a little to his mother and wrote that it was not nice to be so far away from her and to be continually sailing on further. He opined that he wished the silly old war would end as he felt that the Germans surely must see that they couldn't win, especially as the news from the Front was rather grand and that he thought it was the most encouraging of the war. He closed by saying again that he hoped that the war would soon be over and poignantly to his mother that it was her love that brought him back last time and that he believed that it would do so again. 'For I can still say Mother dear, that you are my best girl. Au Revoir and may we soon meet again.'

The voyage continued from Bombay to Aden through the Suez Canal and then to Port Said where a number of the officers were off-loaded to a troop ship. The ship's passage through the Canal was always interesting for the ship's passengers and Lyle described both sides having troops on them, mostly Australians who would rush and line the sides and deliver loud 'Cooee's' to the passing boats. He watched the local boys diving for pennies and also related that during his trip he had seen whales, flying fish and big sharks. It was at this point that it came to Lyle's attention that as all the Australian officers were being offloaded with all their belongings, all of his luggage had also been accidentally included as well. This meant that until the luggage hopefully caught up with him in London in at least a fortnight, he had no spare uniform to wear and only the clothes he was wearing!

Despite this inconvenience he disembarked at Port Said to visit Lady Strangford's Hospital to visit a friend, but as in Aden where he had done the same thing for another acquaintance, both patients had been discharged from their respective wards.

Ever the tourist Lyle took some pains to describe the north Algerian town of Bona controlled by the French and which he saw as an awfully pretty spot and where he was surprised to see a number of sights. He had preconceptions of Algeria that it would look something like the barren landscape and desert near Suez, but was surprised to note a huge range of 'refreshing' green cultivated mountains just inland from the town and beach. Flying was never far from his thoughts and he also noted some sea-planes flitting about and wished that he could have gone for a flight in one.

Perhaps one of the most interesting features of Lyle's voyage on the *RMS Medina* was the number of distinguished passengers and Lyle makes mention of some notable people including the champion Australian tennis player, Norman Brookes. In 1907 Brookes had become the first overseas male to win the Wimbledon singles championship and was also to repeat that feat in 1914 and in 1907 also won the doubles and mixed doubles championships. He had also won the Australian singles championship in 1911 and had partnered with the New Zealander

Anthony Wilding to win the Davis Cup in 1914. On the outbreak of war Brookes, who suffered from stomach ulcers, was rejected for active service. He became a commissioner for the Australian branch of the British Red Cross in Egypt from August 1915 to late 1916; he resigned in January 1917 and in May became commissioner for the British Red Cross in Mesopotamia. Soon after, he was appointed assistant director of local resources for the British Expeditionary Force there, with the rank of lieutenant-colonel.[99] Brookes appears to have been on his way to take up his position in Mesopotamia and whilst on board the *Medina* played some sport and Lyle noted that he 'is quite a good cricket player and gets a nasty twist into some of his bowling.' Lyle also reported in Ceylon that Brookes who had been around the world several times, had told him that Colombo was the most beautiful place he knew. After the war Brookes went on to win the US doubles championship in 1919 and the Wimbledon doubles in 1924 at the age of 47. He was a member of nine Australasian Davis Cup teams, was decorated with the French Legion of Honour for his services in WW1 as a Captain in the British Army, was knighted in 1939 and was President of the Lawn Tennis Association of Australia from 1926 – 1955. He died in 1968.

Lyle also mentioned that Professor Gibson of the Brisbane University was a passenger although he does not record any personal interaction. Alexander James Gibson (1876-1960), was an engineer who in 1910 was appointed foundation professor of engineering in the University of Queensland, where he designed and built the engineering laboratories, then the finest in Australia. Commissioned in the Corps of Australian Engineers in 1904, Gibson transferred to the Australian Intelligence Corps in 1908 and was promoted to captain in 1910. From August 1914 he was assistant censor and temporary censor in Brisbane. Gibson was travelling to England on the *Medina* to take up his position as a temporary major working on Professor(Sir) Henry Barraclough's munitions scheme for the Commonwealth Department of Defence. Returning to Australia in 1918 he became the acting general manager and chief engineer of the Australian Arsenal.

Amongst other distinguished passengers were two members of the British aristocracy, Lord Montagu and Sir, later Lord, Thomas Carmichael who were both returning to England after work in various roles in India. Lord Montagu the British Member of Parliament, was then working as an adviser on Mechanical Transport Services for the Indian Government with the rank of Brigadier-General (Hon.) Of greater interest to Lyle was that Montagu had been an acting member of the British War Aircraft Committee from March to April 1916 before that committee was wound up. Following the demise of this committee Montagu had spoken with great passion in the House of Lords about the state of military aviation and had proposed the following resolution.

THE AIR SERVICE. *'Moved to resolve, That this House considers that the development of aviation for purposes of war can no longer be efficiently carried on under the present system of the divided control and responsibility of two separate Departments; and that the time has now arrived when the supply of men and materials should be concentrated under single control, at the same time leaving the executive power over naval and military aircraft with the Army and Navy as at present.'* (Lord Montagu of Beaulieu.)[100]

The debate was adjourned and then eventually forgotten in the business of a wartime Parliament, but Montagu had shown himself to be a forward thinker and had indeed anticipated the eventual amalgamation in April 1918 of the Army's Royal Flying Corps and the Navy's Royal Naval Air Service into the Royal Air Force.

Lyle was most excited that Montagu was a fellow passenger and wrote to his mother on 7th April the voyage had been wonderfully interesting and that since Bombay it had been particularly so, after Montagu and Carmichael had boarded. He reminded her that he had hinted at something interesting in his last letter and that although he could not say too much, as the voyage was in its last stage, the need for secrecy didn't matter anymore. Lyle wrote that the interest in the voyage had really been because of the people who had been on board, especially as Lord Montagu, 'one of our peers,' who had taken a great interest in aviation and written several books and pamphlets came on board. He proudly related that someone had told Montagu that Lyle was on board and that the Lord had come to Lyle and invited him to sit at his special table. 'It was awfully decent of him,' and Lyle noted that Montagu had gathered together quite a little crowd of celebrities around him, but Montagu himself was the most interesting to Lyle.

The last passenger of special note was Lord Carmichael, the retiring Governor of Bengal and Madras in India who was returning to England having completed his tenure of office and was naturally carrying all of his possessions and substantial art collection in 80 cases of personal luggage. Carmichael had been Governor of Victoria between 1908 and 1911 and would have been well known to all Victorians, including Lyle who was thrilled to write home that Lady Carmichael had asked him to go and see them in London. The Carmichaels had no children of their own, but had been accompanied on their travels to Melbourne and India by Penelope Carmichael, a young niece who had also promised to write to him. Lyle observed that, 'She is an awfully nice girl and quite a sport,' and that she had promised to come for a ride with him one morning when they returned to England, in 'Rotten Row' a fashionable place for upper-class Londoners to go horse riding. Lyle summed up the unique collection of passengers by stating that there were numerous other interesting personalities on board and that all of them had made their mark in the world or were just setting out to the war. He concluded that here were no people travelling for pleasure and that they really were a wonderful crowd of people.

Along with a number of others he had also chosen to disembark in France at Marseilles and continue his journey by train, thus avoiding much extra time on the ship. 'I paid the extra money and secured a berth on a P&O special express right across France as it seems very foolish to go right around by boat as that will probably take a fortnight longer.' His last letter from the *Medina* is dated 15th April 1917 and his first from England is the 20th April which allowed for his travel time across France.

But it was with mixed fortune that Lyle wrote to his parents on 4th May about the tragedy that unfolded after he left the ship, for on 28th April as, having already called at Plymouth, the *Medina* was heading for London when the German submarine *UB31* attacked at 6.05pm and sank her three miles north-east of Start Point. The torpedo struck her on the starboard side, flooding her engine room and leaving her dead in the water, sinking fast. Distress calls were transmitted and the 411 passengers and crew mustered in readiness to abandon ship. The *Medina* sank less than hour after the attack, but by then the ship had been safely evacuated and the only lives lost were those of an engineer officer and five firemen killed by the initial explosion. Naval vessels took the lifeboats in tow to Dartmouth and Brixham.[101] Ironically the UB-31 which was based with the Flandern Flotilla in the Belgian port of Zeebrugge was herself destroyed by a mine in the Straits of Dover on the 2nd of May 1918 with the loss of all her 26 hands. She had destroyed some 29 ships for a total of 84,350 tons during her 25 patrols since being launched on 16th November 1915.

Lady Carmichael had greatly feared such an attack and so she and her husband had left the ship at Port Said and returned to England by *HMS Sheffield*, but had left all their luggage on the *Medina*. After a visit to Italy in 1885, he had collected works of art voraciously, with the 'eclecticism that characterised many late nineteenth century connoisseurs and his interest ranged over early Renaissance painting, medieval words of art, rare books, antiquities and during his time in India, Asian art. Lord Carmichael had avoided the sinking of the *Medina*, but according to his wife he felt the loss of his collection, especially his Indian possessions to the end of his days.'[102]

Lyle had also avoided the sinking of the ship, but wrote to his parents of the direct implication it had taken on his possessions. 'I had left her at Marseilles and come overland, but a lot of my luggage was on her and went to the bottom. I told you before that some of it had been lost at Port-Said. Well it was my big kit-bag and hold-all that went there and since then I have a telegram that they are following by the next boat. So, the things I lost were the fibre suit case and the leather suit case. The new one I brought overland with me, but was not allowed to bring the others. Perhaps it was a good thing that my things were temporarily lost. But what hurts me is the fact that my books and papers were all on the *Medina* with the exception of a few which I carry with me. All the way over from Australia I spent all my spare time collecting and cataloguing my notes and rewriting them and making them into a book as father asked me. I think that some of them were really decently written. On arriving in England Lady Harrowby said that she would publish them for me and with such backing they would have been sure to sell well, but alas! They are gone with my other things. It's horrible luck.'

How difficult it must have been for Lyle to have lost these precious documents especially when he had made such a splendid contact as Lady Harrowby who was going to be his patron as concerned their publication. In time Lyle's family would also come to greatly lament the loss of these irreplaceable memories of their son and brother, made especially poignant as he had laboured long and hard over their writing, compilation and editing. We can but guess what further insights could have been gained into Lyle's life and experiences had they survived. As Lyle regretted the off-loading of his luggage in Port Said, the loss of some precious documents and possessions in the sinking of the Medina, he also turned his mind to the new phase of his military life away from active service. He carried the thought in the back of his mind that his orders releasing him from the Army and enabling him to return to his medical studies in Melbourne might arrive any day. In the mean-time some new adventures and a wonderful 'Red Letter Day' awaited him in London.

Chapter 11:
Life Just Before Death

Return To England

On the 20th April 1917, Lyle wrote to his younger brother Murray and also to his parents from his accommodation at the Royal Aero Club (RAC) in Clifford Street, London and using the colloquial term for England, immediately informed them that it was a 'meatless and potatoeless Blighty, but Blighty all the same.' He observed that they were all on rations and were only allowed 2oz of bread with a meal, with no sugar and they had to have one meatless day a week. 'Still it is not too bad considering, but the Germans must be worse off,' he wrote.

He also noted that since he had left Port Said that the weather had gradually grown colder with his train journey through France being very chilly indeed. In fact, he said that he arrived at Boulogne in the middle of a snow storm. ('Brrrrrr. That's a shiver!') To add to the cold was the fact that after the offloading of most of his uniform in Egypt, he only had a light uniform of light cotton drill, but soon found that if he wore two pairs of underwear he could cope quite well with the cold. But the good news was that his misplaced luggage had been traced and was now on its way to him in England. He wrote that although lately London had been very chill and cheerless, it was now beginning to brighten up and his friends and acquaintances said that he had brought the Australian sun with him.

Lyle described his new place of residence at the Royal Aero Club (RAC) as a great improvement on the former RAC rooms in Reading which consisted simply of a reading room and lounge with very little comfort. 'But the new premises fairly took my breath away as we have a billiard room, three smoking lounges, a reading room, two dining rooms, a huge hall and eight comfortable bed-rooms furnished in perfect taste. The more I see of the Aero Club the more I like it. It is really something to be able to sit alongside a big fire with a paper and yarn to pals here instead of going out in the evenings and I do enjoy it.'

Lyle continued to encounter people from back home and related his meeting with 'young Woodward from Elsternwick, but by jingo he's changed. When I knew him, he was always very proper and sedate, but I'm afraid that he is not that way any longer. He's a real live Australian now and well he sometimes uses expressions never learnt in a Sunday School. Oh, how shocking!'

Another encounter was with his soldier cousin Jack Gibbs who had been wounded at Gallipoli and had now been posted to the Pay Corps in London. 'When I saw Jack Gibbs, I got another shock which reduced me to a quivering jelly. Jack is ENGAGED. I must make him introduce me to the girl and I'll tell you what I think of our future cousin. I only hope she's nice.'

He spoke of travelling to Scotland to see the Whites again and also noted that his South African Buntine cousins Noelle and Jessie were still in England and that he really should go and visit them again. The next ten days or so held a great surprise for Lyle, but also saw him undertake a round of social engagements with some new friends and acquaintances. On the evening of Sunday

22nd April, he attended St Ethelburga's Church at Bishopsgate and described his experience in the following way. 'I don't think I told you about the little church of St Ethelburga that I went to see which is just opposite Liverpool Station and really is the queerest church I have seen yet. The whole of the front of the church is taken up by two shops, a tailor's shop and a sight-testing shop. The church has got a huge pair of spectacles and a pair of scissors sticking out from the front, which are the signs of the two trades. To get to the church you have to go through the back of the shops, but once inside however, all is different and it is a splendid example of the old churches. When I was there, they had candles burning and the parson was preaching on spiritualism.' The following Sunday he attended church at St Martins in the Fields with Miss Cecilia Douglas, the niece of the Hon. Mrs Edwards. 'Yesterday I went to St Martins in the Fields in Trafalgar Square. They had a musical service which was very beautiful indeed and I am enclosing a program, however, I am not too keen on variety shows in church. Admiral Jellicoe was there and also the French Naval Attache and the Fourth Sea Lord. The lady I was with knew them all and was going to introduce me, but they were with a party.'

By the following Wednesday he was back at the Edwards house where he met two Australian women, Mrs Gray and Mrs Enid Boan and their daughters and was later to be invited to Enid Boan's estate at Leatherhead past Epsom. But later that day circumstances were to lead him to one of the most exciting adventures of his life and one his family would prize amongst nearly all others. Lyle described it in the following way, his letter complete with appropriate underlined words.

A King's Command

'On Wednesday I had what was for me the experience of my life and I shall always remember it as a Red-Letter Day. Well here's the story in brief. Mr Brown, the man you have heard me speak of secured me a ticket to visit Windsor Castle. There were several Australian Officers and Nurses going as well and we went off to the Castle and had a most enjoyable time seeing all over it and enjoying it thoroughly. While we there the King[1] heard that we were there and sent for us. Sir Derrick Capel, the Master of the House came out and informed us of His Majesty's commands and we went inside. The men went first and the nurses and the officers brought up the rear. The men and nurses simply marched past, but The King stopped us and shook hands with each officer in turn. As soon as he saw that I had the MC he singled me out and spoke to me for about 10 minutes. He asked me if I had received the MC from himself. I said 'No, I had got it from the Military Secretary Sir Francis Davies.' He then said, 'Well you must come and let me give it to you personally. So, come on Wednesday and I will present it myself. Give your name to Sir Derrick Capel and he will send you a card.' His Majesty then asked me which part of Australia I came from and several questions and I went on. Not only was The King there, but also The Queen and Princess Mary and I shook hands with both the King and Queen. I was so excited I didn't know whether I was standing on my head or my heels. I have a sort of happy recollection of saluting about five times and standing as stiff as a poker while being spoken to, but of what I did and said I have no idea. You can have no idea of the effect it has on one. When I got outside, I found I was as red as a lobster and beads of perspiration on my forehead and

---

[1] King George V (r.1910 - 1936). He and Queen Mary visited India in 1911, the only King-Emperor to do so. Coincidentally they sailed on the "Medina" which Lyle used on his return to England in 1917. The King made over 450 visits to troops and over 300 visits to hospitals during the war. In 1917 anti-German feeling led him to adopt the family name of Windsor. He started the annual Christmas radio broadcast by a reigning monarch in 1932 and celebrated his Silver Jubilee in 1935.

I was trembling all over with excitement. The King received us in plain clothes and looked a splendid and smart little gentleman. The Queen was very gracious and had a lovely little soft white hand. When she gave me her hand, I didn't know whether to kiss it or shake it and I'm afraid I stood and looked at her and did nothing. Then they gave us tea at which Lady Minto presided and we continued on our ramble around the castle. Altogether it was a most enjoyable day. P.S. I haven't washed my hands yet and may not have by the time you get this letter!'

Social Activities

Two days later he received a letter from Mrs Enid Boan inviting him to her family estate at Leatherhead the next day and, 'I jumped at it and left on Saturday morning. They have a lovely big place out beyond Epsom. It used to belong to Sir William Vincent and is one of the biggest places I have seen. The grounds must be about 2 square miles all covered with small trees and undergrowth, which makes it a splendid shooting preserve. They have asked me to go down for the shooting soon and try a shot at pheasants and partridges. In front of the house are big lawns and gardens and I had a ripping time. It is in a most beautiful situation, and one of the prettiest things about the house is Enid Boan. The day I was there we played golf, clock golf and croquet. There were several people there and I wasn't popular because I won all three. It really does seem terrible the way our family scoops the pool when they go anywhere.'

On his return a telegram from the Lord Chamberlain was waiting for him instructing him to go to Buckingham Palace the following Tuesday to receive his MC from the hands of the King. In the mean-time he continued his round of social engagements and wrote of visiting Lady Harrowby, the wife of the 5th Earl of

Harrowby. It would appear that not all of his writings had been lost in the *Medina,* as she had been very interested in Lyle's tales of flying and had asked him to bring some of his written work to her as she was intending to have some of them published. He went for a visit to Westminster Abbey and then had tea with Lady Frances Ryder, the daughter of Lady Harrowby. After his decoration by the King he also planned to visit Scotland, but first he had some serious dental work to undergo and he wrote that, 'for the next week I shall be very busy with the dentist. I have had a tooth out and have three more to be stopped. I had a great old time in the chair. The tooth was very much jammed and took nearly 1 hour to get out. Finally, he split it and got the top off and one root out and had to dig the other out with a small crow bar. My jaw is still aching pretty badly.' But his painful dental work soon faded away in light of the events of Tuesday 1st May 1917 as he wrote in a letter to his mother three days later.

A King Awards the MC

'A tremendous lot has happened since I last wrote to you. You know I went to Windsor Castle and was received by the King who asked me to come up to Buckingham Palace and let him present the MC to me himself. Well I received a telegram from the Lord Chamberlain telling me when to come, so I duly turned up at Buckingham Palace. When my turn came, I was ushered into the Presence and the King pinned the cross on and shook hands with me. He said, 'I am very pleased to give you this cross myself. I had remembered telling you to come at Windsor.' He then asked who had given me the cross at first and I told him Sir Francis Davis. I did not think that His Majesty would have remembered me, but as soon as I reached the palace, I had evidence that he had. For as soon as I arrived a man came along and said, 'Are you Mr Buntine? and told me that arrangements had been made and I handed the cross to him. He then put it on the table with the others so that I received the same one back from King George.'

For Lyle and especially his father, both ardent supporters of the British Empire this ceremony and encounter with the King must have marked a particularly high point in Lyle's life.

A Tourist Again

Lyle then travelled north to Scotland and spent time at the home of Mr Douglas who owned a huge house with a beautiful garden. He had received the invitation to visit there as Miss Cecilia Douglas was the niece of the Hon. Mrs Edwards whose estate he had previously visited. As a tourist Lyle visited Stirling Castle and the Wallace Armament and pointed out to his father that the old jousting ground at the castle was now given over to being a flying ground. He also visited a Mr James M Bontein who was the Sherriff of North Berwick, but was not received in a very warm fashion at all. Mr White had introduced Lyle to Mr and Mrs Brownlee Young and their daughter Ailsa, who had then invited him to spend a weekend at their place in the Scottish countryside. He described Ailsa as being about two months younger than himself and a splendid girl, quite like their cousin Helen Gibbs, and who had been nursing in France. When he later wrote to his brother Murray about the weekend trip, he remarked that he had spent it at the Youngs' place on the coast at the Maidens; 'they were damn scarce though!'

His round of social engagements continued and he reported staying at the Inshaws and then travelling to London and Edinburgh again. But the realities of his situation caught up with him as he wrote that he had not as yet reported to the War Office for further duties and that they had been scouring the country for him, so he thought he had better report at once. 'Still on the loose, although I have a feeling about me that a paternal government is going to get anxious over one of its children if I don't report mighty soon.'

His mother had also expressed her concern for his welfare in a letter he received in early May and in a rare display of written emotion he responded in a pensive vein. 'In your letter you seem to be worrying as to what is going to happen to me. I really don't think there is much need to worry. You know a bad penny always turns up in the end and I'm sure to turn up some time when this beastly war is over. I am beginning to wonder myself when it will be over. It is really much more serious than people in Australia think and we seem to have come to a dead-end, with no chance of moving till after the winter. I am sitting writing this in the Sunderland Club. It is really a very nice place indeed and I am very grateful for the use of it, as we can't get any other place to write and read in quiet, and I have not made any friends in Sunderland yet. I am playing a lone hand over here at present and my only relaxation is to get down to Harefield Park, Middlesex and see Dr and Mrs Allan. It is now about 2 months since I was there so I am going down next Sunday when I am in London. Goodbye and much love from your wandering boy, Lyle.'

But he was not without any company and social life as he related to his brother Murray on May 12th. 'I have been having 'SOME TIME' lately and enjoying myself hugely. This afternoon I went to the London Zoo in Regent's Park with Lord and Lady Carmichael and Miss Carmichael. It was awfully interesting and Penelope Carmichael is a very nice girl. While I was up in Scotland, I got a letter from her asking me to go and see them when I had a few minutes to spare. I don't know if I told you that I had found a little place in London just like the Palais at St Kilda. Well it's jolly good. In fact, there were two of them, the Chelsea Town Hall and the McKenzie Club at Holland Park and they are made more interesting by the fact that if any Officers are caught dancing, they get court-martialled. There was a raid at Chelsea the other day and about fifty officers were caught. There were seven colonials there, South Africans and Australians and they were the only ones not caught. But I'm starting work again soon now and chucking all this sort of foolery.'

But other life opportunities were always present and he related a conversation with a Colonel James of the Cameronians, who turned out to be an Australian and an old Wesley College boy. 'As soon as he met me, he asked if I was a relation of Dr Buntine VC. He was awfully decent and tried for about half an hour to get me to promise to leave the RFC and join his regiment. He promised me another star at once and plenty of chances for promotion and also offered me a commission in the Regular Army which sounds very alluring and nice. You know it is really very difficult to make up one's mind what to do just now; because if I stay here, I shall probably be a captain soon and get a job on the instructional staff for a while. I can only wait and see how things turn out.'

Posted to Turnberry

By the time he wrote to his mother on 3rd June, Lyle had reported to the War Office in the intervening period, received his orders and was now ensconced at his new posting, a location which was a remarkable coincidence for in all of his travels he had already been there. 'Here I am again in the same spot where I spent such a nice week-end with Ailsa Brownlee Young. This time however I am here to work. I told you in a former letter that the little village of Maidens is just alongside Turnberry in Ayshire, which is an even smaller village; but has a huge hotel there. This was formerly used as a popular golfing resort, but now it has been taken over by the RFC and I am there doing a special course in aerial gunnery.

I had a Medical Board some time ago and have been waiting to be posted to a squadron or to some work. The Medical Board marked me permanently unfit as a pilot or observer and recommended that I should be allowed to return to Australia to finish my Medical Course. This recommendation is being considered by the War Office and meanwhile I have been appointed to a job on the staff as an Instructor in Aerial Gunnery. I believe that I shall be a captain very shortly now or at least I hope so anyway. The course is really very good; but there are some funny parts about it. For instance, this afternoon we all had to go and listen to a lecture on aerial fighting. I don't know why, but I had to go as well and the lecturer was a man I flew with in France. At present I am writing in my room and as I raise my head and look out through the open window, I see the coast line stretching away on the right, and inland all the earth is a most beautiful green, while there is not a ripple on the sea or a breath of wind in the air. It is a real Australian spring Sunday and it is beautifully warm. All the week the place has been disturbed by the sounds of machine gun fire and the continual roar of aeroplane engines as a hundred men practised shooting and flying. Today however the only sound is that of the birds singing in the sun and in the distance a piano playing and someone singing. What a pity it can't be like this all day; but no – at eleven o'clock we must start off to work and then the usual sounds will start again. Just as I wrote the last sentence a man passed under my window carrying a huge 12lb salmon which had just been caught. Salmon is one of our commonest dishes up here and fresh too.'

Financial Worries

Other mundane matters were also part of his letters, but the question of his meagre finances raised its head once again as he wrote to his mother. 'The weather has been very cold and dull lately; but as soon as it gets warm again, I am going out to try and shoot a seal which comes up and lies on the beaches in the evening. It is nearly three weeks since I cabled asking for some money to buy kit with as all mine was torpedoed; but I have had no answer at all. When I came up here to work, I had to buy several things and consequently I am in a terrible hole for money till I get more pay.' He lamented the lack of money more than once and after some travelling in early June to Glasgow to visit the Inshaws and Youngs, he wrote that although his short trip was a nice change, it would be his last for a long time as he was in rather a hole for money. As before he asked if his father had not received his cables seeking a cash advance and whether he had lost the address of his bank. 'If I can manage to hang out for another month, I will be all right; but I am still only getting half-pay. Well, I mustn't worry you with my little troubles mother dear so don't worry I'll come thro' somehow, like I have before.'

But in a letter to his father on 15th June Lyle wrote that, 'Today being Saturday I would have liked to go to Prestwick; but could not spare 5/- for the fare. I'm in an awful hole for cash and cabled twice last month; but have received no reply. Perhaps you have lost the banker's address it is, Messrs Cox and Co, 16 Charing Cross London SW. You see although I found that I had about 30 pounds in London the loss of my luggage upset all my calculations and consequently I have not enough to carry on with; but if I can scrape through July and August successfully, I shall be quite fixed again for my pay will be more then. At present I only receive 12/- per day. I am living absolutely on nothing now in order to save so as to meet my debts for clothes, kit etc which amount to £20. It is strange that I've had no reply to my cables and I cannot understand it at all. Well I must drop this subject now. I was awfully glad to receive this last letter from you and it cheered me immensely, as I had received no letters for a month and no answer to cables so imagined you had all forgotten me. Please give my love to Mother and Girlie. I will write to you soon, your affectionate son.'

Thoughts of Home

To add to his woes, he noted again that to date he had not received many letters from home. 'Something seems to have gone wrong with the mail service lately. I wonder if many boats have been sunk! Do you know, I received some letters from home about ten days after I landed, and since then I have had none at all. It's just like the first time I came over here. Do you remember the long wait I had before letters arrived last time? Just about two years ago isn't it?'

His thoughts were often of home and in his letter to his brother Murray on 10th June he wrote from Turnberry of CGS and matters of personal business and underlined his key desire. 'Now first of all, before I start to say too much, I want to ask you to send me a couple of copies of the school magazine, the one that came out while I was there with my photo and the extracts from the letters. Also, I want to ask you if Matheson sold my bike for me or not. Did he get what he expected for it? I told him to give the money to Arnold and he would give it to Dad. By Jove! I wish you could be here with me today. It's a splendid spot.'

A Secret Revealed

But he also revealed to his brother alone, and not his parents, that he had flown again despite being 'grounded' by the Medical Board. 'This afternoon I went out in a bus and flew over to Ailsa Craig which is about 14 miles out to sea. I flew out there and looped over it. Then on the way back I looped four more times and tried some Immelman turns and spirals just to see if I could stand it. You see the Medical Board marked me as permanently unfit as a pilot or observer and I thought they might be wrong, but I'm afraid I'm not much good now and it took a terrible effort of will not to jump out of the bus. When I came down, I had a splitting headache and generally felt giddy and knocked up. I am turning my attention to gunnery now and will concentrate on that in the future as it is very interesting and work that I like.'

Work at Turnberry

Lyle was applying himself with great vigour to his new role and wrote to his younger sister 'Girlie' that, 'I wonder where you are and what you are doing now. I suppose you will be in the second term at school now that is if they have the three-term system at your school. I myself am at school again; but not such a quiet one as yours. I am at the School of Aerial Gunnery and am endeavouring to master as much as I can of this difficult subject in a very short time. I expect to be going off to a wing or Squadron soon to teach gunnery and it is very interesting work indeed.' To his father in a letter headed 'The School of Aerial Gunnery, Turnberry, Ayshire,' he wrote that, 'As you can see by the 'local' address I am back amongst the machines again. All day long we hear nothing, but the continual roar of engines and the rattle of machine gun fire. I am not flying at present, but am on the gunnery staff and I am taking a special course up here.' And to his younger brother Murray at the time of the latter's medical exams he said, 'You talk in your letter about swotting for exams. I suppose by the time you get this letter you will have finished them. Well I wish you the very best luck possible and hope you come out with honours, a thing I'm sure I couldn't do. As a matter of fact, I am swotting damn hard myself as I am going to be a gunnery instructor, so I've got to know absolutely everything about the different kinds of guns we use in the air. Also, the sighting arrangements which are very different to the ground. Also, I've got to know several different arrangements for firing guns through the propeller. My exams come off in about ten days or a fortnight so I'm swotting up for them damn hard at present.'

11 Squadron Memories

Another topic of great interest to Lyle a former member of 11 Squadron was the death of Captain Ball VC, a former squadron comrade. He wrote to Murray that, 'I suppose you know by this time that Johnny Ball has been killed, poor chap. I met an observer who was at the same aerodrome yesterday and he told me about his death. It appears that the Huns sent over a wireless and said that the British Government had offered 'permission to keep his machine, the VC and 2000 pounds to any pilot who brought down 'the travelling circus' as the RFC call Baron von Richtofen. They call him this because he always has a crowd of machines round him or as we call it his circus. He is easily recognised because he flies a blood-red machine with silver tips to his wings. Of course, the wireless was a fake; but it riled Ball that he went up in the evening and swore to bring him down if it was possible. He only had about 3 hours petrol with him at the time and when the Huns saw him coming, they all went down. He waited over there for two hours and a half and then Richtofen and four others came up and between them they bagged Johnny. Afterwards a Hun flew over and dropped his tunic and identity disc to show that they had got him. I'm damn sorry that he's gone as he was a really decent chap and I knew him quite well.'

By contrast Lyle wrote about the exploits of a Canadian RFC pilot who was making a name for himself as a flying ace, although he just wrote 'This man with the 48 Huns is a Canadian called (B........). Well I suppose I better not mention names just yet.' He then went on to relate the 'daring do' activities of the pilot. 'But what do you think; there is another pilot who has brought down even more machines than Johnny did. In fact, the chap Russell who told me about him said that he has got 48 Huns. And another man has bagged 28 Huns, so although Johnny is gone, there are others to take his place. The man with 48 Huns on one evening went out and hovered over a Hun aerodrome at about 3000 ft; but they wouldn't come out and fight, so he went down to 1000 ft and peppered their hangars with bullets until they had to come out. They then sent out 4 machines. He caught the first before it was 50 ft from the ground and crashed it, got the next one when it was only about 10 ft up, the third he strafed just as it was leaving the ground and killed the pilot and observer of the fourth as it was taxiing out. Some man what? Then as his petrol was getting low, he came down and landed just at our trenches riddled with bullets; but himself still unhurt. I think he deserved a tripe medal with a fringe of onions.'

Advice and Concerns

But Lyle was also in a reflective mood and wrote to Murray on 16th June, 'It is awfully decent of you to spare time to write to me and I value letters from home very much indeed. By Jove, those photos of yours make me wish I was home again. It's rather rotten being so far away although I am fairly happy and have some nice friends here. I got a letter today from Penelope Carmichael, the niece of Lord Carmichael. She is an awfully decent girl and with lots of other English girls is doing farm work now.'

Murray had written to Lyle and mentioned a concern about their father. Lyle replied, 'I don't quite catch what you mean when you say Dad is worried, because things haven't been going too well. What is wrong? Tell me what is the matter?' But then Lyle admitted something of his own behavior whilst home at Christmas and reflected that he was afraid that he hadn't spent his time very quietly while he was in Australia. 'As a matter of fact,

I don't think my example was too good while I was out there and I'm damn sorry; but the excitement of seeing you all again drove every other thought out of my head. But I have now seemed to have lost all inclination to gad about now and in addition am forcing myself to be quiet and do a lot of work.'

As the eldest brother he felt entitled to provide some wise advice to his younger siblings and wrote about Arnold the second youngest boy that Murray was not to, 'Let Arnold get too much of a swelled head and get out of hand as you say he is beginning to do. I think it was a wrong move of Father's to let him go to the Training College and he doesn't realise he's miles above that crowd or ought to be. If Arnold wants to go to the War try and get Dad to let him come over here and I can get him a commission in anything he likes Guards, Artillery, Infantry, Cavalry, Engineers or RFC. You see I know Generals and Colonels in all of these and can get him any sort of job he wants, safe or otherwise. In addition, the War Office will refund his passage money when he gets his commission. Also, a little of the English life might teach him to be more of a Gent as you say.'

It was in a letter to his father on 15th June that he laid bare the state of his situation and his anxiety at waiting for his discharge. 'With regard to my discharge I have already written to you twice; but in these days of submarines it is perhaps best to do so again. So please excuse me if you have got my other letters. I was examined and the Medical Board on the strength of Genl. Fetherston's letter recommended that I should get it. At first, I thought I should be put out of the army at once, but the Major in charge of services decided that the papers would have to go to another department to be confirmed and in the meantime a friend of mine in the Gunnery work asked me to take that up. So here I am. And I cannot say for certain when I will know the decision re: discharge. I wish I could get to Melbourne again.

Please give my love to Mother and Girlie. I will write to you soon. Your affectionate son, Lyle.'

And so, in mid-June 1917 Lyle knew that he was not permitted or supposed to fly again. Having tried the experience himself by flying to Ailsa Craig, he had to reluctantly agree with the decision of the Medical Board that had 'grounded him.' His nerves and judgement were incapable of him being an effective pilot again. His short-term future in the RFC looked to be secure and safe as a gunnery instructor and even if he was posted back to a squadron it would have been in a non-flying capacity. But most importantly, his discharge papers were in the system and it was just a matter of time before they arrived and he would be free to return to the University of Melbourne to continue his medical studies. The extensive social contacts he had made amongst the English aristocracy, would stand him in wonderful stead should he decide to pursue his medical career in England and who knows, perhaps even a marriage into one of the titled families. All the conditions were in place for Lyle to patiently wait for the creaky wheels of military bureaucracy to process his papers and he would be free to return to studies at the University and to the safety and love of the family and home that awaited him in East St Kilda.

Chapter 12:
His Death and Immediate Aftermath

CableGram
Postmarked Caulfield North, Victoria.
School Aerial Gunnery Turnberry Scotland.
20 June 1917

To WM Buntine
Melbourne (sic) Grammar School
Glen Eira Rd, East St Kilda.
*19/6/17 Regret notify you 2nd Lt W.H.C.
Buntine killed aeroplane accident today.*

How shattering this brief telegram must have been to the Buntine family and especially to his father Walter, who it was reported appeared in the dining room of the CGS Boarding House still clutching the telegram to tearfully bring the devastating news to the boys. In those days before the instant communications of modern telephones, iPads, Facetime and international air travel, the manner of receiving such sad news and being able to respond was just not possible and the quickest form of communication was a reliance on the telegram. There followed an exchange of these between the Buntines, the Whites and the School of Aerial Gunnery in Scotland to try and find out more information about the circumstances of Lyle's death. In the first instance, Walter sent a telegram to the Whites in Glasgow which read,

> 'Lyle killed Turnberry Tuesday. Please inquire burial and particulars.'

It is here that a letter dated 22nd June 1917 written by Matthew White to the Buntines related what took place next. 'To begin with we knew nothing of the tragedy till I got your cablegram a few hours before his funeral. My wife and I were staying for a few days in Troon, with my son Matthew and his wife. My son got a telephone message from Glasgow that a cablegram had arrived for me from Melbourne and he asked it to be opened and read to him and we heard the sad news first from you. I read of the accident in the morning paper, but no names were given and no place named which is the custom with all such accidents. We phoned from Troon to the Commanding Officer at Turnberry as we knew that Lyle was there, having had a letter from him about two weeks ago. He at once said he could not give particulars over the phone, but asked us to attend the funeral at 4 o'clock that afternoon if we could do so. It was 1 o'clock when we got our cable, so we had not much time, however we got a motor car and covered the 25 miles to Turnberry to be there in time. It was a most impressive sight. There is a large camp pitched here of about 800 Flying Corps men and 200 officers and it is the second largest aerodrome in the United Kingdom. The officers are all billeted in the large hotel and the men and hangars are spread over the Golf Course.

We were received by the Commandant in his room, also the Adjutant and heard all the particulars, then in a few minutes we went out to find the funeral procession all arranged. Lyle's coffin was placed on a motor gun carriage covered with the Union Jack flag and two large wreaths, one placed by the Officers and the other by the Non-Com. Officers. The Officers above the rank of Captain were in a motor car following the bier, then our car came next, myself and Jessie and Matt and Dorothy, followed by the bearer party, all Lieutenants and then other members of the staff. The flags were all at half-mast, the 800 men were drawn up on parade and all the remaining officers not going to the cemetery, were drawn up on either side of the carriage drive from the hotel and as the cortege slowly passed them, they all remained at the salute. The weather was not favourable enough for a flypast of aeroplanes in tribute to Lyle. We had five miles to drive to the cemetery which is in Girvan, a seaside resort on the Ayrshire coast. It is prettily situated on the very shore and Lyle was laid to rest in a lair in a quiet corner beside another officer who was killed some months ago by a similar accident. The burial service was Church of England and the rector officiated himself. He was very kind to us and asked us to the Rectory for tea, but we had to refuse, as the Commandant wanted us to return with him to Turnberry to fill out some particulars as to registering Lyle's death and about winding up his affairs and disposing of his assets.

The first thing was the lair, which I said would be purchased and not to be used for strangers again. The Commandant said the titles would be made out in your name as the nearest of kin, the purchase money I think will not exceed two or three pounds. All Lyle's effects, uniform, papers, Military Cross etc, were to be sent to you at once and he also said he had wired you and had prepaid a reply asking if you would pay any preferential claims against him, if there were no funds at his credit in Cox's Bank. All this had taken place before we arrived for the funeral. I told him that all claims preferential, that is his funeral and burial expenses and his officer's mess expenses would be met and the grave purchased, but for any other debts owing, I could not say at the moment and they of course did not know of any meantime. This guarantee allows them to send on all his effects at once to you. I have his sword which was left by Lyle in my custody until the war was over as he had no need of it in active service and I shall arrange to get it sent on to you.'

Matthew White also sent a telegram which briefly stated that Lyle had been buried at Girvan on the 21st of June, that he and his wife Jessie had attended the funeral and that he would write more fully to the Buntines. He further telegrammed on the 28th to advise the Buntines that,

> 'Lyle's effects all collected also King's decoration. Will forward after war.'

The twelve-page letter which eventually arrived from Matthew White was not received for a number of weeks after Lyle's death and in the meantime a flow of telegrams between Scotland and the Buntine home in East St Kilda provided more information, but also raised some questions at the same time. A telegram from the RFC at Turnberry to the Buntines dated 21st June, stated, *'Lieut. Buntine as passenger killed instantly while carrying out gunnery practice. Funeral today at Girvan. Letter following tonight. Will you pay all preferential claims against your son? Reply urgent.'*

It would appear that Walter replied with a telegram to inquire as to the nature of the meaning of 'preferential claims,' as five days later he received a reply from the RFC authorities at Turnberry which baldly stated, *'Preferential claims are only ordinarily military expenses.'* It was not until Walter received a lengthy letter from a Captain Frank Steel writing on behalf of the Commandant of the Aerial Gunnery School dated 21st June, that a full explanation of 'preferential claims' was given.

'With regard to my question as to whether you will pay all preferential claims against your son, I would like to explain the regulations which cover the circumstances of an officer's death. Whenever an officer dies or is killed, a Committee of Adjustment is formed to settle up his affairs and all the necessary expenses incurred by him before his death and all the expenses incurred in the funeral arrangements have to be paid for out of the estate of the dead officer. If no relation comes forward and expresses a willingness to meet all preferential claims, the personal effects have to be sold and claims thereof met by the sale. Knowing, however, that some of the belongings of your son will be of sentimental value to you, I asked the question, as by paying all these claims you will greatly simplify the difficulties attendant on the settlement of your son's affairs. I am having the title deed of the lair made out in your name and the grave if you will express your willingness to meet all the claims as I ask, will be your own private property, even though the lair will hold three coffins. I cannot do anything of course, until I receive your answer as to this payment of claims, but I have explained the position to Mr White and he will doubtless also be writing to you. The difficulties of the case are added to you because you are so far away and you will doubtless feel it unfair that an officer who dies for his country should not be buried at public expense, but being an officer, he is controlled by Army Regulations, which must be enforced. Be assured that I will do everything in my power to get his affairs settled as quickly as possible and will act at once on any instructions you might like to send me.'

The questions about the exact circumstances of Lyle's death in the flying accident were further answered in later letters received from Captain Steel of the School of Aerial Gunnery and

Matthew White dated on the 21st and 22nd of June respectively. Steel noted that, 'Your son was here as a Gunnery Instructor on probation and was just up to carry out one of the practices laid down at this School. He had been here a very short time and I must confess that I did not know him as well as I should have liked to have done, but one could see with the first glance that his was a charming personality and that friendship with him was an honour.'

Steel introduced his letter however, by outlining the circumstances of the accident. 'It is difficult to describe in a wire the full details of the accident and I am enclosing some of the evidence which was forthcoming at the Court of Inquiry held on the accident. This explains far more fully than I can do the circumstances of the accident. You will probably not understand all the flying technicalities and I would say that to 'stall' means to lose the flying speed necessary to keep the machine in the air. Had the machine been higher up in the air, the pilot Sgt Appleton, would have been able to avoid the accident, but owing to the hilly nature of the country, the machine was not so far off the ground as was indicated by the aneroid. There is no doubt that both the pilot and passenger, your son, were killed instantaneously by the fall, as the engine was behind them and must have crushed them before the fire broke out.'

The pilot of the machine was Sgt Stanley Chalmers Appleton, a former plumbing engineer from Warrington, who had enlisted at age 19 in the Royal Flying Corps on 15th February 1915 at Farnborough. He had worked his way through the ranks and on 1st February 1917 had been graded as a 1st Class Pilot at the Central Flying School but had never been posted to an Active Squadron. An unmarried man he was buried in a military grave in his home town of Warrington in Cheshire.

Captain Steel also included copies of some eyewitness statements from the Court of Inquiry held immediately after the accident.

Court Of Inquiry Evidence

Lieut. N. Sales. KOYLI and RFC states (1st Evidence)

'At about 3.45pm June 19th 1917, I was piloting a BE2c on camera practice with Lt Roth as passenger. I agreed to work with Sgt Appleton and Lt Buntine over Kirkoswald. I was flying at 900ft over a hill which was about 400ft high and Sgt Appleton was flying roughly 200 yards behind me on my tail, 100ft below me, being therefore about 400ft above the top of the hill. Suddenly Lt Roth called my attention to the ground, shouting, 'they have crashed.' I immediately turned to see the machine nose-dive and at once burst into flames on impact with the ground. I then flew over the wreckage at about 200ft and the whole of the centre part of the machine was entirely enveloped in flames. I then landed on the aerodrome and reported to Capt. Stookes as I considered it was of no avail to land by the wreckage.'

Lieut. J.B. Roth, Lancs. Fusiliers attached to the RFC, states (2nd Evidence)

'At about 3.45pm I was taken up by Lt Sales in a BE2c to do Camera Practice 6. After circling round the aerodrome and on reaching a height of about 900 ft, I saw an FE2b approaching and on sighting it at a distance of about 200 yards or 300 yards, it appeared to stall on a turn and then nose dive. In a moment or two flames shot up. I leaned over and shouted to the pilot, 'He's crashed.' We immediately turned and flew towards the wreckage which was on fire, with the exception of the wing tips. We immediately returned to the aerodrome and reported the matter, as in my opinion nothing could be possibly be done by landing besides the wreck, which was lying in a potato field about 30 yards from the edge of a wood.'

No. 50069. 2/AM. Kirk, E. states (3rd Evidence)

'I am the fitter in charge of 120 HP Beardmore engine W.D. No. 1325, Maker's No. 259, which was fitted in FE2b No. 817. Just before the last flight Sgt Appleton told me that the engine was running perfectly and giving her correct number of revolutions per minute. The machine started off all right and I watched it flying along above the hill. I saw the machine stall twice and then get into a spinning nose-dive. I did not see the machine actually reach the ground as it was hidden by the trees and hill. A column of thick black smoke arose and I immediately ran to the place of the accident. I found the machine burning and the pilot and the passenger both pinned under the wreckage. It was impossible to get near the machine on account of the flames.'

Captain J.B. Stevenson MC, RAMC states,

'While at the reception hospital shortly before 4.00pm I received a telephone message from Captain R.T. Leather that a machine had crashed and was burning in a field on the hill east of the aerodrome. I immediately proceeded in the ambulance car to the wreckage which was burning. It took me about 5 minutes to reach the spot. The other ambulance car and RAMC orderly were already there. I found that the machine was completely burnt. The bodies of the pilot and the observer were lying partially under the wreckage. The officer was on his back; his head, face, chest and abdomen were completely burnt and charred. The back was not so much affected. I consider that his death was caused by the fall and was instantaneous. The pilot was lying on his side with his elbow on the officer's body and his body was almost completely burnt. There was evidence of a serious fracture of his skull. Death must in his case also have been instantaneous.'

Matthew White who had spoken to the Commandant on the day of Lyle's funeral also provided some additional information to the Buntines in his letter of 22nd June under the heading,

'Particulars of the accident. Lyle and a pilot went up in an aeroplane on Tuesday 19th June at four o'clock in the afternoon. The pilot a Sgt. Appleton was one of their best experienced men. Lyle was practicing camera-gun fire. Appleton was steering the machine when about 100ft up and just over a ploughed field something went wrong. The technical name is 'stalling.' The machine plunged and they were not high enough to right it before it struck the earth only 400 ft over this field which was on a hill. Had they been several thousand feet up, the pilot could easily have righted the plane before it reached the earth. Both men were killed instantly and part of the aeroplane took fire. In 8 minutes after the accident, men were there but the bodies were under the aeroplane and quite dead. Appleton's body was sent on to his people in Lancashire England. It is a very sad story, for the Commandant told me Lyle was appointed an instructor at Turnberry on anti-raiding gunfire and would in all likelihood have been located there for some time, perhaps till the war was over and have escaped the terrors of air fighting in France, alas! How soon his brilliant career has come to an end. He was so proud of his Military Cross and we were so proud of him. We asked him last time he was with us on May 4th to tell us all about his presentation to their Majesties the King and Queen at Windsor, also the formal presentation of the Cross at Buckingham Palace by the King. He was modest about it. He went down to the 'Maidens' for the weekend with James Brownlee Young and Mrs Young (Nellie Murray) and what a co-incidence he was killed within a stone throw of where they were staying just 6 weeks after. The Maidens is a little fishing village at the foot of Turnberry Hill where Mrs White and I are going to spend the month of August.'

The unanswered question for all of Lyle's family and friends was to try and explain what on earth he had been doing in the aeroplane in the first place, as the Medical Board he had undertaken in February at Victoria Barracks in Melbourne had expressly forbidden him to fly again. By his own admission in his very recent letters home his solo flight offshore to Ailsa Crag had also convinced him that the Medical Board were absolutely right to have grounded him. So, what was he doing in the plane? Sadly, this question remains unanswered.

Condolences

It was only a week after his death that an anonymous hand-written poem of tribute to Lyle was received by his mother Bertha Buntine in East St Kilda. This poem was later published in the June 1917 edition of the Caulfield Grammar School magazine, the only such instance of a memorial poem being printed in honour of a fallen Grammarian. With the heading 'One who has Fellowship with you in your sufferings,' the poem was entitled 'A Humble Tribute to the Memory of Walter Horace Carlyle Buntine.' Although the author is unknown, it is quite possible that it was written by Bertha's sister Helen Gibbs who had also lost her eldest son, and Lyle's cousin, 'Mac' Gibbs at the Battle of Fromelles in early 1916.

> Tread softly through the night of gloom,
> Away with worldliness and mirth.
> T'is meet to 'weep with them that weep.'
> A noble son has fall'n to earth
> A son of tender love and care
> Of spirit great and talents rare

He needed no recruiter's voice
His Empire's need he clearly saw,
And leaving all his heart held dear
He bravely faced his country's foe
For her he nobly fought, and won
A token of his King's 'well done.'

'Good night' beloved sunny smiling face
The school-boys' hero for long years to come
Long will the record of his flight in space
'Live in their memory – Lyle well done.'
Kindest of brothers, loving hearted son
Rest from thy labours, 'Dear Lyle, well done.'

We bid thee not 'farewell – Adieu!'
Thy loved ones did at God's behest
Offer their sacrifice 'to Him'
Braved the fierce storm and stood the test
Lived unto Him each loyal life
Dwells in God's heart above the strife.

It can be seen that the first verse alluded to the flying accident and indicated the depths of the grief felt by his family and friends. The second verse made reference to his willingness to enlist and to face all kinds of danger as well as the official acknowledgement of his bravery in battle by virtue of his winning the Military Cross; personally presented to him by the King. The third verse depicted Lyle as an example to younger Caulfield Grammarians and even made reference to the school motto, 'Labora Ut Requiescas' which was translated as being able to rest content from your labours knowing that you have done your best. The final verse confirmed the Christian view of the promise of eternal life with

God and the reward of being with Him following the sacrifice of one's own life in a noble and just cause. The poem was handwritten in black ink and was mailed to Lyle's mother anonymously and was signed, 'One who shares your grief.'

Matthew White, Walter's cousin ended his letter of 22nd June to the grieving Buntine family with the words, 'We deeply sympathise with you, his dear mother and brothers and sister and he used to talk so lovingly of you all and how happy he was when home last Christmas and showed us photos taken then. Words avail little in presence of such great sorrow and we mingle our sorrow with yours.'

Mr Brownlee Young in a seventeen-page typed letter brought a personal perspective to Lyle's passing as it had only been a few weeks earlier that Lyle had joined them for a holiday, ironically not far from where he was killed.

'On the evening of 3rd May Mr White came across with Lyle and surprised us greatly by announcing to my wife, here is an Australian cousin or second cousin and one who has done his bit. Lyle had just arrived after paying you a visit home and the Whites were closing down for a day or two and it was a real pleasure to be of some service in asking him to stay a day or two with us. Strange to say Mrs Young and my daughter Ailsa were going off to next day to The Maidens in Ayrshire, a half a mile from Turnberry, or rather Ailsa had taken the small cottage and her Mother was to join her part of the time, and some of her friends other parts of the time and myself the finishing visitor. At the moment of my writing I know you will be too grief stricken to listen to this story, but by the time this reaches you, which I hope it will do safely, you may be interested to hear of our little experience with your boy. Ailsa was leaving next day for Maidens and it was decided that her Mother would follow on the Saturday. Lyle stayed with us at Kingsborough on the

Friday night and then went down to the Maidens with us on the Saturday and the arrangement was that he would stay till the Tuesday or Wednesday and then come back to us for a day or two more here.

On the Monday evening I got a phone message from him from town saying he had come up as he had to go off to London. I tried to persuade him to stay that night, but he went out to friends Inshaws in the country and said he would look in on the Tuesday en route for London, which he did and called on the Whites then also. To say that both Mrs Young and Ailsa were charmed with Lyle is to put it mildly. Neither Mrs Young nor Ailsa take particularly quickly to new friends no matter who they are, but Lyle had gone to their hearts instantly, perhaps because they found him so full about his parents, their home and his family. He was so extremely natural and he wasn't in the house many minutes until he was showing photos of your home, his father and mother, his brothers and sister. So natural that while in some it might almost have appeared brag and boasting, it was in his case his own true love of family. His Mother was a brick, the best in the world, his Father, brilliantly clever.

That's by the way, but Lyle wasn't allowing any misconception of his family and yet it was with boyishness naturalness. The one thing he wouldn't talk about was his own success except the episode with the King of which he was rightly proud. Mrs Young raved about him on her return. They were living the simple life at Maidens, no maid and he did the wiping as Mrs Young washed up, anything, everything. One funny remark Mrs Young quoted many and many a time. It was Ailsa's house and they were invited down yet, when they did arrive her Mother, as usual got the work to do and Lyle helped her, Ailsa sitting in the 10ft by 7ft garden sewing. She was really getting her uniforms in order for relief duty this month, but Lyle's remark to

Mrs Young as she washed and he wiped was 'Where's the lady of the house, we are guests.' Ailsa had delightful rambles with him and they fed in the kitchen and they could have fed in the coal cellar for all Lyle cared.

I never saw such a change in anyone in a week-end and he was bronzed with the sun, I have seen less good done in a fortnight. They lived out of doors the whole weekend. Of course, it wasn't summer heat morning and night and here again Lyle displayed his simplicity of character. Wasn't above wearing a thin jersey of my wife's under his jacket, though it was a lady's and didn't mind taking off his jacket and being seen with this on when the sun scorched at mid-day. If he had been my wife's own boy, she couldn't have taken a greater interest in him. The next we heard was only a handful of days ago. A phone message and it was a surprise. To tell he was up to town for the evening with two Australian fliers and would come out to see us next day before returning. How strange, what a surprise he had been sent to Turnberry of all places, a place he had seen for the first time in his life a week or two before. I couldn't fix an hour next day so Mrs Young met him in town for a half hour.

He was full about being at Turnberry as he thought it was the finest place he had seen in this country. He hadn't been many hours in it before he had rushed off to the Maidens to see if Mrs Young and Ailsa were there. AND NOW! To think that Turnberry which in pre-war days had had such glorious memories of splendid holidays and rest-cures and golf matches, for we stayed a lot there at the very hotel which was converted into Flying Corps quarters, to think it should have also so sad a memory. It has been having a sad-like memory during the past eight months to read of the brave bright young men who have had mishaps, but the one of Tuesday last overshadows them all and will be the lasting one.'

How poignant it must have been for the Buntines to think of Lyle and these happy times with the Youngs at Turnberry, although they would always associate the names with the death of their beloved eldest boy. Brownlee-Young's letter whilst providing words of comfort and sympathy also provides a further insight into Lyle's state of mind especially as it concerned flying. 'Dear Parents, be consoled by the nature of his passing away, for King and Country, your country, mine, and for something more, for civilized life itself. Hard lines that he should not have lived to enjoy his decoration in after years but if he had to answer his Call, no better way that in teaching others to defend their Country. Remember also, he was a volunteer, not a conscript. In after years your present sadness will give way to pride, a justifiable pride in this fact. Lyle seemed as physically well as he possibly could be but he wasn't quite right, that's why I never expected he would have been flying yet. Yet the nature of the boy would be to force his superiors to let him resume before they wanted him to, I fear. Let me tell you this. It is strange that our short acquaintanceship with him should have so much crowded into it and it is strange that he should see Turnberry for the first time through us. When the question arose would he stay in town with me or go down to Maidens, I said most certainly the Maidens as I thought he will want to see the Flying School. I said to Ailsa you must take him to Turnberry, introduce him to the Manager, introduce him to Butler, they will introduce him to the Commandant, they will proudly welcome their MC comrade. Strange also that an Australian school of fliers arrived during our stay. Lyle said 'Yes, that will be splendid' – but when he got there, he didn't want to see any of Turnberry, he didn't care to see the machines in the air. His nerves were not quite right, partly that, partly, he told me afterwards, '…if I had gone there, I would have coaxed some of them to let me go up.' There was just that nervy feeling that he didn't know what he wanted to do. A feeling that nothing but time and good feeding would wear off. No sooner at Maidens than he must get to Edinburgh, for he went to Edinburgh on the Monday before phoning me from town. No sooner some-place else than he wanted to be some other place. Perhaps partly his good nature that made him promise to make more calls and stay here and there more than he had time for. Tuesday night 8th May he called to get his bag and say au revoir to me, en route for London and yet he had half promised a few hours before to spend another evening with the Inshaws. He asked if he might phone before leaving and say that he couldn't get out that night, but must get back to London. I know that feeling, I have seen it in others after a time of stress, my daughter had it on her return from nursing in France. I don't know of anything else I can tell you about Lyle. I hope what I have told you has been interesting.'

Perhaps these prophetic words can help to explain why Lyle flew on the afternoon of his death. With the thought of his discharge papers arriving any day, with the thought of returning home to continue his medical studies, perhaps he had indeed coaxed someone in authority into letting him fly with Sgt Appleton '... perhaps for the last time as I'm going home to Australia.' We may never know.

It might be that Ailsa Brownlee-Young and Lyle shared much in common as she had worked for six months as a volunteer in France with the French Red Cross.

George Inshaw also wrote a letter of condolence which also contained some details of Lyle's visit to the Inshaws only a few days before the fatal accident. 'Mrs Inshaw, self and family beg to convey to you our deepest sympathy and condolence in your sad bereavement. Indeed, we all are exceedingly grieved as your son was so much liked by us and he had really become quite attached to us and our home. He would tell you all about the happy times he spent with my young people when he paid his last visit to Lockwood. I was pleased to have him with us knowing that he was so far away from you and when he was wounded, we all were so anxious about him and were pleased to know he had been able to travel home on leave, hoping his voyage would help to restore health after the wonderful work he had done at the front. Soon after he returned to England, he came to see us and spent a pleasant time and afterwards returned to London. I met him in London with my son George who took him to see the works and he was looking much better. He wrote and told us he was coming to Turnberry which is about 60 miles from here. A fortnight last Friday he came and spent the night with us and he returned to Glasgow with me on Saturday morning, promising to come back to Lockwood in the afternoon if he could get leave. He phoned saying he had to return to Turnberry and this is the last I saw of him. We learned the sad news on Wednesday 20th when the Commanding Officer phoned and indeed it was a great shock to us all.'

Other tributes came from unexpected sources, in this case a letter in mid-August to Walter from Mr H McKenna the Postmaster at Girvan, where Lyle had been buried. 'You will no doubt be rather surprised on receipt of this letter, still I hope it will help to comfort you in some way from the great loss you have sustained through the death of your dear boy. I am sorry I did not know him personally still I came in contact with many of the Flying Corps during their stay at Turnberry. It was a sad ending for such a brave lad and the only consolation is that he is resting in our village churchyard after having given up all that is dear in this world. The thought struck me that if I could get a photograph of his grave it was the least I could do to send you a copy. The grave with the wreaths is where your boy is buried and it was taken on the day after the service. The cross indicates where an F.C Pugh is also laid, he having succumbed to a similar accident. I do hope this packet reaches you unless the Huns come across the mail boat.'

Mr McKenna also wrote again in June 1919, 'I am very sorry for being so long in sending the enclosed which I know will bring sad memories to your home again. I thought you would like to see that the boys have not been forgotten in dear old Scotland where a good many lie at rest. These were taken on Anzac Day and the cutting from the local paper will give full details.' The newspaper article under the heading, 'Anzac Day, Ceremony at Girvan Cemetery. Flowers on Heroes Graves,' outlined the proceedings of the day at the section of the cemetery devoted to those who had died whilst serving at the Turnberry Training School. It read in part, 'In recognition of Anzac Day arrangements were made for a party of leading citizens to visit Doune Cemetery and lay floral tributes on the graves of the three Anzacs who lie buried there.' In addition to Lyle and two other Australians, the cemetery contained the graves of five Americans, three Canadians and twelve Britishers.

Other letters from overseas arrived and from Ceylon the Gordons who had hosted Lyle at their tea plantation on his return voyage to England only a few months earlier wrote, 'Just a few lines to convey to you my deepest sorrow at hearing of the sudden death of poor old 'Billy.' At a time like this, words do not convey much, but I may tell you, I loved the lad. My sincerest condolences to you all.'

His wife Vera wrote to Lyle's mother and apart from expressing her sympathies also provided an insight into Lyle's state of mind about the prospect of flying again. 'I cannot tell you how terribly shocked we were to hear of your poor boy's death. We had heard from him only ten days before, telling us that he was not going to the front again, but was to train pilots in Scotland.

We were so relieved when we heard this as your son had such a rooted presentiment that he would be killed if he flew again. I expect he told you that he came up to see us when he was in Colombo on his way home. It was so nice to see him again, but both my husband and I felt very worried about him. When he said goodbye to me, he added that he would never see me again if they made him fly when he returned to England. We tried to cheer him up, but could not dissuade him from the idea. When we heard from him that he was going to train at home, we never dreamed that the end would be just the same. We hadn't known your boy for long, but had grown very, very fond of him and were great friends. Your boy was so well liked by all who met him here and everyone was so shocked to hear of his untimely end.'

At home in Australia, details of Lyle's death reached some newspapers, but first his obituary appeared in the AGE.

'On Active Service.

BUNTINE – On the 19th June, through aeroplane accident at School of Aerial Gunnery, Turnberry, Scotland. Lieutenant Walter Horace Carlyle Buntine. MC. Dearly loved eldest son of Mr and Mrs Buntine of Caulfield Grammar School.'[103]

In the same edition under the heading 'Australia's Soldiers, Casualty Notifications,' was the sub-heading, Flight Lieutenant Buntine killed and the following article. 'By cable message received last evening, Mr W.M. Buntine of Caulfield Grammar School, was informed of the death by aeroplane accident of his son, Lieutenant W.H.C. Buntine of the Royal Flying Corps. Lt. Buntine had only recently returned to England after spending two months at home, having been wounded during operations on the Somme in September last, in connection with which he was awarded the Military Cross for conspicuous gallantry and skill.'[104]

Further afield Lyle's clergyman uncle's local newspaper in NSW also reported the tragic accident. 'The Rev. H.S. Buntine of Armidale (NSW) received a wire on Thursday night conveying the sad news that his nephew, Lieut. W.H. Carlyle Buntine had been killed in an aeroplane accident at the Gunnery School, Scotland. The young officer was only 21 years of age and had a most distinguished career in the army. He first of all on enlisting joined up with an English regiment in which he soon won his commission. His great penchant was however to become an aviator and leaving the regiment in question he entered an aviation school and speedily became proficient being one of the youngest to gain his pilot's certificate.

He was then transferred to France and there soon acquired a splendid record for daring and most effective air fighting. He had in all 15 thrilling combats with enemy aircraft and downed several. It was on one of the latter occasions that he displayed such devotion to duty that the Military Cross was awarded to him. His modest description of this incident appeared in the 'Express' some months ago in the course of a letter he wrote from the front. He received a severe bullet wound in the arm while disposing of his antagonist and made a wonderful trip back to the Allied lines with one arm hanging useless by his side. The news of his death is therefore particularly sad and to be regretted.

He was the son of Mr W.M. Buntine, head of the Caulfield Grammar School, Melbourne and prior to enlisting was a successful student of medicine. He had already accomplished two years of the University course. His country's call however came first and he freely and willingly sacrificed all his excellent prospects and now in the very flower of his early manhood he has made the supremest sacrifice of all.'[105]

The Melbourne Herald June 30th 1917, reported,

'On June 19 Lieutenant Walter H.C Buntine MC, lost his life through an aeroplane accident. He was the eldest son of the headmaster of Caulfield Grammar School and soon after enlisting joined the air service, gaining his commission and the Military Cross. He was injured and returned on furlough, but he valiantly resumed his duties and was engaged at the School of Aerial Gunnery in Scotland when the fatal accident occurred. Athletically he first came into prominence during the visit of the American team. On the Melbourne Cricket Ground on February 17 1914, he tied with R.R.Templeton (snr) in a pole vault handicap. The height was 11ft 2in. and Buntine was receiving 2ft and cleared 9ft 2in. In the Victorian championships of 1915 he cleared 9ft 6in, gaining second place to R.Rodgerson (9ft 9in). As he was quite a lad there was every prospect of further advance. There is general sympathy with his parents in his loss.'

The student publication of the Medical Faculty of the University of Melbourne reported his death in the following manner. 'Lieutenant Walter Horace Carlyle Buntine, MC, was killed on June 19th last at Turnberry in Scotland. We learn he had been appointed to the Instructional Staff temporarily, at the School of Aerial Gunnery. He met his death by aeroplane accident whilst a passenger. Lyle Buntine was educated at the Caulfield Grammar School, where he took a large share of the honours in work and sport. Proceeding to the Melbourne University, he was attending lectures in medicine when war broke out. He immediately volunteered, but being only 18 years of age had to obtain his parents' consent, which was not given until 1915, when he left with AAMC as a corporal.

In England he transferred to the English Army, obtaining his commission first in the Sherwood Foresters and later in the Royal Flying Corps. In July 1916, he left with his unit for

France and saw service during the Somme offensive and at Pozieres, where he won his Military Cross. He was shot down six times by anti-aircraft guns and was wounded in the arm at Gommecourt. After some weeks in hospital he returned for a few months to Australia and then left again to report for duty, when he met his death. To his people we offer our very sincere sympathy and those of us who knew Lyle felt that he would always give of his best for Australia and the Empire. A very gallant gentleman.'[106]

Finally, the Caulfield Grammarian school magazine paid tribute to him in their June 1917 edition under the heading 'Killed on Active Service.' No doubt his father Walter had either written or edited the seemingly perfunctory article and the irony of losing his life in such circumstances whilst awaiting a recall home was writ large for all to see.

'Lieutenant W.H.C. Buntine, MC, Royal Flying Corps, was killed at Turnberry, Scotland on June 19th last. He had been home during the Christmas holidays on leave, recovering from wounds received in France. He returned and reported to the War Office in May, and it had been decided to send him back to Australia to finish his medical course. In the meantime, he had been appointed temporarily to a staff position as an instructor in aerial gunnery. It was when in an aeroplane as a passenger instructing a beginner that the fatal accident occurred.'[107]

Tributes and other memorials were to come later, but of immediate concern to Lyle's family was to gain some closure to his life and to ensure that all 'loose ends' had been dealt with especially with regards to his possessions. On 11th August in a letter from Matthew White to the Buntines from his holidays at the Maidens, he lamented that he was still awaiting instructions from them as to what to do with Lyle's remaining property.

'Rocklea' Maidens Ayrshire

Dear Friends,

You will see by the above address where we are at present spending our summer holiday. It was in a field not far from here that poor Lyle was killed. We are only 1 and a half miles from the Turnberry Aerodrome and 6 miles from Girvan where Lyle lies buried. I have had no letters from you since the tragic death of poor Lyle and expect one daily now unless the mail has been torpedoed as many mail boats have gone down.

   I am waiting your instructions what I am to do with Lyle's effects. I have them all collected at Princes Terrace and an inventory taken by the Commandant at Turnberry attached to them which I signed for on delivery. I placed Lyle's affairs in the hands of my solicitors, Donaldson and Alexander, 186 West Regent St Glasgow. There was a good deal of correspondence with the War Office and others to get matters arranged. The ground in the cemetery was bought and paid for and Donaldson and Alexander have got the title deeds which are down in your name. Funeral expenses and mess bills were also paid and the total at present paid out amounts to over £12. There were a few pounds in his possession at the time of his death and a balance of about £7 in his credit at Cox's Bank and the War Office were due pay him a balance of his salary which has not yet been paid to anyone. It will be necessary for you to authorise Donaldson and Alexander to take out confirmation and act for you as next of kin to get these sums due to Lyle's estate paid into it. There will be a good deal more money than is necessary to pay his debts which as far as is known yet are almost nil.

   You might send a letter to me authorising Donaldson and Alexander to act for you and for all sums due the estate to be paid to them and all debts to be paid by them which are preferential. We will retain his effects here till the war is over when we will ship them to Melbourne by your instructions and register his Military Cross. It is necessary that someone has power of attorney to act for you here and Donaldson and Alexander are a firm held in the highest repute in Glasgow. I consider it best to put the affairs in the hands of the solicitors as there are legal points which might crop up in course.

I hope your good selves and family are recovering from the great shock and sad bereavement which you have suffered and now living and resting on the proud memories of a brave son who did his bit for humanity and the cause of freedom. We came to Maidens for our holiday as it is a small fishing village with few houses about and a most restful place. My wife was in a nursing home with a serious illness and is now convalescing and gradually improving and our two daughters Hetty and Meg are also with us at present. When this terrible war is over, we look forward with pleasure to the time when you and Mrs Buntine will pay a visit to Scotland and do homage at the grave of your brave son. With kindest regards and respects, I remain, Your sincere friend, Matthew White.'

The Buntine family however, were keen to recover Lyle's luggage which had been inadvertently unloaded in Cairo, and which Lyle himself had believed was in transit to him, but in response to inquiries from the family were unable to locate them at all. In response to their requests the Australian Military Forwarding Officer at Suez in a letter dated 28th of August to the Military Forwarding Depot at the Suez Docks wrote in regards to Lt WHC Buntine of the 11th Wing, RFC: 'The above-named officer who is from Melbourne, Australia, but serving in the English Army, passed through your hands about three months ago as a passenger on the 'SS Mandria.' A portion of his kit was mislaid. This officer has since been killed and I should be obliged if you would prosecute enquiries as to the missing kit, and give me any information possible regarding the matter. If his belongings are found will you please forward them to this office.'

A brief handwritten note from a Lt Pobson at the Military Forwarding Depot at the Suez Docks and dated 30th August 1917 stated in reply, 'I regret to inform you that I have no trace of the missing kit, but am of the opinion that an enquiry of Headquarters AIF Cairo would in all probability produce the desired information.'

A brief letter from the Headquarters of the Australian Imperial Force in Egypt located in Cairo and dated 5th September 1917, stated, 'It is regretted that we have no information re the missing kit. As Lt Buntine is not a member of the AIF, the treatment of his kit would not pass into our hands at all.' The letter then suggested that they might try the Officer's Kit Bureau in Mustapha.

The last that is heard of the missing luggage is in a letter dated 24th September from Mrs Pauline de Gay to Whites acting as Lyle's executors in Glasgow, in response to a request from Lyle's mother for more information. 'Some days ago, I received a letter from Mrs Buntine asking if I would make enquiries about poor Lyle's effects. I have been to the Aero Club and was told that you were acting as executor and that all the things had been forwarded to you. Would you kindly let me know if you have received everything, if not I could make further enquiries? Mrs Buntine also requested me to ascertain if any mention was made in any of the daily papers re. Lyle's investiture by the King at Windsor for his Military Cross. If you have any such notice would you kindly forward a copy to her. I am making inquiries also. Poor dear Lyle, we cannot realise it yet. Mrs Buntine wrote to my daughter Sylvia, but she is still in Egypt, I (her mother) am answering the letter as it would take too long if I were to send it on to Egypt. My daughter is making inquiries in Suez regarding some of Lyle's lost luggage there. Yours very truly, Mrs Pauline de Gay.'

The archival records are not clear as to whether Lyle's missing luggage was ever recovered, but given that the name of the ship was given to authorities as the *SS Mandria*, instead of the *Medina*, the chances were not that high to begin with at all.

In the meantime, the family pursued some further lines of inquiry in an attempt to settle some other matters and on 12th September Mr Harold Perrin, the Secretary of The Royal Aero Club in response to a letter from Walter wrote, 'I duly received your letters of the 26th June and 4th July and am sorry I have no particulars in regard to the accident to Lieut. WHC Buntine. If you communicate with the Office Commanding, Royal Flying Corps, Turnberry Scotland or the Department of Military Aeronautics, Air Board Office, Strand, London, WC2, you would probably be able to obtain full details. On receipt of your cablegram the three bags left by the late Lt WHC Buntine at the Club were collected by Messrs. Thos.Cook and Son for despatch to you, but owing to it being necessary to procure a licence from the Board of Trade for their despatch the goods were not forwarded. A few weeks later we received a communication from Messrs. Donaldson and Alexander, 186 St Vincent St, Glasgow, who informed us that they were acting for the executors and asked us on behalf of Mr Matthew White Snr, 45 Hope St Glasgow to instruct Messrs. Cook and Son to forward the luggage belonging to the late Mr Buntine to them; they also informed me that Mr White was acting on your behalf and had written and cabled you on the matter. In accordance with these instructions Messrs. Cook and Son were asked to forward the articles to Messrs. Donaldson and Alexander. I have no information regarding Mr Buntine's Military Cross and should think he had it with him at

Turnberry. With sincere sympathy in your loss, Yours faithfully, Mr Harold Perrin, Secretary.'

The next day a letter was sent to Walter from Cox and Co. in London which in many ways almost finalised Lyle's financial affairs. 'We beg to acknowledge the receipt of your letter of the 4th July and to express our deep sympathy with you in your sad loss. We have written to the Officer Commanding at Turnberry requesting him to communicate direct to you, details of your son's death. The balance in our hands is £7 - 11. This does not include the £50. mentioned by you, which we are unable to trace having received on Lt Buntine's behalf. We shall be obliged if you can furnish us full particulars to enable us to trace the amount. We have been in communication with Messrs. Donaldson and Alexander Solicitors, 186 St Vincent St Glasgow, who we understand are acting on your behalf, to whom we are giving full particulars and details of any monies to which your son may be entitled and where to obtain such sums. The Military Cross, Will or other documents were not lodged with us for safe custody. We are sir, your obedient servants.'

The final word on matters financial came via a telegram on 21st October from Glasgow. 'Fifty pounds returned bank Melbourne October 3rd. Require formal power of attorney from next of kin to James Donaldson to settle estate. Post at once. Donaldson.'

But apart from settling these financial matters and attempting to trace his missing luggage the family still felt that they did not have final closure about Lyle's tragic accident. Having received no further details from the Royal Aero Club or Cox and Co., an answer finally arrived in a letter in early October from the Military Aeronautics Directorate section of the Air Board Office.

'In reply to your letter, the following are the circumstances under which your son met his death. He was flying in a machine with Sergeant S.C. Appleton as pilot. The accident was due to the machine stalling on a turn at a height insufficient for recovery to be made from the ensuing nose dive and both pilot and observer were killed. His death is very much regretted inasmuch as the Medical Board told him that he was not to fly. He was well aware of this fact and was given a note to this effect. All arrangements had been made for him to return home to resume his medical studies in accordance with his wish. I can only say that we all deplore his death and Lt-Gen. Sir David Henderson desires me to express his deepest sympathy with you in your sad loss. Yours faithfully, Lt.Col. W.W.Warner.'

Having exhausted all available channels for some closure as to Lyle's death, all that was left for the Buntine family now was to mourn his passing and grieve for what might have been.

In the meantime the family dealt with the many cards and letters of condolences by replying with their own black edged card which read, 'Mr and Mrs W M Buntine and Family desire to thank you very sincerely for your kind expression of sympathy in the sad loss of their son and brother, Lieutenant W.H.C.Buntine, MC, (RFC), who met his death during aerial gunnery practice at Turnberry, Scotland on June 19th 1917.'

Other letters of condolences came from James S Bontein in North Berwick, Scotland who wrote, 'He was in this house not so very long before his fatal accident and his attractive personality greatly impressed us. This is yet another of her many fearless sons which both Australia and Scotland feel they can claim with pride.'

Even a year after Lyle's death his memory was still being invoked in a poem published in the Caulfield Grammarian magazine and was unique in that it was written by Phyllis Mollison, the sister of some former School friends and said by some members of the Buntine family to have been a special friend of Lyle; perhaps even a girlfriend.

By Daryl Moran

A year to-day!
Since thou, brave spirit, bravely winged thy way
Up, up into the azure sky –
The canopy of God on high!

The triumph was short
In that thy splendid flight should come to nought,
For, all unseen, Death hovered aft
Round the frail pinions of thy craft.

One moment more
Ere thy proud course was stopt by unknown law;
Did crippled lever fail to heed
Thy tightened grip in hour of need?

The end came soon,
For hurtling downwards like some meteor flame,
Sped thy machine on slanting wing,
And, falling, crashed to earth a shattered thing!

Thy race was run,
Thy heart-beats stilled - but duty nobly done;
They found thee lying on the sod
Who triumphed then? - Not Death! – Nay, God!

A year to-day!
Since thy brave spirit swiftly passed away;
And, passing, soared to higher realms above;
To Him who reigneth there in Peace and Love.

In addition to his name being placed on the Honour Board at CGS and the University of Melbourne, Lyle was also remembered on the Roll of Honour at the Melbourne Swimming Club and in the planting of a Memorial Tree by the City of Caulfield and the Town of Brighton. At a Public Demonstration, this tree was planted by Walter Buntine during the ceremony at 3.00pm on Saturday 3rd August 1918, along with eighty-one others on the north side of North Road on the section from Point Nepean Road to Fuller Avenue.

A simple white cross with his name and date of death had initially marked his grave in Scotland and Matthew White had written to the family in January 1920 and assured them that the grave was being kept in order by the cemetery people and that it was easily found when visiting. He suggested that it was wise of them to delay the erection of a tombstone until prices became more reasonable as he had heard of £500 being charged for an ordinary sized obelisk. 'Surely normal times will arrive soon.'

Eventually the Buntines made the necessary arrangements for the simple white wooden cross to be replaced with a splendid marble headstone, engraved with his life's key details and a tribute which read;

> 'In Loving memory of Walter H Carlyle Buntine, MC. 2nd Lieut. Sherwood Foresters and Royal Flying Corps. Aged 21 years. Born at Melbourne Australia 10 August 1898. Left on Active Service 17 July 1915. Accidentally Killed at Turnberry 19th June 1917. Jesus said, I Am the Resurrection and the Life.'

On a card dated Anzac Day April 25th, 1924, the Annual Pilgrimage to Australian and New Zealand Soldier's and Sailors' Graves throughout the United Kingdom, in grateful remembrance of the brave sons of Australia and New Zealand who fought and suffered, died and conquered, on many battlefields, visited Lyle's grave. A handwritten note on the back of the card says, 'We remembered him with a floral tribute, in simple praise of him, and for our honour and your comfort.'

On 23rd November 1921 the War Office forwarded to the Buntines, Lyle's British War and Victory medals and the letter concluded, 'In forwarding the Decorations I am commanded by the King to assure of His Majesty's high appreciation of the services rendered.'

Lyle's name was to be remembered in Scotland on one more unique memorial, which was the Turnberry War Memorial opened on 28th April 1923 and dedicated; 'To the memory of the Officers, Non-Com. Officers and Men of the Royal Flying Corps, Royal Air Force and the Australian and United States Air Services who gave their lives for their country while serving in the School of Aerial Gunnery and Fighting at Turnberry, 1917 – 18. Their name liveth for evermore.'

Lyle was listed under the Royal Flying Corps and his name was one of 37 listed on the impressive granite obelisk. What was especially unique about the memorial was that the local residents and community of Turnberry had raised the necessary funds to construct the memorial, at the time the only such 'public funded' memorial in Great Britain. The Marquis of Ailsa who unveiled the memorial said in part that, 'The memorial which we have just unveiled has been erected by the exertions of the people of Turnberry, in admiration and affection, it is true, not to their own kith and kin born and brought up here in this parish, but as a spontaneous tribute of admiration and honour to those who came here at the call of duty and to the gallantry and self-sacrifice of the air services of our King and country. They came here, not on pleasure bent, but in the grim happiness and pride of their youth and high resolve to fit and quit themselves here like men for the greater part to which they felt the call, of fulfilling the destiny of their race and worthily of their blood. It is raised in the highest honour to those members of the Air Force whose names are recorded upon it. Heroic lives heroically rendered are not lives lost.'

Sadly, Lyle's former companion observer from 11 Squadron, the Irishman 2nd Lt Archibald James Cathie, survived the fighting at the Battle of the Somme, but was also tragically killed in a flying accident in Gloucestershire, just three weeks after Lyle's death.

Although nothing could ever bring Lyle back from the grave, in reading these words and coming to understand the sentiments of the people of Turnberry in raising the funds and seeing the project through to its conclusion, the Buntines must have taken some small comfort that his death had been seen by others in the light of a glorious sacrifice for the greater good of the Empire.

Chapter 13:
'Years May Pass On, But Memory Remains'

(A line from the Caulfield Grammar School Song)

Australia Mourns for its War Dead

The families of the men killed in the Great War were deprived of the traditional mourning rituals of their culture, because their dead lay far away, as was the case with Lyle Buntine; it not being entirely feasible or financially possible to transport the bodies of the dead soldiers back to Australia for burial by their families, historian Ken Inglis noted.[108] In the case of Australia this 'memory keeping' had begun during war time with the compilation of Honour Rolls in work places and schools which at first sought to encourage young men to enlist, but later came to become a stark visual and public record of those who had died. Caulfield Grammar School had instituted its own Roll of Honour in early 1915 to mark the enlistment and sacrifice of its Old Boys by naming each enlisted individual and in time constructing a special central section for those who had died. This Roll was completed and finally unveiled in October 1919.

Australians needed some tangible form of a memorial to the dead and what did become an issue was the form that the memorial should take. Inglis outlined in some detail the variety of common forms of memorial that were used and amongst these are a cenotaph (empty tomb), a treed Avenue of Honour, a Memorial Arch, a cross, an obelisk, a statue of a 'digger' on a pedestal, a symbolic female figure and even captured enemy weapons of war displayed as trophies.[109] But once again different communities and associations used a further variety of forms including the endowing of scholarships, specially dedicated buildings, purpose built structures in public places such as bandstands or shelter places, memorial gardens, memorial tablets in local churches and in some extreme cases, the construction of empty graves in family cemetery plots.[110] Whilst these memorials went some way to providing a site for mourning, both public and private, it was no replacement for a grave at which families could pay their last respects. In many cases the absence of a grave was compounded by the vast numbers, perhaps some 20,000 out of 60,000 deaths of Australian soldiers who had no known grave. As a small sample, CGS had lost 70 of its Old Boys during the Great War and of that number, 28 had no known grave.

Families remembered their own dead in many small ways and it became important to them to recover the dead man's possessions and belongings as it gave them a direct link with something he had owned or touched. In some cases, grieving families erected shrines of these artifacts, photographs, letters and other ephemera, so that there was always a tangible reminder of the person to hand. In this context, it becomes much clearer as to why Lyle's family tried so desperately to find his missing luggage in Egypt. Author Ross McMullin provided an example describing the grief displayed by a father for a lost son.

'But in 1916 George (the father) still had another decade and more of alert life ahead of him. He devoted much of it to commemorating Geoff (his son). This obsessive devotion reflected the intensity of the father's never-ending grief by turning Geoff's bedroom into a perpetual shrine, by cherishing his medals and mementos, by installing a memorial window at his local church, by compiling commemorative verse, by seeking his personal effects, by sketching his faraway grave, by locating the cemetery site, by pursuing posthumous awards and by spending hours and hours transcribing Geoff's wartime diary and letters, even re-sketching the accompanying drawings.'[111]

Many bereaved Great War families in Australia also strove to preserve the memory of the lost loved one through the keeping of artifacts, letters and photographs, in some cases as a shrine in the family home. Writer and historian Tania Luckins suggested, 'Wartime loss was responded to with a series of personal and social acts. This included writing letters, making scrapbooks, wearing mourning black and being part of a crowd of these mourners. It also involved focusing on an object and investing it with the memory of an absent body. According to Luckins these acts were both personal and official.'[112] She further observed that, 'Small items, such as wallets, photographs, coins, postcards, letters and diaries were in many instances, the only material things left for relatives, and they became important in the process of accepting loss and memory-making.' As Luckins noted, 'Personal effects were considered substitutes for the absent body and thus became treasured, even sacred objects of memory, kept in a 'Drawer of Remembrance' or placed on display on a mantelpiece, drawer or bedside table inside the home.'[113]

Following Lyle's death in a flying accident in June 1917, the Buntine family observed this practice through the keeping of a large collection of Lyle's letters, memorabilia and associated artefacts and thus the role of material culture in the families' commemorative process managed to preserve his memory. A special wooden glass-fronted display case was constructed which held many precious objects associated with his war service such as his medals, 'flying wings,' rank insignia and his 'Dead Man's Penny,' which was a special medallion given by the King to the families of the deceased. This treasured icon was wall mounted and displayed in the family home. Incredibly, the German machine-gun bullet that had wounded him and the propeller tip from his crashed aeroplane were also kept as treasured artefacts.

At CGS the process went further with Lyle's father, WM Buntine, the Principal, even naming a House at the school in his memory. In this way, the underlying ethos of the school had come full circle where deaths of the 'Empire warriors' it had helped to create, were used as a means of justifying and confirming the correctness of the ideological approach underpinned by the ethos of muscular Christianity, imperialism, athleticism and militarism at the public school.

But the war brought much sorrow on a deeply personal level to the wider Buntine and Gibbs family. Walter Murray Buntine, the Principal of CGS was a family man with a devout Christian faith, but this deeply seated religious belief must have been sorely tested as a result of the tragedies that befell his own immediate Buntine family and that of the Gibbs family, his wife Bertha's relatives, as a direct result of the Great War.

His oldest nephew Richard Horace Maconochie (Mac) Gibbs (1908 – 11) was the eldest son of Dr and Mrs Richard Gibbs of Colac and entered CGS in 1908 as a boarder and continued until 1911. He was in his fourth year of medicine at the time of his enlistment in 1915 and was a prominent athlete, and had distinguished himself as a half-mile runner and footballer. He played 35 games and kicked 3 goals from 1912 - 1914 with the University team in the VFL (now AFL) team. He was twenty-four years old when in his very first battle, he lost his life in an attack upon the German trenches at Fromelles, in France, on July 19th 1916. He was reported to have led his men of the 59th Battalion gallantly in the face of heavy fire from machine-guns, but was eventually killed in action within a few yards of the enemy trenches and was awarded a posthumous Military Cross for this bravery. This was the début action of the AIF on the Western Front and the Australian War Memorial described the battle as the worst 24 hours in Australian history as over 5,000 casualties were suffered with 2,000 dead and the 59th and 60th Battalions were practically wiped out.

We already know the story of Walter's eldest son Walter Horace Carlyle (Lyle) Buntine (1903 - 13) tragically killed in a flying accident in Scotland whilst waiting to return to university in Melbourne.

Walter's youngest nephew John (Jack) Harbinger Gibbs; (1912 – 1914) was the youngest son of Dr and Mrs Richard Gibbs of Colac a boarder at CGS for three years, the younger brother of the late Lt. Richard (Mac) Gibbs and was Lyle Buntine's cousin. He served in Egypt and Gallipoli and after being invalided out from Gallipoli with a chest illness, was compelled to rest in Egypt and eventually took a clerical position in the Army Pay Office. Later he was sent to London and continued in the same work, became engaged to an English girl, and met up with Lyle while he was recovering after his wounding in France. Jack developed a bad cough and showed symptoms of serious chest trouble and arrived back in Australia to recuperate during the school vacation in September 1917. He was first admitted to the Military Hospital at Caulfield for treatment for tuberculosis, but was later transferred under his father's care at Colac. He began to improve in weight and his friends and family were encouraged to believe that he soon be much stronger, but he succumbed very suddenly to the condition and died on 13th October, just a month after his arrival in Australia and is buried in Colac.

Walter's older brother Robert (Uncle Bob) Andrew Buntine also attended Scotch College and was an uncle to all the Buntine and Gibbs boys. He lived in South Africa, served as a medical officer in the Boer War and later represented the city of Durban in the South African Parliament. A widower, Robert's two daughters Jessie and Noelle attended boarding school in England during the war and spent a number of holidays and visits with Lyle in Scotland and England respectively. It was when he was returning to South Africa with them in mid-September 1918 that their ship the *Galway Castle* was torpedoed by a German submarine. The life boats were launched with women and children first, but when the lifeboat with his two daughters tipped over, he dived in to rescue them, but only the youngest daughter Noelle was found alive. Ironically the ship survived the sinking and was able to return to England. Robert was held in the highest esteem by the residents of Durban who subscribed to a hospital ward named in his honour, as well as erecting a plaque to his memory in the South African Parliament.

Walter's oldest niece Jessie Buntine aged 18 had been attending the Hamilton School in Tunbridge Wells with her sister Noelle and had corresponded with and holidayed in Scotland with Lyle and other family members during the war. She drowned with her father Robert in the aftermath of the torpedoing of her ship, whilst her younger sister Noelle survived and eventually returned to live in South Africa, having lost all her immediate family.

Walter's brother in-law and oldest school boy friend Richard Horace Gibbs, attended Scotch College with Walter Buntine and Walter had married Richard's sister Bertha. Amongst others he was an uncle to Lyle and Jessie Buntine. He became a medical practitioner and surgeon at Colac and ministered to his son John, but after his son's death at home from tuberculosis gave up his private practice and as Major Gibbs became the senior surgeon at Macleod Military Hospital in Melbourne. However, on 13th July 1919 at the intersection of St Kilda and Domain Roads in Melbourne, he fell from the rear platform of a cable tramcar where he struck his head on the road, losing consciousness and dying later that evening.

Walter Murray Buntine had lost six close family members to the Great War in a three-year period between mid-1916 and mid-1919.

War and Memory at Caulfield Grammar School

From the listing in the June 1915 magazine of the first Grammarian casualties at Gallipoli, which were accompanied by obituaries and photographs acknowledging the dead; aspirational and noble characteristics were clearly spelt out in many of the tributes to Old Boy soldiers. A pattern of reporting on these lives and deaths had by now been set early in the war by the magazine and the obituaries in nearly almost every case highlighted the dead Old Boys' noble characteristics, their schoolboy achievements, especially sporting, at CGS, their working life, military careers and sometimes the precise circumstances of their death. This pattern could be seen as a coping strategy for dealing with the increasing amount of deaths and woundings of these 'noble' Old Boys. The noble, unselfish and committed characteristics of Old Boy soldiers was also highlighted; Lyle Buntine no exception.

Trying to make some spiritual sense of the tragic deaths, for example, was highlighted in a letter to the clergyman father of Private Robert Nash, who had enlisted aged 16 and had been killed on the Western Front aged just 17 years and 26 days old.

The language used was a means to try and mask the awfulness of the war and promise some positive outcome, in this case immortality with God. The language used in the obituaries in the school magazine, especially that of Nash, also seems to be chosen to point to the nobility of the men's lives and deaths in the service of a great and important cause, perhaps to act as a coping mechanism and to help assuage the deep feelings of grief and mourning.

The scholarship founded in another Old Boy's memory was clearly designed to not only perpetuate his memory, but to be used as a means of inspiring younger Caulfield Grammarians to emulate his life and actions, especially if called to serve on the battlefield. Selflessness and sacrifice were highlighted in a number of articles and references about Old Boy soldiers and casualties and mention was made of Old Boys who had been wounded or invalided home. The title of these articles and the tenor and tone of the language seemed designed to highlight the bravado and adventure of war, but at the same time mask its pain and tragedy. The pattern of letters outlining the military service and circumstances of the subsequent deaths of some Old Boys continued to be published during the war, with ethos reinforcing principles in mind. In all of these cases it would appear that CGS had raised very good soldiers indeed, ones who were admired by their comrades and although some had been killed, they were nearly all described as having died in a 'painless' and 'instantaneous' manner.

In all of these letters and tributes could be seen the need to sanitize the deaths, '... killed instantaneously and suffered no pain,' '... he suffered no pain as he was killed instantly.' In addition, deep regrets and sorrow were expressed, but also the aspects of their glorious lives and deaths are mentioned, ''... your son's supreme sacrifice for his country,' '... the finest and best are taken,' 'a good comrade and a gentleman,' '... doing his job gallantly,' '... courageous conduct, which set a fine example to all.' It was important for the school to acknowledge these letters and deaths, especially given that not only did they reflect on the school's ethos and fine record, but in some cases that they tragically took place so close to the end of the war. The letters also reinforced the rhetoric of sacrifice and a glorious end, a painless death with no suffering, the loss of the best of humanity and always being remembered, all encompassed in the school ethos of supporting the military tradition of CGS. In turn, the grief of the Principal at the many losses in his own family and his extended school family had begun to be fed into an emerging school ethos of commemoration wrapped up in the context of 'War and Memory.'

Old Boy soldiers returned from their war service to speak at various school assemblies, with great interest being shown in the topics and messages by the youthful listeners. But bigger lessons were being taught to the boys through the medium of the visitors and their addresses. Despite the restrictions of censorship, CGS was assertive in highlighting its Old Boys' military service during the conflict and forthright in its commemorative practices of their sacrifice both during and after the Great War. This was due to a number of reasons.

Firstly, the war provided a practical 'proving ground' for the ethos of 'service to God, King and Country' that the school had instilled into its students, notably through celebrations of empire, sport and cadets since its foundation. In this context, the lives of Lyle Buntine and other Old Boy casualties were held up as examples to be aspired to by a younger generation of Caulfield Grammarians. Secondly, the larger numerical weight of Australia's involvement in the Great War provided a greater immediacy and scope of numbers to the servicemen and casualties than had been the case in the South African 'Boer' War of 1899 – 1902 or other conflicts. Thirdly, the school's practices may be regarded as typical of such institutions and other 'brother schools' given the times and circumstances. Finally, the CGS Principal Walter Buntine had lost his eldest son as a war casualty, as well as five other extended family members.

Because of Lyle's standing in the CGS community and the Principal's personal loss, it may be the case that both Walter Buntine and the school remembered the war dead with a greater intensity and closeness, believing that their sacrifice should never be forgotten, especially as an example and lesson to the younger boys at the school. It should be noted that Lyle Buntine did not die in combat or battle, but in a flying accident in Scotland. Nevertheless, his death was marked equally by CGS with others who died of illness or combat unrelated-causes and ranked alongside those who 'made the supreme sacrifice' in the circumstances of battle. The school's Honour Roll for the Great War noted all of these deaths without exception.

Lyle Buntine's Death and Commemoration at CGS

It is Lyle's story that became pivotal to the way that CGS commemorated their war dead. The manner of reporting his tragic death in June 1917 however, departed from the usual pattern of the magazine as it provided scant information and any reference to his 'noble characteristics,' his schooldays at CGS, his life as a medical student and had only brief contemporary details of his military career included to explain the circumstances of his death. Thus, we read,

> Lt. WHC Buntine, MC, Royal Flying Corps, was killed at Turnberry, Scotland, on June 19th last. He had been at home during the Christmas holidays on leave, recovering from wounds received in France. He returned

and reported to the War Office in May, and it had been decided to send him back to Australia to finish his medical course. In the meantime, he had been appointed temporarily to a staff position as instructor in aerial gunnery. It was when in an aeroplane as passenger instructing a beginner that the fatal accident occurred.[114]

This very matter of fact style of reporting actually concealed the real tragedy lying beneath the circumstances, and it is possible that Lyle's father, Walter, may have wanted to downplay his personal grief in the context of setting a dignified example of mourning to the school community. In 1918 an article about the Anzac Day service at CGS read in part,' 'Everybody stood and at Mr Buntine's request, Rev Langley then read the list of those who had made the supreme sacrifice for their country. Sympathetic reference was also made to Mr Buntine on his own recent sad bereavement; the death of his eldest son, Lyle. The glorious Roll of Distinctions, which we are convinced, will yet be greatly lengthened on by old CGS boys at the front, was then read.'[115]

The publishing of a poem in 1926 to mark the ritual of the One Minute's Silence, clearly affirmed the CGS message that when duty for the Empire called, the boys of the school had to be prepared to defend the liberty of the Empire and Australia, no matter if the cost was to be their death. It was clear that the responsibility of those left behind was to always honour the proud memory of those valiant men. In other words, the school had set the ethos for the sacrifice and in turn the sacrifice reaffirmed the school's ethos. These various messages delivered in a solemn, meaning laden annual format to the boys of Caulfield Grammar School at these Anzac and Remembrance Day services were designed to ensure that they were always reminded of the place in the national setting and story of the sacrifice of former Grammarians.

In addition, an emphasis was made of the challenge to lead lives that followed their examples and to use the standards set by the Anzacs as their life's benchmark. Wherever possible, links were made both by the context of the ceremony and by the speakers to ensure that boys received clear messages about the life lessons to be gained from sport, education and military life.

But from the perspective of Walter Buntine, there was always an aspect to be emphasized, even if it was never voiced publicly, and that was the personal loss of his eldest son Lyle, a fact brought home each Anzac and Remembrance Day when his name was read out amongst the other sixty-nine dead Grammarians. In many ways, the story of the life, death and commemoration of Lyle Buntine is reflected in the way that War and Memory has been marked at CGS. Once again Walter Buntine was making a connection between the debt owed by his schoolboy audience to those who had died in war and the efforts needed to repay that in the manner in which they led their future lives. Walter Buntine was very clear about emphasizing the war service, sacrifice and significance of Caulfield's Old Boys and was keen to relate these achievements and events directly back to their time as school boys at CGS. This was done at a time when he was grieving for Lyle, and when he was eager to justify the sacrifice that these men had made and the life preparation for that sacrifice made during their education at their old school. Walter Buntine's public utterances in this area always seem to carry a hidden agenda, that of the life, example and loss of Lyle, who had also addressed a school assembly whilst convalescing from wounds received in battle.

Walter Buntine explained to his audience that, 'In the field of action abroad, the school has been well represented – no less than 431 have been accepted for service and all but a very few have sailed from our shores. And if from amongst them men have been found with powers of leadership, courage and devotion to duty, men who have been found capable and reliable in times of great crisis, it is because these qualities have been developed in the earlier, quieter days, when under the regular influence and discipline of the school. Some idea of how real a thing the war has been to our school will be gathered from the fact that sixty-two (later revised to seventy) have laid down their lives for their country. This could not but make a very deep impression upon those at home, and awaken in them the noblest of ideals of service'. Here it seems that Walter Buntine of behalf of CGS is linking sacrifice, loss and a sense of the nobility of the cause as a means of justifying the supreme sacrifice made by these Old Boys, Lyle included.

Lyle's grave in Scotland had been marked and his name recorded forever on the Turnberry War Memorial. The City of Caulfield had expedited the planting of trees in memory of their fallen citizens, Lyle amongst them. The Melbourne Swimming Club and the University of Melbourne had placed his name on their respective Rolls of Honour as had Caulfield Grammar School. In time, his name would also be placed on the Commemorative Roll at the Australian War Memorial in Canberra; this book commemorates Australians who died during or as a result of service in wars, identical with the Roll of Honour (which marks service in Australian forces), but who were not serving in Australian forces at the time. In time Caulfield Grammar School would construct an impressive War Memorial Hall in 1958 and commission a magnificent stained-glass window at its entrance. Designed to illustrate a student's path from school to a life of service it also illustrated various contemporary military events, especially those in which Old Boys had participated. High up in one corner is depicted a single biplane from the Great War to symbolise the life and sacrifice of Lyle Buntine.

Whilst these tributes are what would be expected from a grateful country, organisations and his former school, the most amazing and poignant instance of commemoration was carried out by Lyle's family themselves in the custodianship of his memorabilia, documents and letters. Lyle Buntine's short life and legacy provides a notable and well documented example of how his former school and family dealt with his loss. Remembered as *'A Noble Son of Empire Fall'n to Earth,'* in a tribute poem published in the June 1917 CGS magazine, Lyle Buntine's correspondence and associated papers reveal him to be very much an 'Australian-Briton,' whose short life and death were held up as an example to all at Caulfield Grammar School, an institution whose ethos very much reflected the traditions of Empire.

By using Lyle's own words as a basis, this story has explored how the life of Lyle Buntine informed the ethos of the school; an ethos based on factors such as athleticism, militarism, muscular Christianity, British-Australian identity and loyalty to God, King and Empire. This ethos was in large part constructed during the pre-Great War period by his father Walter Buntine as the owner/principal of CGS and the commemorative war practices instituted at CGS in the context of a Principal mourning for his lost son, Lyle Buntine.

CGS ensured that the names of the War dead were listed on the prominently displayed Honour Roll and that at appropriate times wreaths were laid. These physical reminders of the War were juxtaposed with annual Anzac and Remembrance Day services with their reminders of the valorous sacrificial deeds of the Grammarian dead and calls for students to emulate their example in life. The grieving Principal Walter Buntine, who consciously or otherwise established the parameters of 'War and Memory,' was instrumental in ensuring that the sacrifices and stories of the dead would never be forgotten. With the retirement of Walter

Buntine from CGS in 1931, the mantle passed to following generations who ensured with the construction of such edifices as the War Memorial Hall and its evocative and meaning-laden stained-glass window, that the memory of these dead Grammarians would be always present in the life of the school. Significantly, the life and sacrifice of the name of Lyle Buntine was noted in the naming of a House, depicted in the stained-glass window, listed on the Honour Roll and in the trophy for Inter-House competition. These actions clearly bear out the words of the CGS school song, 'Time goes Forever, but Memory Remains.'

In the final analysis, perhaps the depth of grief that Walter Buntine felt at losing his eldest son in such a tragic and seemingly pointless manner, especially as he was so close to being recalled to civilian life, was compounded by the multiple tragedies experienced by his extended family. When added to the keenly felt war deaths of so many of his former CGS pupils, it is not surprising that the family cherished every trace and memory of Lyle and honourably moulded the school's memorial rites and practices.

The final written words of a fallen German soldier who was killed just five days after Lyle was severely wounded, help to encapsulate the feelings, emotions and actions of Walter Buntine and the CGS community as they mourned their many personal losses.

> Farewell. You have known all the others who have been dear to me and you will say goodbye to them for me. And so, in imagination, I extinguish the lamp of my existence on the eve of this terrible battle. I cut myself out of the circle of which I have formed a beloved part. The gap which I leave must be closed; the human chain must be unbroken. I, who once formed a small link in it, bless it for eternity. And till your last days, remember me,

268 ✧ Empire's Noble Son

I beg you with tender love. Honour my memory without gilding it, and cherish me in your loving, faithful hearts.

Letter written by German soldier Otto Heinebach, the night before he was killed on 14 September 1916 [116]

Published Sources

Almond, P. Aviation the Early Years. 1st ed. Koln: Konemann verlagsgesellschaft mbH, Bonner Str 126 D-50968, 1997.

Ashmead-Bartlett, E. Australians at the Dardanelles. *Argus* 8 May 1915 1915. p, 8.

Barker, R. A Brief History of the Royal Flying Corps. London: Constable and Robinson Ltd, 2002.

Bean, C.E.W. Anzac to Amiens. Australian War Memorial, 1983.

Bean, C.E.W. The Official History of Australia in the War of 1914 - 1918. Volume 1. The Story of Anzac. St, Lucia, Queensland. University of Queensland Press, 1981.

Bishop, W. Winged Victory. New York. Ace Books. 1967.

Bou, J., Dennis, P., Grey, J., Morris, E., Prior, R. The Oxford Companion to Australian Military History. 2nd ed. South Melbourne. Oxford, 2008.

Bowen, E. Knights of the Air. Chicago, Time-Life Books, 1980.

Brown, D. Athleticism in Australia. St Peter's College, Adelaide: A Case study in the diffusion of a Victorian Educational Ideology. Unpublished paper, University of Queensland, Dec. 1986, p, 7. Cited in Mangan. p, 392.

Chant, C. The Pictorial History of Air Warfare. London. Octopus Books Ltd, 1979.

Clark, A. Aces High. The War in the Air over the Western Front 1914 - 1918. Glasgow. William Collins Sons and Co Ltd. 1973.

Clements, M.A. Adamson, Lawrence Arthur (1860 - 1932). Australian Dictionary of Biography. Vol. 7. MUP, 1979.

Cole, C. (ed). Royal Flying Corps Communiques 1915 - 1916. Tom Donovan Publishing Ltd. London. 1990.

Cooksley, P. G. The RFC/RNAS Handbook 1914 - 18. Stroud. Sutton Publishing Limited, 2000.

Crouch, T. D. Wings. A History of Aviation from Kites to the Space Age. 1st ed. New York. W.W.Norton and Company Inc., 2003.

Feltus, P. Bombing During World War 1. 2005. US Centennial of Flight Commission. Available: www.centennialofflight.gov/essay/Air_Power/WW1_Bombing/AP3.htm.

Franks, N. Aircraft Versus Aircraft. The Illustrated Story of Fighter Pilot Combat from 1914 to the Present Day. London: Grub Street, 1998.

Frederick, W.H. Brookes, Sir Norman Everard, (1877 - 1968) Australian Dictionary of Biography, Volume 7, (MUP) 1979.

Fussell, P. The Great War and Modern Memory. Sterling. New York. 1977.

Gammage, W. The Broken Years - Illustrated Edition. Carlton. Melbourne University Press, 2010.

Gliddon, G. Somme 1916. A Battlefield Companion. The History Press. Gloucestershire. 2009

Hanson, N. The Unknown Soldier. The Story of the Missing of the Great War. London. Doubleday, 2007.

Hart, B. L. History of the First World War. 1914-1918. London. Pan Books. 1972.

Hart, P. Aces Falling - War above the trenches, 1918. Phoenix. London. 2008.

Hart, P. Somme Success. The Royal Flying Corps and the Battle of the Somme 1916. Pen and Sword Books Ltd. South Yorkshire. 2012.

Hayley, B. The Healthy Body and Victorian Culture. 1978. Cambridge. Harvard University Press.

Haythornthwaite, P. J. The World War One Source Book. 4th ed. London. Brockhampton Press, 1998.

Holmes, R. Tommy. London. Harper Collins. 2005.

Hook, A. World War 1 Day by Day. Rochester UK. Grange Books. 2004.

Hooten, E.R. War Over the Trenches. Air Power and the Western Front Campaigns 1916 - 1918. Midland Publishing. Surrey. 2010.

Hutchison, G. Remember Them. A Guide to Victoria's Wartime Heritage. Prahran. Australia. Hardie Grant Books. 2009.

Inglis, K.S . Sacred Places. War Memorials in the Australian Landscape. 3rd ed. Melbourne. MUP, 2008.

Insall, A.J. Observer – Memoirs of the RFC 1915 – 18. Kimber. London. 1970

James, L. The Rise and Fall of the British Empire. 2nd ed. London. Little, Brown and Company, 1998.

Jefford, C.G. Observers and Navigators and other non-pilot aircrew in the RFC, RNAS and RAF. Grub Street. London. 2014.

Jones, H.A. The War in the Air. Being the story of the part played in the Great War by the Royal Air Force. Volume Two. The Naval and Military Press Ltd. East Sussex and The Imperial War Museum. London 1928.

King, H.F. The World's Fighters. Bodley Head Ltd. London. 1971.

Levine, J. On A Wing and A Prayer – The untold story of the pioneering aviation heroes of WW1 in their own words. Collins. London. 2008.

Lewis, C. Sagittarius Rising. Harrisburg. Penn. Stackpole Books. 1963.

Luckins, T. The Gates of Memory. Australian Peoples Experiences and Memories of Loss and the Great War. Curtin University Books. Fremantle. 2004.

MacIntyre, S. and Selleck, R.J.W. A Short History of the University of Melbourne. Carlton, Australia. Melbourne University Press. 2003.

Mangan, J.A. Manufactured Masculinity. Making Imperial Manliness, Morality and Militarism. (Sport in the Global Society - Historical Perspectives). Routledge. Abingdon. 2012. ISBN13:9780415677189. p, 9.

McCudden, J. Flying Fury – Five Years in the Royal Flying Corps. Wren's Park Publishing. London. 2000.

McIntosh, P. Physical Education in England since 1800. London, 1968. Cited in Mangan.

McMullen, R. Farewell Dear People. Scribe Publications Pty Ltd. Brunswick. Victoria. 2012.

McKernan, M. The Australian People and the Great War. Melbourne. Nelson. Australia 1980.

McQuilton, John. Rural Australia and the Great War. From Tarrawingee to Tangambalanga. Melbourne. Melbourne University Press. 2001.

Meyer, A.R. CSKLA Annual General Meeting. Baylor University. 2010. Journal of Sport and Social Issues.

Morris, Joseph. The German Air Raids on Great Britain 1914 - 1918. 1925. Dallington. UK. The Naval and Military Press. 1993.

Nesbit, R. C. An Illustrated History of the RAF. Battle of Britain 50th Anniversary Commemorative Edition. 1990. 2nd ed. Hong Kong. Colour Library Books. 1991.

Parsons, I. The Encyclopedia of Air Warfare. London. Salamander Books. 1975.

Penrose, H. Outside the Square - 125 Years of Caulfield Grammar School. Carlton. Melbourne University Press. 2006.

Preston D. A Higher Form of Killing. Bloomsbury Press. London. 2015.

Revell, A. Fall of Eagles - Airmen of World War One. Pen and Sword. UK. 2011.

Robertson, J. Anzac and Empire - the Tragedy and Glory of Gallipoli. Melbourne. Hamlyn Australia. 1990.

Robson, L.L. The First AIF - a Study of Its Recruitment. 1914 - 1918. Carlton. Melbourne University Press. 1982.

Saunders, H. St. G. Per Adua. The Rise of British Air Power 1911 - 1939. London. Oxford University Press. 1944.

Selleck, R.J.W. The Shop. The University of Melbourne, 1850 - 1939. Carlton, Australia. Melbourne University Press, 2003.

Sherington, G. Athleticism in the Antipodes. The AAGPS of New South Wales. History of Education Review, 12(2) (1983).

Skeet, M. RFC Pilot Training. 29 August 2001. The Aerodrome. Available: www.theaerodrome.com/contrib/training.html.

Spartacus. Zeppelin Raids. 2005. Available: www.spartacus.schoolnet.co.uk/FWWzeppelinraids.htm.

Steiner, Z., and Neilson, K. Britain and the Origins of the First World War. 2nd ed. Hampshire, UK. Palgrave MacMillan. 2003.

Stockings, C.J.A. The Torch and the Sword. The History of the Army Cadet Movement in Australia. Sydney. University of New South Wales. 2007.

Strachan, H. The First World War. London. Simon and Schuster. 2003.

Taylor, A. The First World War and Its Aftermath. London. The Folio Society. 1998.

Tyquin, M. Little by Little. A Centenary History of the Royal Australian Medical Corps. Loftus, Australia. Australian Military History Publications. 2003.

'Victorian Government Gazette.' March 6 1885. p, 710.

Webber, H. Years May Pass on - Caulfield Grammar School 1881 - 1981. Clayton. Wilke and Company, 1981.

Werner, J. Knight of Germany. Oswald Boelcke, German Ace. Casemate. UK. 2009.

Westwell, I. World War 1 Day by Day. Singapore. Brown Partworks, 2000.

Wilkinson, I. The Fields at Play - 115 Years of Sport at Caulfield Grammar School. Sydney. Playright Publishing, 1997.

Williams, D. Wartime Disaster At Sea - Every passenger ship loss in Worlds War I and II. Patrick Stephens Ltd. Somerset. 1997.

Williamson, J.A. The Foundation and Growth of the British Empire. 5th ed. New York. MacMillan and Co. Ltd. 1916.

Wilson, Trevor. The Myriad Faces of War. Oxford. Polity Press, 1988.

Winter, J.M. The Experience of World War 1. New York. Oxford University Press, 1999.

Archival Sources

Caulfield Grammar School, Victoria.
Caulfield Grammar School Magazines (various as referenced)
Caulfield Grammar School Speech Day programmes (various as referenced)
Caulfield Grammar School Prospectus - 1883
Caulfield Grammar School Founder's Day Address - 2008.
Papers, letters and photographs from the WM Buntine Collection - (as referenced)

Newspapers, Magazines and Other Such Publications

The Argus (Melbourne)

The Daily Telegraph (Launceston)

The Daily Mail (London)

The Herald (Melbourne)

The AGE (Melbourne)

The Armidale Express (NSW)

The Church of England Messenger (Diocese of Melbourne)

The Victorian Government Gazette (as referenced)

The Speculum - The Journal of the Melbourne University Medical Student's Society (as referenced)

Digital Sources

National Archives (UK) (as referenced)
House of Lords (UK) Debate in Hansard (as referenced)
Miller G.M. (ed) 'WW1 – The Medical Front.' www.vlib.su/medical/index.htm
http://cunard//www.cunard-whitestarline.net/id16.html
www.theaerodrome.com
www.centennialofflight.gov/essay/Air_Power/WW1_Bombing/AP3.htm.
www.spartacus.schoolnet.co.uk/FWWzeppelinraids.htm.

Notes

1. Wilkinson. I. *'The Fields at Play - 115 years of Sport at Caulfield Grammar School.'* Playright Publishing Pty Ltd. Sydney, 1997. ISBN 0949853607 p, 51.
2. Wilkinson. I. (ibid) p, 54.
3. Caulfield Grammar School magazine. June 1919, p, 408.
4. Caulfield Grammar School Prospectus 1883. File 8 - Item 0039: The W.M. Buntine Acquisition.
5. Webber H. *'Years May Pass On - Caulfield Grammar School 1881 - 1981.'* Wilke and Company Ltd. Clayton. Victoria. 1981. p, 20
6. Wilkinson. I. (ibid) p, 17
7. Wilkinson. I. (ibid) p, 65
8. Victorian Government Gazette. March 6 1885. p, 710
9. *The Argus.* 18 March 1884. p, 7
10. Stockings C.A.J. *'The Torch and the Sword.* The History of the Army Cadet Movement in Australia.' UNSW Press. Sydney. 2007. p, 33
11. Durie M. Caulfield Grammar School Founder's Day Address. 2008
12. Caulfield Grammar School magazine. *'The Cricket'* October 1888 Vol.1 - No 2. Page, 9
13. Wilkinson. I. (ibid) p, 31
14. Webber. H. (ibid) p, 40.
15. *'The Church of England Messenger.'* December 26 1930, p. 621 (Diocese of Melbourne, pub)
16. Letter from Rev E.J. Barnett to CGS Parents; March 23rd 1896: The W.M. Buntine Acquisition. File 2 - Item 017

17	Brown D. *'Athleticism in Australia: St Peter's College, Adelaide: A Case study in the diffusion of a Victorian Educational Ideology'*. unpublished paper, University of Queensland, Dec. 1986, p.7. cited in Mangan. p. 392
18	Brown D. (ibid) p, 7. cited in Mangan. p. 393.
19	Mangan J. A. *'Manufactured Masculinity. Making Imperial Manliness, Morality and Militarism. (Sport in the Global Society – Historical Perspectives)'* Routledge. Abingdon. 2012. ISBN13: 9780415677189 p, 9.
20	McIntosh. P. *'Physical Education in England since 1800.'* London, 1968, p.70. in Mangan (ibid) p.67.
21	Meyer. A. R. CSKLS Annual General Meeting. Baylor University. 2010. Journal of Sport and Social Issues.
22	Haley. B. *'The Healthy Body and Victorian Culture'*. 1978. Cambridge: Harvard University Press. p, 119.
23	Mangan J.A. (ibid) p, 15.
24	James L. *'The Rise and Fall of the British Empire'*. London. Abacus. 1982. p, 329
25	Steiner Z. and Neilson K. *'Britain and the Origins of the First World War'* (2nd Ed) Palgrave MacMillan. Hampshire. UK. 2003 ISBN 0333736467 p, 168
26	McKernan M. *'The Australian People and the Great War.'* Nelson Australia. 1980. Melbourne. p, 1-2. ISBN 0170057658
27	Steiner Z. and Neilson K. (ibid) pp, 167 - 8
28	Clements M.A. *'Adamson, Lawrence Arthur (1860 - 1932)'* Australian Dictionary of Biography, volume 7, (MUP), 1979
29	McKernan M. (ibid) p, 101
30	Webber H. (ibid) p, 58
31	Webber H. (ibid) p, 60
32	Brown D. (ibid) p, 7 cited in Mangan, (ibid) p.393
33	Sherington G. *'Athleticism in the Antipodes: The AAGPS of New South Wales,'* History of Education Review, 12(2) (1983), p,7.
34	McKernan M. (ibid) p, 95
35	Penrose H. *'Outside the Square – 125 years of Caulfield Grammar School.'* MUP. Carlton. 2006. p, 19
36	Penrose H. (ibid) p, 14

37 Webber H. (ibid) p, 88
38 Caulfield Grammar School magazine. December 1909, p, 5
39 Caulfield Grammar School magazine. June 1910, p, 23
40 Caulfield Grammar School magazine. December 1910, p, 44
41 Webber H. (ibid) p, 81
42 Webber H. (ibid) p, 80
43 Stockings C. (ibid) p, 7
44 Stockings C. (ibid) p, 42
45 Stockings C. (ibid) p, 55
46 Stockings C. (ibid) p, 44.
47 Caulfield Grammar School Speech Day programme. 17th December, 1906
48 Caulfield Grammar School Speech Day programme. 12th December, 1913
49 Caulfield Grammar School magazine. December 1914 No.11. Vol. 1. p.178
50 The ARGUS Monday 7th September 1914. p.182
51 Caulfield Grammar School magazine. June 1912. p. 108
52 Caulfield Grammar School magazine. December 1913. p. 118
53 Eulogy to Lyle Buntine written by his father WM Buntine. Buntine Collection. CGS Archives
54 Selleck R.J.W. *The SHOP. The University of Melbourne, 1850 - 1939*. p, 528 MUP, Carlton, 2003
55 Selleck R.J.W. (ibid) pp, 527 - 8
56 Preston. D. *A Higher Form of Killing*. p, 4. Bloomsbury Press. London. 2015.
57 Preston. D. (ibid) p, 163.
58 Dennis P., Grey J., Morris E., Prior R., Bou J. *The Oxford Companion to Australian Military History* (2nd ed) South Melbourne, Australia. 2008. ISBN 9780195517842 (hbk) p, 38
59 *The Argus*. Saturday 8th May 1915. p, 8
60 Dennis P. et al. (ibid) p, 424
61 Robson L. L. *The First AIF. A study of its recruitment 1914 - 1918*. Melbourne University Press. Carlton. 1982. ISBN 0522842372 p, 44
62 Robertson J. *ANZAC and Empire - The Tragedy and Glory of Gallipoli*. Hamlyn Australia. 1990. Melbourne. ISBN 094733419X p, 23

63	Caulfield Grammar School magazine. December 1915. Vol.12 No.2 p, 229
64	Caulfield Grammar School magazine. June 1915. p, 213
65	Bishop W. 'Winged Warfare' New York Ace Books. 1967. P, 21
66	Clark A. 'Aces High. The War in the Air over the Western Front 1914 - 1918.' Glasgow: William Collins Sons and Co Ltd Glasgow, 1973. p, 16
67	Lewis C. 'Sagittarius Rising.' Harrisburg, Penn. Stackpole Books, 1963. pp, 11-15
68	Barker. R. *A Brief History of the Royal Flying Corps in World War 1.* Constable and Robinson Ltd. London. 2002. ISBN184119470-0 p, 167 - 9
69	Barker. R. Ibid. p, 180-81
70	King. H.F. *The World's Fighters.* p, 18. Bodley Head Ltd. London. 1971. ISBN 0370108078
71	*Daily Telegraph.* (Launceston, Tasmania) April 9th 1915. p, 7
72	Hart P. *Somme Success. The Royal Flying Corps and the Battle of the Somme 1916.* Pen and Sword Books Ltd. South Yorkshire. 2012. ISBN 978 1 84884 882 5 p, 83
73	Hart P. (ibid) p, 100
74	Hart P. (ibid) p, 109
75	Hart P. (ibid) p, 116
76	Hart P. (ibid) p, 127
77	Hart P. (ibid) p, 131-2
78	Hart P. (ibid) p, 137
79	Hart P. (ibid) p, 141
80	Jones H.A. *THE WAR in the AIR. Being the story of the part played in the Great War by the Royal Air Force.* Volume Two. The Naval and Military Press Ltd. East Sussex and The Imperial War Museum, London. 1928. (originally published) p. 251.
81	Jones H.A (ibid) p, 226
82	Barker R. *RFC at the BATTLE of the SOMME. A Brief History of the Royal Flying Corps in World War 1.* Constable and Robinson Ltd. London. 2002. ISBN1 – 84119-470-0 pp, 166 – 7
83	Barker R. (ibid) p, 166
84	Barker R. (ibid) p, 167
85	Barker R. (ibid) p, 167

86   Jones H.A. (ibid) p, 255-7
87   Cole C. (ed). *Royal Flying Corps Communiques 1915 – 1916*. Tom Donovan Publishing Ltd. 1990. ISBN 1-871085-03-9
88   Cole C. (ibid) p, 228
89   *Daily Mail* 1916.
90   Werner. J. *Knight of Germany: Oswald Boelcke, German Ace*. Casemate (UK). 2009. ISBN 978-1-61200-0435 pp, 2-3
91   Barker R. (ibid) p, 167
92   Barker R. (ibid) p, 250 -1
93   Barker R. (ibid) p, 251
94   National Archives (Britain). 3rd Brigade RFC, Recommendations for Decorations.
95   The *ARGUS* (Melbourne) Tuesday 28 November, 1916, page 4
96   Caulfield Grammar School magazine. – No 15, Vol 1. December 1916. pp, 289 – 29
97   HERALD (Melbourne) 22 November 1916
98   Miller G. M. (ed) *WWW1 – The Medical Front*. www.vlib.su/medical/index.htm
99   Frederick W.H. *Brookes, Sir Norman Everard, (1877 – 1968)* Australian Dictionary of Biography, Volume 7, (MUP) 1979.
100 House of Lords (UK) Debate in Hansard. 23 May 1916. vol 22. pp, 101-26
101 Williams, D. *Wartime Disaster at Sea – Every passenger ship loss in World Wars I and II*. Patrick Stephens Ltd. (Somerset). 1997. pp, 51 – 2.
102 http://www.cunard-whitestarline.net/id16.html
103 *AGE* Thursday 21st June 1917. p, 1
104 *AGE* Thursday 21st June 1917
105 *The Armidale Express* (NSW) Tuesday, June 26 1917
106 *The Speculum* – The Journal of the Melbourne (University) Medical Students' Society. No. 99 September 1917 – pp, 115 - 116
107 The Caulfield Grammar School magazine. No.16, Vol.1. June 1917, p, 300
108 Inglis K.S. *Sacred Places – War Memorials in the Australian Landscape*. MUP. 2008. Melbourne. p, 93
109 Inglis K.S (ibid) pp, 148 - 195

110   Inglis K.S. (ibid) p, 101
111   McMullin R. *Farewell Dear People*. Scribe Publications Pty Ltd. 2012. Brunswick. Victoria. p, 95
112   Luckins T. *The Gates of Memory: Australian People's Experiences and memories of Loss and the Great War*. Curtin University Books. Fremantle. 2004. p, 18 ISBN 1920731741
113   Luckins T. Ibid. p, 213
114   Caulfield Grammar School magazine. June 1917. No. 16. Vol. 1. p, 300 (Obituary for 2nd Lt WHC Buntine)
115   Caulfield Grammar School magazine. December 1917. No. 17. Vol. 1. p, 347
116   Hanson N. *The Unknown Soldier. The story of the missing of the Great War*. Doubleday. London. 2007. Preface. ISBN 9780552149761

Photographs

(All photographs are from the Buntine Collection held in the Caulfield Grammar School Archives; unless otherwise noted)

Walter Murray Buntine. Principal of Caulfield Grammar School 1896 – 1931 and father of Walter Horace Carlyle (Lyle) Buntine.

Lyle Buntine as a young Caulfield Grammar schoolboy.

1911 CGS SAAAV Champion Athletic team.

Back Row - L to R: Lyle Buntine, Roy Scott, 'Mac' Gibbs, Arthur Meyer, Mr Frank Archer (Sportsmaster), Harrie McGuigan, Murray Buntine, Alan Wilson.

Middle Row - L to R: Vivian Worrall, Hugh Rose, Allan Southey, John Robinson, Victor Sheppard, Colin Simpson, Rupert Berry, Charles Davis.

Front Row – L to R: Henry Rusden, Russell Keon-Cohen, Robert Prendergast, Robert Little, John Fawckner, John Gardiner.

Lyle Buntine, Rupert Berry, John Gardiner and 'Mac' Gibbs were killed in the Great War. Lyle Buntine, Charles Davis, John Gardiner, 'Mac' Gibbs and Colin Simpson won the MC, whilst John Robinson won the DCM. Both Robinson and Simpson were Mentioned in Despatches. 'Mac' Gibbs was a cousin to Lyle and Murray Buntine. Allan Wilson later married their sister Mary, (Girlie). All team members except Fawckner, Keon-Cohen, Meyer, Prendergast and Rusden enlisted.

1913 CGS SAAAV Champion Football team.

Back Row – Arnold Buntine, R.G. Nankivell, William Coulson, Charles Joynt, Mr Frank Archer (Sportsmaster), N. Elliott, T. Melhuish, Cecil Linton, D. Evans.

Middle Row – J. Tyson, Lyle Buntine, Jack Gibbs, Murray Buntine, Allan Chaffey, Allan Wilson, C.A. 'Jerry' Masterton, C Stewart, John Gardiner.

Front Row – Wilkie Lum, Don Kenley, Alexander Drew, A.E. Lee.

This team contains three of the four Buntine brothers as well as their cousin Jack Gibbs and a future brother-in-law, Alan Wilson. Of this team Lyle Buntine, John Gardiner, Cecil Linton and Jack Gibbs died on active service. The team's win in 1913 began an unbroken sequence of 18 consecutive football premierships until 1930.

Cpl Lyle Buntine (Left) and three fellow medics photographed in June 1915 at the Broadmeadows Camp just after their enlistment. (AWM DA09253)

Portrait photographs of Cpl Lyle Buntine as a medic in the AAMC.

Lyle (seated third from left) at camp at Seymour

Lyle with his sister Mary (L) and mother Bertha (R)

Family on the hired motor boat farewelling Lyle as he departed Melbourne on board the Orsova in July 1915.

Family and friends at Troon, Scotland at Easter 1916. Left to right, Jessie Buntine, Murray Richardson, Sheila Richardson, Noelle Buntine, Cousin Mima Frame.

Lyle (extreme left) and fellow officer trainees making a raft.

Lyle (third from left) with fellow 11 Squadron members, 'somewhere in France.'

Lyle (standing at front) with his observer and aeroplane on active duty with 11 Squadron in France.

Photograph of Lyle flying a BE8 on active service at the Battle of the Somme.

Portrait photograph of Lyle in the uniform of a 2nd Lieutenant in the 4th Battalion of the Notts and Derby Regiment of the British Army.

Lyle (seated) with his observer Lt Cathie.

An artists' impression in the publication 'Deeds That Thrill the Empire,' of the aerial battle in which Lyle won his MC and was badly wounded.

The German machine gun bullet that wounded Lyle

Lyle in a happy mood pictured at home in East St Kilda at Christmas 1916 after his repatriation to Australia having been wounded in aerial combat.

Most likely the last photograph taken of Lyle upon his return to duty in Scotland. Note his worn expression and MC ribbon.

The telegram that brought the tragic news of Lyle's death to the Buntines.

Lyle's original marked grave at Girvan in Scotland.

Lyle's grave in Scotland marked with the headstone erected by his family.

Lt 'Mac' Gibbs MC and Lyle's cousin. KIA at the Battle of Fromelles in 1916

Cpl Jack Gibbs, Lyle's cousin and brother of 'Mac,' who died of Tuberculosis at Colac in September 1917

Dr Robert Buntine, Lyle's uncle and Walter's brother who drowned in the torpedoing of the Galway Castle in September 1918

Jessie Buntine, the daughter of Robert, was Lyle's cousin who drowned with her father in the sinking of the Galway Castle.

Dr Richard Gibbs, father of 'Mac' and Jack, brother in law of Walter and Lyle's uncle who died after falling from a Melbourne cable-car in 1919.

Index

0-9

11 Squadron, 142-148, 159-160, 169, 175, 177, 217-218, 252

A

A'Becket, Thomas, 86
Adamson, L.A., 14, 18
Ailsa Craig 215, 220
Aircrafts
   BE2C 133, 159, 227, 228
   DH2 175
   FE2B 143, 177, 227, 228
   Fokker, biplanes 175, 176
   Fokker, Eindecker 133, 163, 167, 169
   Jagdstaffeln (Jastas), 174
   Maurice Farman S.11 (Shorthorn) 121-124, 127
   seaplane 57
   Sopwith Camel, 28
   Sopwith Tabloid, 28-29
   Vickers FB5 'Gunbus,' 143
Allan, Dr (at Harefield Hospital) 52, 68, 74, 89, 90, 119, 134, 165
Allen, Harry, 29
Appleton, Sgt Stanley Chalmers, 226, 228
Ashmead-Bartlett, Ellis, 31
Australia Day, 52-53, 55
Australian Army Medical Corps, 187
Australian Imperial Force (AIF), 33

B

Ball, Lt Albert, 144, 187, 217
Barker, Ralph, 139
Barnett, Rev. Ernest Judd, 10-11
Blogg, Val, 182
Boan, Enid, 206, 208
Boelcke, Oswald, 174-175, 187
Broadmeadows Camp, 33-38, 50, 96, 175, 176
Broadmeadows Depot.
  see Broadmeadows Camp
Brookes, Norman, 197-198
Brownlee-Young, Ailsa, 212, 232-236
Brownlee-Young, James, 229, 232-236
Brownlee-Young, Nellie, 229, 232-236
Buntine, Bertha Florence (mother), 24, 230, 256, 259, **286**
  letters from, 80
Buntine, Bertha Mary Gladys (sister), 24, **286**
Buntine, Carlyle, 1, 2
Buntine, Collection, The 2-3
Buntine, Jessie (cousin), 59, 64, 80, 86-87, 258, 259, **287, 292**
Buntine, Martin Arnold (brother), 24, 151, 219
Buntine, Noelle (cousin), 64, 80, 86-87, 258, **287**
Buntine, Richard Murray (brother), 24, 149, 217-219

Buntine, Robert Andrew (uncle), 59, 64, 86, 258, **292**
Buntine, Robert Douglas (brother), 24, 151
Buntine, Walter Horace Carlyle (Lyle)
    11 Squadron and, 142-144, 217-218, **288**
    academic, 24
    active service Squadron and, 130-134
    advice and concerns for family, 218-220
    and Archibald Cathie, **289**
    as an athlete, 25-26, 27
    at Seymour Camp, **285**
    awarded a Military Cross, 180-181, 209-210
    Battle of Somme, combat and, 156-168
    billeted with the Grimwade family 75 - 78
    Broadmeadows Camp, **284**
    cadet's training and, 26, 33
    Ceylon (Sri Lanka), travel in, 194-195, 198
    combat at the Battle of Somme, 160-172
    commemoration of his life and death, 256, 262-268
    comments about Australia, 96-97
    condolences and, 230-242, 248
    convalescing in England, 182-183
    Court of Inquiry re death of, 227-229
    cricket matches, 75, 193
    death and funeral of, 221-227, 257
    death reported of, 262-263
    departure to the front, 139-140
    describes life and conditions 144-147
    early Army days, 66-67
    early days in England, 62-63
    England, observations of, 94-96
    enlists in the AIF - AAMC, 30-34, **285**
    factors for enlistment of, 30-32
    first flight at Hendon, 67-68
    flying training experiences, 121-129
    in France, 140-142
    friendships and, 83-86
    getting Military Cross from the King, 209-210
    Indian Ocean experience, 51
    letters to and from home, 3, 38, 40-45, 80-81, 117-119, 134-138, 135-138, 140-142, 148-155, 179-182, 202, 205-220
    life in France, 144-148
    managing estate of, 242-248
    Medical Board appearance at, 187-189, 191-192
    medical studies at Melbourne University, 29-30
    meeting the King and Queen, 206-208
    meets other Caulfield Grammarians, 43-44, 69-70, 81-82, 129-130, 182
    meets other 'Shop' boys, 52
    money matters and, 74-75, 90-91, 134, 213-215
    news from home, 148-152
    newspaper interviews and, 186-187
    newspaper obituaries of, 239-242
    Notts and Derby Regiment, 74, 105, **289**
    officer training at Ipswich, 105
    officer training in the British Army, 68, 73-76, 105-112
    personal matters and, 152-155
    posted to Hospital Ship, 33
    posted to Seymour Clearing Hospital, 37
    recovering at home, 189-190
    return home to Australia, 184-186
    return to England, 192, 204-206
    RFC and, 68-69, 112-113
    RFC training and, 116-117
    school days at CGS, 24-27
    School of Military Aeronautics and, 114-115
    secret venture of, 215-216
    with sister and mother, **286**
    social activities in England, 208-209
    solo flight and, 126-129

sports and, 8, 27
as a student, **282**
thoughts of home, 215
a tourist in England, 64-65, 77, 93-94, 210-212
training at Broadmeadows, 33-37
training squadron and, 119-121
transfer to Seymour, 37-45
tribute poems to, 4, 230-232, 248-249, 266
at Turnberry, 212-213, 216-217
various photographs of, **286-287**
wounded and shot down, 177-182
Zeppelin raids and, 70-73, 98-99
Buntine, Walter Murray (father), 1, 2, 4, 8, 11, 17, 23, 28, 32, 103, 135 - 136, 185-186, 190, 221, 222, 234, 239-240, 242, 250, 262-267, **282**
  birth and childhood, 15
  cadet unit, support of, 19-20
  Hawksburn Grammar School and, 15
  Melbourne University, 15
  Morrison, Dr Alexander, 15-16
  mourning family member's death, 190, 256-259,
  Ridley College, 17
  Scotch College, 15, 16
  University of Melbourne, 15, 17
Buzzard, J, 44, 47, 52

C

Capel, Sir Derrick, 207
Carmichael, Penelope, 200, 211, 218
Carmichael, Sir Thomas, 199-200, 202, 211, 218
Cascader, Col. G.W., 187
Cathie, Archibald James Lt, 146-147, 182, 252, **289**
Caulfield Grammar School (CGS), 1, 4, 7, 8, 15, 17, 33
  cadet unit, 9-10, 18-20, 26, 100-101
  Christian emphasis, 9, 10, 12-13, 23
  foundation and early years, 4, 8-12
  Great War declared and its immediate effects, 20-21
  hero's welcome for "Lyle" Buntine, 184-185
  Honour Roll, 3, 104, 135, 253, 266, 267
  life at, 21-23, 100-104
  Life at CGS in 1914 21 - 22
  Life at CGS in 1915 100 - 101
  Old Boys of, 4
  philosophy of, 4, 12
  playing fields, sport, 9-11, 16
  purchased by W M Buntine, 11
  school life in 1915, 100-104
  War and Memory into modern times, 4, 259-262
Caulfield Grammarian School Magazine, 26, 100, 104, 134, 135, 184-185
  articles about Old Boys and the Great War, 10, 100-101, 104
  cadet unit stories in, 19, 26
  condolences/death of Old Boys mentioned, 102, 104, 259-260
  Lyle Buntine mentioned in, 3-4, 184-185, 190, 230, 242, 249, 262-263
  Lyle Buntine requests for the, 134, 215
  obituary/condolences for Lyle Buntine, 242, 262-263
  poem in remembrance of, 230-231, 248-249
  sent to Lyle Buntine, 81
  support of the war, 20-21
  tribute poem in, 230, 266
Caulfield Grammarians' Association (CGA), 2
Caulfield Grammarians members
  deaths at Gallipoli, 32, 102, 104
  deaths in the Great War 1915, 102-103, 189-190
  meet at Sargent's Café, 22-23
  reunion of Old Boys, 103-104
Caulfield Tally Ho Harriers Club, 27
Cecil Hugh, Lord 69
CGS. *see* Caulfield Grammar School (CGS)

CGS SAAAV Champion Athletic team (1911), 7-8, **283**
CGS SAAAV Champion Football team (1913), **284**
Commonwealth Military Cadet Corps (CMCC), 19
Coombes, Bertrand, 22
Cox and Co, 148, 163, 214, 247
Croker, B, 130
Crossley, Ada, 153, 182

D

Daily Mail article, 172-174
Davenport, George, 82
Davies, Joseph Henry, 8-10
Davies, Sir Francis, 207
Davis, Sydney, 83-86, 90
de Gay, Pauline, 153-154, 245-246
de Gay, Sylvia, 153-154, 182, 205-206
Deakin, Alfred, 19
deG Gill, Gunner W, 104
Dimant, Roy, 190
Donaldson and Alexander lawyers, 243-244, 246, 247
Douglas, Cecilia, 206, 210
Duntroon Royal Military College 22

E

Enlistment Factors 1915, 30-32
Evans, Gilbert, 190

F

Fethers, Noel Lt 102-103
Fitzpatrick, Captain Sam, 52
Fitzurze, Reginald, 86
Fowler, Robert (Bob) Capt. 23, 130
Frame, Mima (Cousin) 79, 89, 94, **287**
Fremantle, voyage to, 50

G

Gardiner, John 47, 70
Gardiner, Keith 70, 82
Gartcash, the Inshaws at, 91-93, 130
German Air Force 133, 156 - 158, 169, 174-175
Germany, attitudes to, 30-31, 49

Gibbs, Horace Richard Dr (uncle), 257-259, **292**
Gibbs, John (Jack) Harbinger (cousin) 135, 155, 182, 205, 257-259, **284, 292**
Gibbs, Richard Horace Maconochie (Mac) Lt. (cousin) 118, 181, 190, 256-257, **283, 292**
Gibbs, Richard (Mrs), 257
Gibson, Alexander, 198-199
Girvan 223, 224, 237, 243
Grant, Frank, 47
Grimwade, Edward, 75, 77

H

Hagelthorn, F, 101
Hampton, H, 47
Hardy, Roy, 52
Harefield Hospital, 68, 89-90
Harton, Horace, 82
Hawker, Harry, 28-29, 171
Hawksburn Grammar School, 15
Hayward Cedric, (RFC), 192
HMAT Orsova
    arrival at Plymouth, 60-61, 62
    Fremantle to Aden, 54
    in the Mediterranean, 60
    in the Suez Canal, 56
    nurses on board 46, 52-53
    University of Melbourne medical students on, 47
    voyage to Fremantle, 50-51
Holst, Frederick, 190
Honour Rolls, 253
Hopkins, Jesse, 75

I

Immelmann, Max, 133-134, 174
Insall, G. S. M., 144
Inshaw, George, 236
Inshaws, at Gartcash 91-93, 130, 214, 236-237
Ipswich 75, 77, 98, 105

J

Jutland, Battle of 131-132

K

'Kaiser-I-Hind' voyage, return to Australia, 184
King Edward VII, 17-18
Kitchener, Horatio Herbert 19, 131-132
Kyarra SS
    controversial passengers on, 48-49
    return of, 48-49
    wounded soldiers on, 48-49

L

Langlands, Alec., 190
Laughlin, Austin, 182
Le Bas, Owen Vincent Lt, 133
Leather, Captain R.T., 228
Libby, Frederick, 144
Little, George, 135
Lonie, A.M., 23
Luckins, Tania, 255
Lyall, Mary, 89
Lyall, Murray, 89

M

Maguire, Major 39, 44
Maguire, Dr T Miller, 112
Maidens, The, 210, 212, 229-230
Male, Lindsay, 47
Mathy, Heinrich, 72
McCowan, Douglas, 56
McCubbin, George, 134
McCullough, Lt 19-20
McKenna, H, 237-238
McKernan, M, 16
McMullin, Ross, 254
Medical Board, 191
Medina RMS
    Brookes, Norman, 197-198
    Carmichael, Sir Thomas, 211, 218
    Carmichael, Penelope, 200, 211, 218
    Gibson, Alexander, 198-199
    Hayward Cedric, (RFC), 192
    Lyle leaves the ship, 201
    Montagu, Lord, 199-200
    notable passengers on, 197-201

    sinking of, 201
    Travel in Ceylon (Sri Lanka), 194-196, 198
Melvin, John, 32
Mollison, Phyllis, 248
Montagu (Lord), 199-200
Morrison, Dr Alexander, 15-16
Moran, Rod 3
Morton, Sgt Godfrey Julian, 177, 181-182
Murray, Noel, 103-104
Murrell, Charles, 190
muscular Christianity, 4, 13-14, 23, 27, 256

N

Nash, Robert, 259
Nelson, William, 47
Newbolt, Henry, *Vitae Lampada*, 14
Nineteenth Century Education, background of, 12-15
Notts and Derby Regiment, 74, 106, **289**

O

Osler, Sir William, 188-189

P

Patterson, Donald, 88
Perrin, Harold, 247
Phillips, Ernie, 52
Preston, Diana, 31

R

Reid, George, Sir 69
Reade, Lloyd, 82, 135
Richards, Willie, 47
Richardson, Murray, 89, **287**
Robinson, J, 130
Rodgerson, R, 27
Roll of Honor, Caulfield Grammar School (CGS)'s, 3, 102, 135, 253
Royal Aero Club (RAC), 120, 129, 150
Royal Flying Corps
    and the Battle of Somme, 156-160
    Communiques, 159
    newspaper article about, 172-174
    No 11 Squadron, **288**

S

Sargood, Lt Col. Frederick, 9–10
School of Military Aeronautics, 114–115
Schools Amateur Athletic Association of Victoria (SAAAV), 7, 26
Schools' Association of Victoria (SAV), 11
Scotch College, 15, 258
Seelenmeyer, Dudley, 70
Seymour Camp, 34–43
Shell-shock. see traumatic neurasthenia
Sherington, G, 16
Shorthorn. see aircrafts
Somme, Battle of, 142, 144, 156–160, 174–175, 192
    11 Squadron's role, 159, 169, 177, 217–218
    phases of the, 158–159
    RFC Communiques, 159
    RFC role, 156–160, 159. see also Buntine, Walter Horace Carlyle (Lyle)
    Trenchard's strategy, 158–159
Southey, Captain Marcus, 129
Southey, H, 130
Sproule, George, 135
Staughton, Eric, 135
Steel, Captain Frank, 224, 225–226
Stevenson, Captain J.B., 228–229
Stock, Tom, 102
Syme, Col. G.A., 187–188

T

Templeton, R.R., 27
Thomas, W. Beach, 172
Traumatic Neurasthenia (PTSD), 188–189
Trenchard's strategy, 158–159
Troon 222
Turnberry, 212–213, 216–217, 221–223, 230, 234–235, 237, 239, 241–243, 246–248, 250–251
Turnberry War Memorial, 251, 265
Tunbridge Wells 59, 80, 87, 89
Tyrer, Henry, 190

U

University of Melbourne, 8, 17, 27, 29–30, 149, 220
    medical students on the *HMAT Orsova*, 47

V

Vincent, Sir William, 208
Vines, Ernest, 69
Vines, Geoffrey, 52, 69
Vines, Jack, 69
Vitae Lampada (Newbolt), 14
Von Below, Fritz, General 158

W

War and Memory
    Australia finds ways to mourn, 253–255
Warnock, Joe, 52
Watt, Thomas, 47
Weather, in England, 78–80
Webber, Horace, 16
White, Hetty 64, 88
White, Jessie 64, 88
White, Matthew, 64, 86, 222, 224, 226, 229, 232, 242, 250
White, Meg 64, 88,
Wilding, Anthony, 198
Wilson, Robert Capt. 175
Wilson, R.G., 34
Wood, Arthur O'Hara, 68

Y

Young, Arnold, 69, 135
Young, Nellie. see Murray, Nellie

Z

Zeppelin Raids, 70–73, 98–99

Locators with "**bold**" refer to pictures.

www.ingramcontent.com/pod-product-compliance
Lightning Source LLC
Chambersburg PA
CBHW070508120526
44590CB00013B/778